The Clerical Library.

EXPOSITORY SERMONS

ON THE

NEW TESTAMENT.

THE CLERICAL LIBRARY

I. Three Hundred Outlines of Sermons on the New Testament.
II. Outlines of Sermons on the Old Testament.
III. Pulpit Prayers. By Eminent Preachers.
IV. Outline Sermons to Children. With numerous Anecdotes.
V. Anecdotes Illustrative of New Testament Texts.
VI. Expository Sermons and Outlines on the Old Testament.
VII. Expository Sermons on the New Testament.
VIII. Platform Aids.
IX. New Outlines of Sermons on the New Testament. By Eminent Preachers. Hitherto unpublished.
X. Anecdotes Illustrative of Old Testament Texts.
XI. New Outlines of Sermons on the Old Testament. By Eminent Preachers. Hitherto unpublished.
XII. Two Hundred Outlines of Sermons for Special Occasions.

EXPOSITORY SERMONS

ON THE

NEW TESTAMENT.

REV. NICHOLAS J. KREMER

HODDER AND STOUGHTON
LONDON NEW YORK TORONTO

34/29,625

PREFATORY NOTE.

The following expositions are all gathered from fugitive or unpublished sources.

AUTHORS OF SERMONS.

Right Rev. WILLIAM ALEXANDER, D.D., Bishop of Derry.
Rev. STOPFORD A. BROOKE, M.A., London.
Rev. HUGH STOWELL BROWN, Liverpool.
Rev. J. OSWALD DYKES, D.D., London.
Ven. Archdeacon FARRAR, D.D., F.R.S., Westminster.
Rev. CANON H. P. LIDDON, D.D., D.C.L., London.
Right Rev. J. B. LIGHTFOOT, D.D., D.C.L., Lord Bishop of Durham.
Rev. ALEXANDER MACLAREN, D.D., Manchester.
Very Rev. J. J. S. PEROWNE, D.D., Dean of Peterborough.
The Late Rev. W. MORLEY PUNSHON, LL.D.
The Rev. CHARLES STANFORD, D.D., London.
Very Rev. C. J. VAUGHAN, D.D., Dean of Llandaff.
The Late Right Rev. S. WILBERFORCE, D.D., Lord Bishop of Winchester.

I. The Virgin Mother. MATT. i. 22, 23. *"Now all this was done, that it might be fulfilled which was spoken of the Lord by the prophet, saying, Behold, a virgin shall be with child, and shall bring forth a son, and they shall call His name Emmanuel, which being interpreted is, God with us."*

MANY readers of the Bible must be struck by the reason which St. Matthew here gives for the occurrences connected with the birth of Christ. "All this was done, that it might be fulfilled which was spoken of the Lord by the prophet." We are, perhaps, tempted to whisper to ourselves that the event predicted is, after all, more important than the prediction; that it would have seemed more natural to say that the prophecy existed for the sake of the event, than the event for the sake of the prophecy; more natural to say that Isaiah's utterance was meant to prepare the world for Jesus Christ, than that the Birth of Jesus Christ was designed to justify Isaiah by fulfilling his words. But, in truth, both the prophecy and its fulfilment were from God; and the independent and higher importance of the event does not really interfere with its also being a certificate of the Prophet's accuracy. There were other reasons, no doubt, for the birth of Jesus Christ of a Virgin Mother; but one reason for it was this—that it was already foretold, and on Divine authority. And it fell in with St. Matthew's general plan throughout his Gospel to insist on this particular reason. He is writing for Churches made up almost, if not quite, exclusively of converts from Judaism; and he is concerned, at almost every step of his narrative, to show that the life of Jesus, in all its particulars, corresponded to what Jewish prophecy, as understood by the Jews themselves, had said about the coming Messiah. So he begins at the beginning, with the birth of Christ; and he says that Christ was born, just as Isaiah had said that Christ would be born, and, among other reasons—because Isaiah had said so. These first Jewish Christians might feel wonder, even scandal, when first they heard of the embarrassment of Joseph and of the angelic assurances; but they had only to open the roll of prophecy to find that the history had been accurately anticipated. "All this was done, that it might be fulfilled which was spoken of the Lord by the prophet, saying, Behold, a virgin shall be with child, and shall bring forth a son, and they shall call His name Emmanuel, which being interpreted is, God with us."

In St. Matthew's eyes, then, Isaiah is almost as much the historian as he is the prophet of our Lord's nativity. But is it clear that when Isaiah uttered the words which are quoted he meant to predict such an event as St. Matthew records?

It has been suggested that this was not really Isaiah's meaning: that Isaiah had in view some other event at once nearer to his own times, and more commonplace and ordinary than the birth of the Redeemer; and that St. Matthew accommodates the Prophet's language by a gentle pressure to the necessities of the supernatural account which he is himself narrating. And a main reason which is urged for this view of Isaiah's meaning is that, if we look to the circumstances under which his prophecy was uttered, it is difficult to think that so distant an event as the birth of Messiah would have at all served his purpose in giving a sign to Ahaz.

What, then, were the circumstances which led Isaiah to proclaim, "Behold, a virgin shall conceive and bear a son, and shall call his name Emmanuel?" Ahaz, the king of Judah, was besieged in his capital by the allied forces of Israel and Syria, under their kings, Pekah and Rezin. These kings were really leagued against the rising empire of Assyria; but they thought that they would best consolidate their own power in Palestine by deposing the reigning family of David from the throne of Jerusalem, and setting up a vassal monarch, "the son of Tabeal," on whose services they could reckon in the approaching struggle with Assyria. Isaiah was sent to encourage Ahaz and his son to make a stout resistance, and to assure them that, notwithstanding the project of the allied kings, God would be faithful to His covenant with David. These associated kings, Isaiah says, need occasion Ahaz no anxiety; they were like brands that are nearly burnt out; there was no Divine force in Syria, and no political future for Israel. Ahaz had only to trust God, and all would be well.

Ahaz was silent—silent, because suspicious and distrustful—and then Isaiah bade him ask for some token which might assure him of God's presence with and goodwill towards him. "Ask thee a sign of the Lord thy God; ask it either in the depth, or in the height above." Had Ahaz, then, asked for a token of God's goodwill towards himself personally, or his immediate descendants, it would, no doubt, have been granted. But Ahaz was bent upon an irreligious policy of his own; he thought that, by the aid of Assyria, he would be able to do without the God and the religion of his ancestors; he looked on God and His prophets as personal enemies, who thwarted his plans; and he did not wish to commit himself, by asking for a sign, to a religious creed and system with which, he hoped, he had parted company for ever. Yet Ahaz, standing before the Prophet, could not refuse to say anything: he must accept or decline the invitation to ask for a sign. He declined to do so; and, as irreligious people often do in like circumstances, he pleaded a religious scruple as the reason for his refusal. The old law had warned Israel against tempting the Lord by asking for new evidences or "signs" of sufficiently attested truth;[1] and Ahaz, who had resorted freely to the forbidden arts of necromancy, gravely produced this entirely insincere reason to account for his resolve—" I will not ask, neither will I tempt the Lord."

Then it was that Isaiah spoke, not without righteous anger, to King Ahaz and his son. "Hear ye now, O house of David, is it a small thing for you to weary men, but will ye weary my God also? Therefore the Lord Himself shall give you a sign." A sign would be given; but Ahaz could now no longer determine its character and drift. It would show that God would be true to His promises to David; but it would not reassure the degenerate descendants of the man after God's own heart as to their dynastic interests. The earthly throne of David

[1] Deut. vi. 16.

might perish; but the promise made to David of unfailing empire would still be safe, though it would be fulfilled in a distant age, and by unthought-of agencies. Just as Moses was assured that God had sent him, by the sign of a future event—the complete deliverance from Egypt—which at the time seemed impossible,[1] so religious Jews of Isaiah's day, for whom Isaiah was really speaking, were to be assured of the safety of the great religious interests intrusted to the race of David, by a predicted wonder, without parallel in history, but designed to persuade them that God might punish the rebellious kings of Judah, and yet work out the promised salvation of Israel and the human race. Behold—Isaiah cries as he gazes across the centuries, at the picture which passes before him—"behold *the* Virgin"—the language shows that he is thinking of one in particular—"is with child, and beareth a Son, and shall call His name Emmanuel."

It was, then, no part of Isaiah's plan to give a sign which should assure Ahaz of present deliverance; he had done that before in plain language. And when he utters the prophecy quoted by St. Matthew, he has other and higher objects before him, the nature of which must be determined, not by the real or supposed state of mind of Ahaz, but by the natural force of the Prophet's words. Here, then, let us consider the importance of the event to which Isaiah thus looks forward, and which the Evangelist describes as fulfilled.

I. This importance is seen, first of all, in the strictly preternatural character of the occurrence itself. "Behold, a Virgin shall conceive, and bear a Son." The foil to this prediction is the universal law by which our race is transmitted, that a child must have two human parents. St. Matthew is explicit in his account of the events which preceded our Lord's birth; but it has been contended that the word [2] which Isaiah uses, and which is translated virgin, really means a young but married woman.[3] If this was the meaning it is difficult to see why there should be any allusion to the mother at all; since the predicted child would only be born like all other children, and would be a poor "sign" in the prophet's sense. But the Hebrew word for "virgin" is used of Rebekah (Gen. xxiv. 43) before

[1] Exod. iii. 12.   [2] עלמה   [3] So Kimchi.

her marriage with Isaac; of Miriam (Exod. ii. 8) the maiden sister of the infant Moses; and in four other places[1] in which it is found in the Old Testament there is no decisive ground for thinking that any but unmarried women are meant. I do not forget the names of scholars, who, moved by whatever considerations, have disputed the accuracy of our present translation; but one fact in connection with it is instructive, and may throw some light upon the motive of recent objections. When the first translation of the Hebrew Bible into Greek was made, about some two centuries before our Lord, in Alexandria, and nothing was supposed to be at stake, the Jewish translators rendered this word by "virgin."[2] But when, in the second century of our era, Aquila, a Jewish proselyte of Sinope, having his eye upon the Christian appeal to Jewish prophecy, undertook a new translation of the Hebrew Scriptures into Greek, he rendered it by "a young woman."[3] The word seems to have been originally employed in a narrower sense than its derivation might suggest. If the point could be decided on grounds of language—without reference to the claims of Christianity, or to the possibility of the supernatural—there probably would not be much room for hesitation.

The birth of Jesus Christ is not unfrequently discussed in our day, as the birth of a great man, but without reference to the virginity of His mother. Isaiah's prediction and St. Matthew's narrative are passed over, as if they were not of much importance to our estimate of the event. My brethren, it is necessary to say plainly, that the account in the Gospel is either true or false. If it is false, it ought to be repudiated by honest men as baseless superstition. If, as we Christians believe, it is true, then it is a momentous truth; it implies a great deal more than is to be expressed by saying that the Son of the Virgin was a great and extraordinary man; it carries us altogether beyond the limits of nature and ordinary experience.

Doubtless, here and there in the heathen world there were legends of sages or poets who were born of virgins; but these legends are related to the history of our Saviour's birth as are false miracles to the true. As the counterfeit

---

[1] Ps. lxviii. 25; Song of Sol. i. 3, vi. 8; Prov. xxx. 19.
[2] LXX. παρθένος. [3] νεᾶνις.

miracle implies the real miracle of which it is a counterfeit, so the idea of a virgin-birth, here and there discoverable in paganism, points to a deep instinct of the human race, and the high probability that the Absolute Religion would satisfy it. Men felt—pagans though they were—the oppression and degradation of their hereditary nature; they longed for some break in the tyrannical tradition of flesh and blood; they longed for the appearance of some Being, who should still belong to them, yet in a manner so exceptional as to be able to inaugurate a new era in humanity. Revelation surely is not less trustworthy because it recognises an instinct which only led men to do it justice, and which was itself in accordance with moral truth.

For here we touch upon a primary reason for our Lord's preternatural birth. If He was to raise us from our degradation, He must Himself be sinless—a sinless example, and a sinless sacrifice. Our Lord Himself and His apostles abundantly insist upon this His sinlessness; but how was it to be secured, if He was indeed to become incorporate with a race which was steeped in a mighty tradition of evil? When by his transgression our first parent had forfeited the robe of grace in which God had clothed him in Paradise, he passed on to his descendants a nature fatally impoverished, and thereby biassed in a wrong direction; so that thenceforth, throughout all generations, evil was inherent in human nature. It descended like a bad name, or a disease, from generation to generation; and though here and there, as with Jeremiah, or the Baptist, there was a special sanctification before birth, yet the millions of mankind had to say with David, "Behold I was shapen in wickedness, and in sin hath my mother conceived me." How, then, was this fatal entail to be cut off decisively—so that all should understand it? The Birth of a Virgin was the answer to that question. The Son of Mary was still human; but in His humanity had inherited none of that bad legacy which came across the ages from the Fall. And truly "such an High Priest became us—holy, harmless, undefiled, separate from sinners."

This, indeed, is not—as you will have felt—the whole account of the matter. The birth of Jesus Christ, as we Christians believe, marked the entrance into the sphere of sense and time of One who had already existed from eternity. At His birth, as St. Paul says, He was "manifested in the flesh";[1] but whether He is here called God or not in the true reading, it is thus, in any case, implied that He existed before His manifestation. The Father "sent forth His Son, made of a woman," as St. Paul again tells us. But the Son existed before He was sent forth—the expression is evidently chosen to imply this. And this previous existence did not date from creation: for "in the beginning was the Word, and the Word was with God, and the Word was God."

How was the entrance of such a Being into this our world so to be marked as to show that He did not originally owe existence to a human parent? We could not have dared to answer such a question beforehand; but we can see how it is answered by our Lord's birth of a Virgin. . . . Was it not natural that nature should thus suspend her laws, to welcome the approach and the blessing of her Maker?

II. The importance of our Lord's birth of a Virgin mother is further seen in its resnlts. At this distance of time it is clear that no other birth since the beginning of history has involved such important consequences to the human race. We Christians have had nearly nineteen centuries in which to form comparisons and to arrive at conclusions. We have had time to take the measure of the great statesmen, soldiers, poets, teachers who have been foremost among mankind. Who of them all has left behind him a work which can compare with that achieved by Jesus Christ? As Napoleon I. once asked, what was the empire of Alexander, or of Cæsar, or his own, compared to that of Jesus Christ? Theirs were transient; His is lasting. Theirs had reached a limit; His is ever extending. Theirs was based on force; His is based on convictions. Who again of the great men of letters has swayed the world like Jesus Christ? Doubtless they too have an empire. Who can dispute the influence at this hour of Plato—of Shakespeare—of Newton? But it is an influence which differs in kind from His; it interests the intellect, while His enchains the will. Nay, compare Him with the great teachers of false religions—with Sakya-Mouni, who preceded, or with Mahomet, who followed

[1] 1 Tim. iii. 16.

Him, in human history. I do not forget the statistics of Buddhism, or the undeniable activities of Islam in certain portions of the Eastern world. But these religions are the religions of races with no real future; Christianity is the creed of the nations which, year by year, are more and more controlling the destinies of our race. And, if it be urged that large portions of these very nations, Christian by profession, are now abjuring Christianity, it may be replied that such an apostasy is in the long run impossible. Man cannot dispense with religion; and when he has come into contact with the highest type of religion he has thereby exhausted the religious capacities of his nature: the Absolute Religion makes any other impossible for free and sincere minds. The present efforts to replace Christianity by an imaginary religion of the future, distilled out of all the positive religions of the world, is doomed to a failure only less complete than the attempt to replace it by mere negations. There are not wanting signs of a rebound towards the faith; there are no signs whatever of a rising religious force capable of superseding it.

Yes? all that is best, and most full of hope, in the civilised world, dates from the birthday of Jesus Christ. Doubtless we owe some things which rank high in the order of nature to the old pagan days. We owe philosophy to Greece, and law and well-ordered life to Rome. But the idea of progress, which, however it may have been misapplied, is perhaps the most fertile and energetic in modern public life, is a creation of the Christian creed; it springs from those high hopes of the future, whether of individuals or of the race, which Christ has taught His disciples to entertain as a matter of loyalty to Himself. And the institutions which make life tolerable for the suffering classes—that is, for the majority of human beings—such as hospitals, these date, one and all, from the appearance of Jesus Christ, from the principles which He proclaimed to men with sovereign authority.

To take one point among many. The position of woman in Christian society is directly traceable, not only to our Lord's teaching, but to the circumstances of His birth. Before He came, woman, even in Israel, was little better than the slave of man. In the heathen world, as in Eastern countries now, she was a slave to all intents and purposes. Here and there a woman of great force of character, joined to hereditary advantages, might emerge from this chronic oppression, might become a Deborah, or a Semiramis, or a Boadicea, or a Cleopatra, or a Zenobia, —might control the world or its rulers; yet the lot of the great majority was a suffering and degraded one. But when Christ "took upon Him to deliver man, He did not abhor the Virgin's womb." In the greatest event in the whole course of human history the stronger sex had no part: the Incarnate Son was conceived of the Holy Ghost, and born of the Virgin Mary. And, therefore, in Mary woman rose to a position of consideration unknown before, in which nothing was forfeited that belongs to the true modesty and grace of her nature, but by which the larger share of influence in shaping the destinies of the Christian races was secured to her in perpetuity. It was the Incarnation which created chivalry, and all those better features of modern life which are due to it; and they are no true friends, it seems to me, to the real influence and usefulness of women, who would substitute for the Christian ideal of womanhood another, in which woman is to compete with man in all the activities of his public life, and in the end to be relegated to some such social fate as would inevitably follow upon unsuccessful rivalry.

But these outward and visible results of the birth of Christ were far from being the most important. It is conceivable that such results as these might have been due to a religious genius of commanding influence, or to a man invested with miraculous powers, but still strictly and solely a man. The birth of Jesus Christ meant much more than this. It was the entrance of the Word made Flesh into the scene of sense and time; it was the manifestation of the Incarnate God.

Before the Incarnation there was a great gulf fixed between God and man. Man could think about God; he could pray to Him; he could practise a certain measure of obedience to His will. But in his best moments man was conscious of his utter separateness from God, as the perfect moral Being. He was conscious of sin; and this meant nothing less than separation from the All-Holy.

The Incarnation of Jesus Christ was a bridge across the chasm, which thus parted earth and heaven. On the one hand, and from everlasting, Jesus Christ was of one substance with the Father, Very and Eternal God. On the other, He was made very Man, of the substance of the Virgin Mary, His Mother. As the Collect says, He took Man's nature upon Him. When He had already existed from Eternity, He folded around Him, and made His own, a created form, a human body and a human soul, to be for ever united to His Eternal Godhead. Through this His human nature, He acts on God's behalf upon mankind. Through this His human nature, He pleads for man before the Majesty of God. Thus there is "One Mediator between God and man, the Man Christ Jesus." It is as Man that He mediates between the Creator and the creature; between sinners and the All-Holy; but His Godhead secures to His mediation its commanding power. If He were not human, we should be unrepresented in heaven, where He "ever liveth to make intercession for us." If He were not Divine, it would be impossible to say why His death upon the Cross should have infinite merit. At one and the same moment, He is as Mediator in the bosom of the Godhead, and in the closest contact with the souls of His redeemed; and this is a result of His entrance in a created form into our human world—as the Everlasting Son, yet withal as the Child of Mary. That this is the deepest meaning of Christmas, and of the birth of Christ, is implied in the name assigned by prophecy to the Virgin's Son—the sublime name, Emmanuel. From the day of the Nativity, God was known to be with man, not simply as heretofore, as the Omnipresent, but under new and more intimate conditions. From the day of the Nativity, men felt a change in the relations between earth and heaven. To be one with Christ was to be one with God; and this union with God through Christ is the secret and basis of the new kingdom of souls which Christ has founded and in which He reigns. Who shall describe the wealth of spiritual and moral power which dates from the appearance of the Incarnate Son in our human world—as our wisdom, and righteousness, and sanctification, and redemption? Here and there, we see, as by glimpses through the clouds, some streaks of the glory of this invisible kingdom of souls; but only in another life shall we understand, at all approximately, what it has meant for millions of our race.

And here, though we are still on the threshold of the subject, we must note two points in conclusion.

(1) Observe the contrast between the real and the apparent importance of the birth of Christ. To human sense, what took place at Bethlehem may well have seemed, at the time, commonplace enough. An infant was born, under circumstances of hardship, in a wayside stall. To those who did not look closely at what was passing, it might have occurred that a like event had happened scores of times before, and would often be repeated. Everybody did not hear the song of the angels, or mark the bearing of the Virgin Mother and of her saintly spouse. The Kingdom of God had entered into history; but certainly "not with observation." Nay, more—even among the worshippers of Christ the full meaning of His birth, as opening a new era in the history of the human race, was not at once practically appreciated. For five centuries and a half, Christians still reckoned the passing years by the names of the Roman consuls, or by the era of Diocletian, just like the pagans around them. It was only in the year 541 that Dionysius the Little—a pious and learned person at Rome—first ranged the history of mankind around the most important event in it, the birthday of Jesus Christ. Christendom at once recognised the justice of this way of reckoning time, and no attempts to supersede it—such as that which was made in France during the first Revolution—have since had a chance of success. But how often do we use the phrase, "the year of our Lord," without reflecting that it proclaims the birth of Jesus Christ to be an event of such commanding importance that all else in human history, rightly understood, is merely relative to it—interesting only as it precedes or follows, as it leads up to or is derived from it. Yet, as I have said, five centuries and a half passed before this was practically recognised. So it has been ever since; so it is at this hour. Real importance is one thing, apparent importance another. The events which move the world are not always those which men think most about. The men who most deeply influence their fellows are not those of whom everybody is talking. The currents of thought and feeling which will shape the future are not those which are welcomed by the organs and interpreters of current opinion. When Christ appeared, the palace of

the Cæsar seemed to be more important to the destinies of the world than the manger of Bethlehem. No, brethren, depend on it, the apparent is not always or generally the real.

(2) There is a question which we should, each of us, lose no time whatever in answering, if it be not answered yet: What is my relation to Him who, for love of me, was conceived of the Holy Ghost and born of the Virgin Mary—my present Saviour, my future Judge?

H. P. L.

II. John the Baptist. MATT. xi. 7. *"What went ye out into the wilderness to see?"*

THIS question was put to a large assemblage of his countrymen by our blessed Lord on an occasion of importance. He had just received and replied to an embassy which we may dare to say would have moved His human sympathies very deeply. John the Baptist, whose baptism Jesus had Himself received in the waters of the Jordan,—John the Baptist, who had so preached repentance as to be in very deed the prophet of the Highest coming before the face of the Lord to prepare His way,—John the Baptist was in prison. He had dared to tell a plain but unwelcome truth to a sensual king, and this king had acted as powerful vice generally does act when it is confronted with weak but inconvenient virtue. Herod Antipas, the capricious, tyrannical, unscrupulous, sensual but weak prince who then, under the title of tetrarch, ruled the Jordan valley and the northern district of Palestine, had actually married the daughter of a neighbouring Arab chief, called Aretas. But this did not prevent him from making overtures of marriage to Herodias, the wife of his own half-brother, Herod Philip, and these proposals were favourably entertained, and then it was that the Baptist pointed out to the king the true moral character of this proceeding; and Herod, who would have killed him had it been politic to do so, shut him up for the present in the gloomy fortress of Machærus, on the Eastern shore of the Dead Sea. It was from this prison that John the Baptist sent the embassy to Jesus. The fame of the miracles of Jesus in Galilee, had reached the ears of the imprisoned prophet, and of the few followers that still clung to him with an affectionate devotion that does them honour. It would seem probable that John had in vain endeavoured to persuade these faithful friends that if they would be true to him they must become disciples of Jesus, that his own ministry only meant to lead men to Jesus, and that the miracles of which they heard so much as being worked in Galilee ought to satisfy them that Jesus was the Messiah of Jewish prophecy. The followers of John still hesitated, and then the Baptist determined to send two of them to Jesus that they might ask Him whether He was what John proclaimed Him to be, and might see and hear for themselves. They put the question to our Lord just as if it had been a message from their master; and our Lord answered them accordingly. He bade them go and tell John the story of their Galilean experience: how the vivid imagery of Isaiah many a century before had been translated before their eyes into the world of fact; how the blind received their sight, and the lame walked, and the lepers were cleansed; how the deaf heard, and the dead were raised up, and, above all, the poor had the good news from Heaven preached to them. And then as the disciples turned away, well satisfied, we may be sure, to carry back this message to their imprisoned master, Jesus turned to the multitude of bystanders with a question of His own, a question which He Himself went on to answer. As they departed, Jesus began to say to the multitudes concerning John, "What went ye out into the wilderness to see?" What, we may reverently ask, was our Lord's motive in asking this question then and there? It is plain from His own answer to it that He asked it in order, first, to repair, and then to sustain the honour in which John the Baptist had been held by the Jewish people. Recent events would have tended naturally enough to diminish that honour. First of all, there was the broad fact—John was in the prison. The days were when he had at his command the love and the admiration of the entire people; now his work was closed, closed, as it seemed, by the mere will and fiat of a weak and immoral king. Depend upon it, the majority of men thought that the sun of the prophet of the desert had set or was setting in humiliation and in ruin. In their mind's eye they traced over the gate of the fortress of Machærus the fatal motto,

"He has failed." This would have been the popular impression at the moment, and our Lord Jesus Christ knew the people as none had ever known them before or since. He knew that the people, if generous in its judgments, is also sometimes precipitate; that it is apt to be misled by mere appearances; that success often, though not always, passes with it as a certificate of merit, and that failure, if not always, yet often is, accounted a proof of moral wrong. John the Baptist was a prisoner; that was the fact before them, and, however honourable to himself might be the reason for which he was imprisoned, the fact was likely, in the long run, to outweigh the reason, and to leave an imprint of depreciation on his name and character in the coming time. Besides this, in sending to ask whether Jesus was the expected Messiah, John, in his noble self-forgetfulness, had sacrificed his credit for the sake of his disciples: that they might learn the better, he was willing to seem as one who had parted with the secret of his inspiration. For years he had been a great teacher and prophet whose utterances, confident, direct, vehement, had awed multitudes into a change of life. Now it might seem the light and strength of heaven had deserted him; he was but one of the many whom he had taught and led; the great teacher, charged with an inspired message to the world, seemed to have become at once only an inquirer hesitating before a difficulty. And this apparent change of attitude on the part of John towards religious truth could not but have affected the imagination of the people. They may well have thought, as modern critics, with less reason, have thought since their day, that the gloomy solitude of the prison had done its work upon that noble soul; that his faith in his mission as the precursor had at last given way, and that the dreadful thought that his life had been devoted to the propagation of a vast mistake had settled down upon him with all the gloom of a misgiving that ushers in the night of an absolute despair. It was, therefore, in order to counteract this unworthy and depreciatory estimate of his great servant, it was to redress the balance of one-sided opinion, it was to rehabilitate the Baptist in the judgment of the new generation that was coming to the front, that our Lord desired His hearers to turn their thoughts back to the time of the great popularity and ascendancy of John. There had been a time when there went out to sit at the feet of the prophet of the desert, "Jerusalem, and all Judea, and all the region round about Jordan, and were baptized of him in Jordan, confessing their sins." Some of our Lord's hearers had been among that multitude, and our Lord bade them ask themselves why it was that they had thus left their homes. Where was the reasonableness of doing so? What was the governing attraction? "What went ye out into the wilderness to see?"

Our Lord's words do, in fact, raise a very large and interesting question, which we may do well to consider—namely, What it is in human character that exerts the most powerful influence over the hearts of men? Is it what we generally call amiability,—the instinct or habit which makes itself agreeable to everybody, which never opposes, never contradicts, never even holds its own when to do so would cause a passing sense of discomfort? Is it, as our Lord puts it, "a reed shaken with the wind,"— a character that bends or that trembles at the first expression of adverse opinion, at a phrase in a speech, or at a paragraph in a newspaper? Is this the character that wins the human heart? Are we really drawn by men who in their intercourse with their fellows conceive one, and one only golden rule of conduct, that of making things easy, and so of voting down principle whenever principle becomes unwelcome or exacting? There are many people to be met with who evidently take this view of life in perfect good faith; they have no principles at all, or none, at any rate, which they care to defend or to make sacrifices for; their one object is to avoid that kind of discomfort which arises from a sense of social collision; and so they go about the world bowing and smiling their unmeaning compliments to all its gathered incompatibilities whom they may chance to meet on their way, and whatever else may be said of them, this most assuredly may be said of them, that they are very amiable people. Undoubtedly such persons are easier to get on with than those who look upon the society of their fellow-men as affording them the same sort of opportunity for distinction which a sea captain might discern in the neighbourhood of a hostile fleet; they are entitled, beyond doubt, to this negative sort of praise, but the question is whether they exert any attractive power upon the heart, and that question can assuredly be answered only in one way. My brethren, what is it we want, all of us, in those whom we really love and respect? If we know anything about ourselves we know this, that we are each of us at times weak, unstable, swayed hither and thither by gusts of feeling, of opinion, of passion, by vacillations, of which in our better moments we are ashamed; and therefore, in our Lord's words, we do not go out into the wilderness voluntarily to see a "reed shaken with the wind." We are, most of us, too familiar with that spectacle at home, to make any efforts whatever to study it abroad. That which really draws us to itself is the sight of a man who knows the value of truth, and who is strong in knowing it—strong enough to be perfectly courteous to its opponents, and to be, withal, entirely unyielding; strong enough to resist the delicate blandishments as well as the calculated ferocities of error or of vice; strong enough to feel that he can afford to be, and that he is bound to be, considerate and tender, and so by this exhibition of a strength in which you and I know ourselves to be so lamentably deficient drawing us to lean on him in quest of a support which we do not find in ourselves. No, most assuredly. If St. John the Baptist had been the man to make himself agreeable under all circumstances to a king like Herod Antipas, the multitudes would never, never have troubled themselves to go out into the wilderness to see him. Are we, then, generally attracted by the attributes of high station and position? John the Baptist was a man of good family. Was it a man "clothed in soft raiment" who drew the Jewish multitudes from their homes into the desert at the time referred to by our Lord? There can be no question, brethren, as to the attractive power of high station and of the circumstances that encompass it in the case, at least, of the great majority of men. Few persons, I apprehend, are really insensible to their influence, and, generally speaking, those men are least of all insensible to it who go out of their way most ostentatiously to disclaim it. Nor is such an influence to be accounted for by supposing that the great and powerful are only sought after for the sake of what can be got out of them. This vulgar explanation of their influence goes a very short way towards accounting for the facts, since we find that in all ages and countries royalty commands the homage of multitudes who never could expect to add one penny to their resources from the bounty of a sovereign. And in truth, the sentiment in question appeals not to the commercial instinct of making money and getting on, but to a wholly disinterested sense and conception of what is involved in what we call a great position. A great position! —it is the product of some form of human enterprise in bygone days which represents the valour, or the wisdom, or, at least, the perseverance, of some among those whom we call the dead. It has accumulated with the lapse of years a vast assortment of associations, each one of which adds to it some new claim upon the feeling of the people; it has been consecrated, we may dare to say, at least in some sense, by the protecting and upholding hand of God; and so it comes down to us as a royal dynasty, or as a great family enriched with a thousand subtle but imperious recommendations. And as we look, you and I, on the man "clothed in soft raiment," we yield to him at least, and quite ungrudgingly, a corner in our hearts. And yet, does he really take possession of us? Surely not. His life may be in contradiction to the ideal expectations that are raised by his position, and where this is not the case, reflection here, as in other matters, if not entirely undoing the work of imagination, at least forces us to keep imagination in check.

After all, what we seek in our most solemn moments is not the position but the man; not the soft raiment, but the mind and heart and will that underlie it. The position —it is not the real man, it is merely the decoration outside the man, and when we have stripped it off, and have looked at what lies beneath we find perhaps what we find elsewhere, what we are conscious of within ourselves—a timid, forlorn soul shivering as it gazes up at the justice and the magnificence of God, and as little able as ourselves to give the sort of satisfaction that is most needed by the human heart and will. No, dear brethren, if we leave our ordinary occupations, if we go out into the wilderness of thought, it is not to see a man clothed in soft raiment. Such persons, as our Lord says, are found elsewhere; they live in kings' houses, they have their own due and assured range of influence and consideration, but it does not include the recesses of the heart.

Is it, then, mental power which most powerfully affects us? Is it some great endowment which at once places a human mind in a rank high above its fellows, whether it be strength of reason or wealth of imagination, or retentiveness of memory, or subtlety and delicacy of intellectual touch?

Certainly, brethren, many a man bows down to intellect who would shrink from being supposed to care for station or for wealth. Intellect, he says to himself, is part of the man himself. Intellect is not like station or wealth—a mere adjunct, contributing nothing to make the man what he really is. Intellect is the most conspicuous ingredient in the composition of the man; intellect, above all things, is power. Sometimes it is power of the very highest order, having decisive influence upon human affairs. Intellect may well, then, he says, prove a powerful attraction, and the gift of prophecy, although spiritually conferred, was in its exercise an intellectual gift which charmed and swayed the minds of men by the play of thought which was involved in its expression, and this was why our Lord asked His hearers whether they went out into the wilderness to see the popular prophet as if in quest of a form, a rare form, of mental enjoyment. Intellect, no doubt, my brethren, is attractive, but the attraction is wanting both in power and in universality. It is not a universal attraction, since, to do justice to intellect, there must be mind enough to take stock of what it is and of what it achieves; and most of us make no pretension to be, in this sense, intellectual. And it is not a very powerful attraction. There are large regions of our nature, and those often the most interesting regions, which intellect does not even remotely touch. How often do we see intellect triumphantly silencing adverse argument, yet quite unable to produce conviction; the truth being that although no answer seems to be forthcoming, there is within the soul a whisper that there is an answer if it could only at the moment be produced. And this whisper proceeds from a district of the soul for which mere intellect has made, and can make, no sort of provision whatever— that district is spirit. Just as real a department of the soul's life as is that in which intellect lives and works; just as real, but only a much higher one.

There were simple Christians in Paris who had no chance in conversation with a master of profane repartee like Voltaire, but then his brilliant sarcasms left them just where they were, because they did not even touch that region of spiritual instinct in which, as in a native atmosphere, faith and love flourish and grow. The truth is, that intellect often forfeits its legitimate power through being divorced from goodness. There is no necessary connection whatever between goodness and the very highest intellectual gifts. Balaam is an instance of lofty prophetic insight joined to a fatal obliquity or weakness of moral character; he died fighting against that truth which he had defended and proclaimed. Bacon, the father of the inductive philosophy, is a sample of the highest scientific intellect, and yet we almost wish that he could have been, for the credit of intellect itself, less wise than he was, if he could not have been less mean. And not to insist upon other instances, what a conspicuous example of this truth is afforded by the great writer who, perhaps more than any other man, has formed the modern mind of Germany. All the world knows that Goethe's works sparkle with an originality that is all his own, and yet it is difficult to name a book that leaves us with a more melancholy impression of the tyrannical and deliberate selfishness of a human character than Goethe's autobiography. Goethe is all very well for educating taste, for stimulating and for refining thought so long as the heart and its needs are kept out of the way, and all that is highest and deepest in life is not in question; but in times of real seriousness or real sorrow Goethe would be intolerable; his cold and polished acuteness says nothing whatever to the finest elements of the soul of man. And here he differs conspicuously from our own Shakespeare—Shakespeare, in whom intellect is constantly in felt alliance with higher qualities, and whose majestic language stutters once and again as he feels himself on the confines of a higher world, as if in instinctive deference to a truth or to a beauty which it is beyond the power of human thought to reach.

But in all probability there is no created intellect so acute, so trained, so endowed with all the apparatus of knowledge, so vast in its capacity, and withal so intense in its power of concentrated application, as is that of the evil and apostate spirit—the king of the children of pride. For many thousand years he has been observing, inferring, correcting his observations and his inferences, accumulating knowledge in a vast field of experience which is only less than infinite ; profiting by man's wisdom, profiting by man's success as well as by man's failure and his folly ; and thus becoming, by a process of unarrested growth, a being of mental powers to which there can, from the nature of the case, be no parallel among the sons of men. And yet when we think of his relation to the all-holy and loving God, of his will stiffened by ancient persistence into determined and irrevocable opposition, and the whole volume of desire in his nature changed from love into a current of malignant hatred, we see how consummate intellectual endowments only in this case enhance our reasons for utterly shrinking from his dreadful approach. No, intellect is not of itself attractive, at least in the long run, and if the multitudes went out into the wilderness to see the last of the prophets, it was because if a prophet, he was more than a prophet, because there was that about him which threw even his great prophetic endowments into the shadow, while it drew to him the inmost hearts of men.

" More than a prophet ! " What was it, this something which transcended thus the highest gifts, and which lured the Jewish multitudes from their homes into the desert ? Was it the report of a supernatural birth ? Was it the spectacle of a hard ascetic life ? Was it the firmness of a great character, the simple majesty of a nature that was conscious of a single aim and indifferent to all besides ? These things, no doubt, had their weight, but beyond them there was the feeling which is always inspired by a great religious soul of whose consistency we are well assured, but which we only half understand. Such a character lives and moves before us evidently in constant communion with God while shrouding from the public eye much which our curiosity would fain, if it could, explore. All this reserve of spiritual power in St. John, his hermit life in the desert, his wild food, his dress of camel's hair, were aptly suggestive ; they showed that this side of existence was repressed for the sake of the other and the higher side, and that to

St. John the other was incomparable, and always the vaster and the more real. Without analysing their feelings, the multitudes felt that in coming near to John the Baptist they were like men who stood at the base of a mountain which buries its summit in the clouds of heaven. Instinctively they knew that a man of no common mould was there, and that he was worth understanding if he only could be understood. This reserve, I say, is inevitable in the case of every great servant of God, and it is a reason, generally it is the main reason, of his attractive force over others. We, too, moral pigmies as we are—we, too, long to catch a glimpse of that greater world in which God's spiritual aristocracy lives and works. We listen for the distant echo of its secrets; we are irresistibly drawn to crave such fellowship with it as we can, if only because it touches a chord in our souls which reminds us that we, too, each one of us, are created for the infinite being, and have before us, if we only will, a destiny of boundless magnificence. It was this quality in St. John which our Lord desired to suggest to the minds of those who listened to him; for if they did understand that, there would be no danger of their thinking that John was a prophet who had been discredited by the cessation of his public utterances or by his imprisonment. If John was a prophet, it mattered little from this point of view whether he still prophesied or not. If John's body was detained by the bars and bolts of the prison house by the lake, those bars and bolts could not confine the activities or narrow the range of his majestic soul; they could only at their best illustrate the puny impotence of the world of sense when it provokes a conflict with the sublime aspirations and convictions of the world of spirit. It was this quality in St. John which explained his office as our Lord's precursor. "Yea, I say unto you, and more than a prophet. For this is he of whom it is written, Behold, I send My messenger before Thy face which shall prepare Thy way before Thee." In truth, such a character as the Baptist's raised expectations which from the nature of the case it could not satisfy; it pointed upwards to the infinite and to the perfect; but as men gazed into the vast azure all became before their eyes vague and indistinct, and the soul fell back upon the dull, concrete realities of everyday existence. If the work of St. John was to be completed and sustained, another and a higher presence was needed—a presence so real, so certain, and yet so unassailable in its majestic beauty that in it the human heart would really find the perfect satisfaction of its highest hopes. It is this quality, depend upon it, dear brethren, which to the end of time explains the attractive power of Churches and of men. Churches do not draw us into communion with them when they ostentatiously profess to have no positive doctrines, and to be only anxious to secure adherents; they do not draw us by the high station of their chief ministers, or even by the intellectual endowments of their most distinguished representatives. The human soul seeks in the Church of God something more than a "reed shaken with the wind," something more than a man clothed in the softest raiment, something more than even an intellectually gifted prophet,—it seeks that felt but indescribable touch of a higher world, which lifts it right above the trivialities of this,—it seeks a temple the threshold of which it may cross, but whose sanctuary lies far away in the bosom of the infinite,—it seeks a life the Divine pulses of which it knows to issue from an invisible heart; but, above all, it seeks that which will lead it itself most effectually, most intimately, to Him its Lord and its God, who alone can satisfy the deep, mysterious yearnings with which He has endowed it. And as with Churches so with men. It is not the easy-going, it is not the highly-placed, it is not the intellectual who win our hearts. The men who really take us captive are the saintly. They take us out of ourselves; they draw us into the wilderness, into some solitude of thought where the common associations of life are not; and then, without a word, by the mere power of their example, they bid us look upwards if we would understand what they are—look upwards beyond themselves to the strength and secret of their life, to Jesus Christ, God and man, incarnate, crucified, risen, ascended. Divine prerogative thus to prepare the way of the Lord! Oh happiness undeserved, unutterable, thus to be drawn to Him, though it be by influences which we only half understand ourselves, and which the world will never understand, and probably will always persecute until all things become clear in the presence of the Judge!

H. P. L.

III. **Trusting in Jesus.** MATT. xi. 25-30. *"I thank Thee, O Father, Lord of heaven and earth, because Thou hast hid these things from the wise and prudent, and hast revealed them unto babes. Even so, Father: for so it seemed good in Thy sight. All things are delivered unto Me of My Father: and no man knoweth the Son, but the Father; neither knoweth any man the Father, save the Son, and he to whomsoever the Son will reveal Him. Come unto Me, all ye that labour and are heavy laden, and I will give you rest. Take My yoke upon you, and learn of Me, for I am meek and lowly in heart: and ye shall find rest unto your souls. For My yoke is easy, and My burden is light."*

OUR Lord Jesus Christ comes before us in this remarkable passage, giving utterance both to His sorrow and to His joy amidst the encouragements and discouragements of His ministry. The passage, or at least the former part of it, is found also in St. Luke's Gospel, although there it stands in a somewhat different connection. There we are told that Jesus uttered the words on the return of the Seventy from their mission; there it is said that He rejoiced in spirit when He heard the tidings of their success, and expressed His joy in these memorable words, "I thank Thee, O Father, Lord of heaven and earth, that Thou hast hid these things from the wise and prudent, and hast revealed them unto babes." Here, on the other hand, they stand in close connection with thoughts of sadness and feelings of depression. He is thinking of His work in the world, and of the way in which it has been received. Culture, fashion, intellect, religious profession, all that is most powerful and all that is most worldly-wise, and all that is most esteemed among men disregards and rejects Him. He is, at the moment, absolutely alone. The voice of His forerunner is silent; the Baptist is languishing in his prison, and even he seems to have misunderstood the Christ to whom he was to bear witness. Jesus has wrought many mighty works in the cities of His native land, but who would listen to so humble a teacher? If he had come as a philosopher or as a rabbi, if he had come with some pretension to the wisdom of the schools or as some teacher of asceticism clothed in sackcloth garb, and with the austere sanctity of a prophet, then they might have listened to Him ; as it was they put Him on one side, and went one to his farm and the other to his merchandise ; for what heed need the wise or the wealthy give to the Carpenter's Son ? And what is the thought that sustains Him as He looks on the apparent failure of His mission ? Where is His consolation in the midst of reflections such as these ? It is that which marks all His ministry—absolute, unhesitating submission to His Father's will; His sorrow is turned into joy as He rests in that supreme will which governs all things, both in heaven and in earth, "I thank Thee, O Father, Lord of heaven and earth, because Thou hast hid these things from the wise and prudent, and hast revealed them unto babes. Even so, Father, for so it seemed good in Thy sight."

In the words I have chosen for my text, our Lord propounds, first of all, the two great laws of His kingdom, and then, as the Sovereign of that kingdom, He issues His gracious invitation. The first law is that which declares that the revelation of God can only be received by the child-like heart, and the second is that God can only be known as He has been pleased to reveal Himself in His Son, Jesus Christ our Lord. The first law of God's kingdom, I say, is this, that God's revelation of Himself is made, not to man's pride, but to man's humility; not to the intellect, arrogantly asserting itself, but to the candid, unprejudiced, childlike temper, to the receptive spirit which is willing to accept the teaching of God ; not to those " who are wise in their own eyes, and prudent in their own sight," but to those who have simple, unprejudiced minds—children crying for the light, and with no language but a cry ; not to those who say, "We have the truth, and others have it not," but to those who long after wisdom, which they feel they have not, and search for it as for hid treasures ; to those who, because they are poor shall be made rich, and because they hunger after righteousness shall be filled. And our Lord rejoiced in spirit as He beheld the moral beauty of this Divine order whereby the hungry are filled with good things, whilst the rich are sent empty away. Christ our Lord did not rejoice because the wise and the prudent failed to understand His revelation. We know, and we thank God for it, that some of the greatest in this world in intellect and in knowledge have also been the foremost and the truest of Christ's disciples; but Christ did rejoice in the thought that it was not by wisdom nor by prudence that man found out God. He rejoiced because He saw the humble and the contrite spirit cleaving to the dust under a sense of its own defilement and sin, lifted up to God, and filled with the light and peace of His Spirit; He rejoiced because he saw this righteous law, written in letters of light over the portals of His kingdom: "Except ye be converted and become as little children, ye shall in no wise enter therein."

But while I have been insisting that it is this Divine law, this Divine order of the world, which called forth our Lord's thankful acknowledgments, you will remind me that He does not here seem to speak of a law. He says, "Thou hast hidden." You will say, "Is not that an arbitrary act? Is it not plain that God has interfered to prevent certain persons from attaining a knowledge of salvation? I know there are those who would cut the knot of all difficulties by a bare reference to the sovereignty of God, but I cannot understand how such a sovereignty differs from the caprice of an arbitrary tyrant." I should be very sorry to suppose that the constitution of the world, of the moral government of the world, were not in the hands of supreme wisdom and love; and if you once admit this, I conceive it matters very little whether you attribute the facts and phenomena of life to the general course of God's providence, or whether you attribute them to the immediate operation of His fingers; it matters little whether you say, "God has done this," or whether you say "this happens as the consequence of the laws by which God governs the world." It matters little, for instance, whether you say, "God hardened Pharaoh's heart," or whether you say, "God has so constituted human nature that if a man persists in wilful rebellion against Him he most assuredly hardens his own heart." And so it matters very little whether you say, "God has hid these things from the wise and prudent," or whether you say, "The wise of understanding will not stoop to God's revelation, and, thinking themselves wiser than God, have drawn a veil over their own eyes, so that those things which pertain to their everlasting welfare are hid from their sight."

Here, then, we see the first law of Christ's kingdom. If any man will enter therein he must enter, not, indeed, by ignoring his intellect, but by putting his intellect in its right place, by doing under religious conditions exactly what men have found to be their true wisdom under physical conditions; not beginning with the assertion that the world ought to be this or ought to be that, and then bending facts to their theory, but sitting down reverently and considering what God would teach them by the facts that lie at their feet. If a man would become wise he must first be a fool that he may become wise. And so it is with God's revelation of Himself in Christ. Whether it be a revelation of Himself in nature, or whether it be a revelation of Himself in His written law, in both cases, it is true, we must receive the revelation as a little child—" Even so, Father, for so it seemed good in Thy sight." This is the first law of Christ's kingdom—" He who would enter therein must enter as a little child." And, brethren, would we have it otherwise? Would you have it left to the exercise of man's intellectual powers to find out God and determine the nature and the limits of revelation? Would you have it be a privilege of the great discoverer or of the wise philosopher to tell the world what they are to believe about God? I say nothing of the imperfections of the human mind or of the terrible moral perversions of the human heart which most cloud men's thoughts of God, and drive them, as it has driven them in all ages, to make God the creature of their own baseness, their own imperfection, their own sin. I say, would we rebel against this law of Christ's kingdom? Would we have this honour put upon man's intellect, and this the sign of its eminence and greatness—that it shall need no help from above; that religion, like philosophy, or art, or science, shall spring from the brain of man? Ah! my brethren, what then will become of the poor, the simple, and the suffering? What then will become of those who lack the intellectual capacity to grasp the high truths which arrogant and self-satisfied reason holds up? What would become of those vast crowds who plod along the dusty highways of the world, carrying each his weary burden of work, and sorrow, and toil? They cannot explore theories, they cannot study systems, they cannot construct theologies, they cannot follow elaborate proofs;

they need the message of a Father's love, they want the sunshine which will stream in upon their hearts and light up their daily lives; they need for their spiritual being, for its temptations, its struggles, its griefs, the same beneficent provision which is made for them in the world of nature. The sunshine and the rain are God's gifts to man by which he lives; they are not in man's power to summon or to destroy.

And now, what is the second law of Christ's kingdom? All that would know God can only know Him as He has revealed Himself in Jesus Christ. There is no other way; He is the perfect and absolute revelation of God. He is one with the Father in His Divine pre-existence, and one with us as having taken our nature in the Virgin's womb; all other revelations of God have been only fragments and syllables of truth; they waited for their completion and fulfilment in Him who was the Incarnate Word. In Christ there has been made, once for all, a perfect and final revelation, to which nothing can be added, and from which nothing can be taken away. And it is just this, brethren, which it is so necessary to insist upon; for men will accept anything but this. They will not accept it, because it rebukes their pride, and compels their submission. Christ, a teacher, came from God, like other teachers, that they will allow—not Christ the Eternal Light, who lighteth every man that cometh into the world. Christ, the beautiful and all but perfect, whose life may be gently criticised and whose death they profess to admire—not Christ the spotless Lamb, the sacrifice for human sin. Christ, the martyr, sealing with His blood the truths which He proclaimed—not Christ the victim and the Priest, through whom alone, man, guilty and sinful, can draw near to God. And yet this is a revelation which we are bound to proclaim. Christ came to manifest God in human flesh. Christ came by His precious blood-shedding to put away for ever human sin; Christ came to open Heaven to all believers; Christ came that, having accomplished man's redemption by His death, He might rise again from the grave the Lord of Life, and ascend into Heaven and live there for ever to plead man's cause with the Father. In Christ, God is manifested to man; through Christ, man can come near unto God.

These, then, are the two great laws of Christ's Kingdom; these that called forth the acknowledgment of our Lord in His communion with the Father, "I thank Thee, O Father, Lord of heaven and earth, because Thou hast hid these things from the wise and prudent, and hast revealed them unto babes. Even so, Father, for so it seemed good in Thy sight. All things are delivered unto Me of My Father: and no man knoweth the Son, but the Father; neither knoweth any man the Father, save the Son, and he to whomsoever the Son will reveal Him."

And, now, following on these two great laws of His kingdom, comes the gracious invitation, "Come unto Me all ye that labour and are heavy laden, and I will give you rest." And what shall I say of these words, brethren? Shall I call them most human, or most Divine? Certainly they are most Divine. Put these words into the mouth of an apostle, and then you will feel what I mean. Let the saintliest, purest, noblest, most loving, and most truly inspired of God's messengers to man, address you in words like these—let a St. Paul or a St. John say unto you, "Come unto me, and I will give you rest," and how many of you would listen to the invitation? Would you not recoil from the human teacher who gave you such a promise,—a rest? Would you not feel instinctively that it must be treacherous on his lips? You cannot trust man; you cannot find rest in man; none but God can say to you, unless in mockery, "Come unto me, and learn of me, and you shall find rest unto your souls." My brethren, if I were asked to point out one passage in the whole of the Gospel which should teach most plainly, which should bring home to the heart most consolingly, the precious truth of the divinity of Christ our Lord, I would choose this; and I would choose it not because of the sublime acknowledgment which it contains of the eternal righteousness of the Father, not because of the sublime witness which it bears to the perfect and intimate union between the Father and the Son, but because of the sublime invitation which falls from the lips of Him who speaks as man never spake, saying, "Come unto Me." I say these words are most truly Divine. He who utters them, utters them in the full consciousness that all things are delivered unto Him of the Father. I see here, God interpreting Himself;

I see in these words the answer to all cavils against the righteousness of God ; I see here the true expounding of the law of His kingdom. But I say, also, these words are most assuredly human. This invitation, so full of Divine power and grace, is also full of human tenderness and pity; so soothing in their matchless sympathy, so precious to the poor, struggling, fainting, human heart is every syllable of that invitation, "Come unto Me." Why ? "Not because I am the Lord of angels and of men ; not because I have all power in heaven and in earth ; not because resistance to Me is vain, and submission to Me is necessary ; but come unto Me, for I am meek and lowly of heart, and ye shall find rest unto your souls." Blessed words ! Sweet as the dews of heaven, precious as the droppings of a summer cloud ! for they fall from human lips, they are the words of One who has wept as you have wept, and whose heart has been wrung with anguish as your heart has been wrung with anguish, He who bids you bring to Him the burden of your sorrow and the burden of your sin, and gives you His precious promise of rest, is One who has taken upon Him your nature, with all its varied experience. There is not a grief that He has not felt, there is not a load beneath which He has not stooped, there is not a temptation which He has not met with. He knows your frame, and He knows it, not only with the omniscience of God, but He knows it with all the loving, tender sympathy of a human friend. He has borne our griefs, He has carried our sorrows, He has suffered being tempted ; He can be touched with the feeling of our infirmities, for they are His.

Mark the largeness of the invitation : " Come unto Me all ye that labour." That invitation is wide as the world and large as the ages. That invitation reaches to every phase of human life ; for where is the life that does not confess its weariness and long for rest ? Where is the man, when he has left the haven of his childhood behind him and has launched upon the stormy ocean of life, who does not feel the weariness of the uneasy tossing of the billows, and long for rest ? Is not the sadness and the weariness of life the constant complaint even of those whom we might be disposed to think most free from the troubles of life ? Men who have been admired and flattered by the world, men who have been happy in their families and beloved and applauded by their friends, cannot repress the cry which goes up from their hearts, as they look upon life and think how weary a burden it is. "I have run nearly to the length of my tether," writes one; "I have grown old, and apathetic, and stupid. All I care for in the way of personal enjoyment is quiet ease, with nothing to do, nothing to think of. My only glance is backward; there is so little before me, that I would rather not look that way."

But that invitation is yet more. It might be large, it might be wide—and yet it might not be winning; the accents might be kingly, but they might be cold and awful, and we might fear to obey them; but here is the blessedness of Christ's invitation—not only its freedom, but the certainty that none can be rejected, none can be misunderstood. "Come unto Me, for I am meek and lowly of heart." Who shall fear to come unto One who thus invites them? It is not so with any child of man. Take your burdens to men, and what will you find? If you are poor, you will find no sympathy, or, at best, but an awkward sympathy from the rich; for they have never been in your place, and therefore, with the best intentions, they cannot fully understand you. If you are in pain a few commonplace words of condolence is all that you can expect from those who are in health; if you are unhappy, if you are miserable, and tell your grief, you may have the shame of feeling that you have bared your bosom to one who could not enter into your feelings; if you are tormented by doubt, where should you carry your perplexity? Your religious friends will suspect you or turn away from you, or perhaps call the anguish of your heart "infidelity." If you are bowed down by a sense of guilt, to whom shall you tell your tale of shame? To the hard judges who in their Pharisaic righteousness can make no allowance for the power of temptation? You shrink from a human judge; you know that you must have either his merciless condemnation or, what is equally bad, his indulgent allowance. Where should you go? Sin lies like a burden upon you, crushing, heart-withering; and you exclaim in the bitterness of your soul, "My iniquities are more in number than the hairs of my head, and my heart has failed me." Who shall help you? You dare not go to God—He is a judge of purer eyes than to behold iniquity; He is a Spirit dwelling in light unapproachable. Who shall bring God near to you? Who shall take away your fear? Man is like yourself—hard in judgment and weak to help; but Christ says, "Come unto Me. I am the perfect revelation of God, come unto Me." Then it is that, repulsed on all sides, lonely and helpless, we turn to Him whose mighty heart understands and feels all; then it is that the soul hearing in the stillness that voice, which says, "Come unto Me," answers, "To Thee, Lord, will I come. Thou callest the weary and the heavy laden, and I am weary—weary with my sin, weary with the conflict of life, weary with my load of unbelief, weary with my temptations, weary with my struggles, weary with my fears, weary with my sorrows, weary with my despair, and I bring all to Thee; for Thou art meek and lowly of heart. I bring all to Thee, for Thou hast promised me rest. Lord, I come to Thee, give rest to my soul." And that rest Christ does give. His promise is not a deceitful promise; He does take away our weariness of life, He does fill the heart with His own mighty peace. But He does so, dear friends, remember, on one condition. Oh, do not let us in wilfulness hide that condition from ourselves. Christ says, " I will give you rest," but He says also, " Take My yoke upon you, and learn of Me." Yes, brethren, it is a yoke and it is a burden which Christ asks us to take up. It is a yoke to lay a restraint upon our natural inclinations, to mortify self, to crucify the flesh with its affections and lusts, to watch over our desires, to curb our unruly, peevish, and irritable tempers; it is a yoke, when we are naturally fretful, when we are naturally proud and overbearing, to give up our own will and our own way, when we are naturally bent upon having our own will and following our own way. It is a yoke to have to say to ourselves day by day, " I will follow a Master who bore for me shame and spitting, the crown of thorns, and the cross, and I must forego my own selfish desires, and my own will, and my own pleasures, and I must be as He was ;" it is a burden to feel the flesh lusting against the spirit, and to know that when we would do good evil is present with us. Not a day can pass without a conflict which, alas! too often brings to us defeat. It is a burden to find by painful experience that when the spirit is willing the flesh is weak; to kneel in prayer and to be chilled and weighed down in heart, instead of rising, as on eagles' wings, towards heaven. It is a burden to see our efforts baffled, our good evilly spoken of, our motives misunderstood, our character maligned; it is a burden to feel that after all we make but little progress ourselves, that we get but a very little nearer heaven, and that others seem little better for our words or for our example.

And yet this yoke is easy and this burden is light, and to have this yoke and this burden is to have the mind of Christ and of God; it is to be on the side of truth and purity and gentleness and goodness and love, in the great battle against wrong and wickedness and selfishness in every form. There is no deeper joy than the joy of self-sacrifice, the joy of self-conquest. Struggle? Yes. Pain? Yes. Weariness? Yes. But their triumph that no words can paint, victory beyond that of kings and of armies—a joy so Divine that it is a foretaste of heaven. This is Christ's yoke, this is Christ's burden. If we take up that yoke and that burden, we shall find that His blessed promise of rest will come to our souls. O, dear friends, He is speaking to you now, and is uttering His invitation now; He is here in the midst of this great congregation, here in the midst of this great city with all its eager, jostling crowds, with all its sin, its folly, its splendour, its crime. He stands, as He has stood for centuries, and still He says with that awful and piercing yet, withal, loving and tender voice—"Come unto Me." Oh, listen to His words, accept His invitation, and then you shall enter into His joy, you shall be made free with His blessed freedom, the burden which presseth upon you now shall be taken away, life shall no more be weariness—"you shall find rest unto your souls."

J. J. S. P.

IV Christ Speaking in Parables. MATT. xiii. 1–3, 10–36.

"*The same day went Jesus out of the house, and sat by the sea side. And great multitudes were gathered together unto Him, so that He went into a ship and sat; and the whole multitude stood on the shore. And He spake many things unto them in parables, saying, etc."*

THE time is especially important and significant here. It was the same day on which Jesus had come to words with the Pharisees of Jerusalem about the cure of demonia. For the first time they charged Him with being inspired by the Evil One. He retorted the charge with what we might call fearful distinctness. Nor is this all. By a touching coincidence when this rupture took place, while the words were on His lips, His mother and brethren came that they might take charge of Him—as they said because He was beside himself. The *same day* Jesus sat by the sea side, sad and alone. Many sorrowful reflections passed through His mind, perhaps, as He watched the pebbles on the seashore, of the result of so much sowing for so little fruit. This had been the result up to then of His ministry.

But the crowds now gathered for instruction, and He went up on a fishing-boat, upon the sunny water, and the people stood by the seashore. And He spake many words that afternoon, but not like other times, for lo! as He opened His mouth He spake in parables. Not pious words, such as the people were wont to hear uttered by those gracious lips, but strange words about treasure, corn and seeds. When He had ended all these sayings, and without a word of explanation, He left them astonished—"for without a parable spake He not unto them." His disciples were confounded for they had never heard Him speak thus before, and as they felt incapable of taking the fruit from the husks, as it were, they sought an explanation; and so when they were alone with Him, their first question was, "Why speakest Thou to them in parables?" and their second question was, "What might this parable be?"

Brethren, there was a deep reason for this change of method. This marks a change in His teaching, it marks a turn in the career of Jesus. The parable had its adaptation, but before we seek to explain this, let us see what are the peculiarities of parabolic teaching. The parable belongs to a class of discourse which has always been familiar in Western Asia. In the Old Testament we have the parable of Nathan, etc.; the veiled, the historical type, the symbol, the entire language of active metaphor—all these abound in Biblical and historical literature. But Jesus so adapted the parable, and wrought it to such a point of beauty that, regarded from the literary standpoint alone, His are the only parables we care to remember. Once or twice it breaks into the allegoric. It is always related in its earthly covering to the spiritual truth it is intended to typify. It takes the widest range; any fact in nature, such as the progress of vegetable growth, or anything in human life, like a supper or a banquet, all these are available for the purposes of parabolic teaching. Only the incident narrated must be possible. It may be a narrative fact, though it does not necessarily follow that it should be so. It must however be true to the facts of nature. But beneath all this lies the real meaning, the religious truth; in other words, the fact or incident of the spiritual world. This is what underlies the outward statement. Only when this is got at is the parable useful; unless you grasp the Divine truth within, it is useless.

Now it is very plainly a most gracious act to begin with, for the Lord Jesus to speak to us men in such accommodation to our earthly speech; and we shall be struck to find that the incidents on which these parables are based are of the homeliest—marriage, fishing, service, the judge, the housewife, and the debtor. Common references and the plainest things, always in order that they might reach the lowest understandings.

It is well for us to mark the value of this parabolic use of the world we live in. Did Jesus put gospel ideas into the natural life of plants and men, or did He only bring these ideas out? Was He the inspirer of nature or only her interpreter? It seems to me quite clear that He spoke here not as the Maker of nature, but as the Son of Man; and that He read from the pages of God's creation lessons which had been written from the beginning—written there, indeed, by His own fingers. As the Maker of nature He inspired these things, but as the Son of Man He interpreted them. Some things which had been written from the foundation of the world did He reveal, but which before men had not seen; while the earth kept in trust that which God had committed to her from the first but which she was prepared to yield up. The parable-making of our Lord was, therefore, no mere witty or skilful application of ideal metaphors. It is quite true that symbols in the hands of priests have often degenerated into this. It is true that a debased poetry has sometimes spoken in this manner. But Jesus did not find any significance in these things which He had not Himself put therein. His words only spoke back to Him His own created thought. If the sun shone on Him every morning enlightening the world ; if the vine by His mother's door showed how the people were to bear fruit unto Himself ; if the corn seeds which He, a Syrian peasant, saw His fellow peasants scatter in the fallow, breathed unto Him the story of the good see[d] which He was scattering, it was because He made the[m] capable of speaking. Constructing nature and human li[fe] on parallel principles with human views, He did that o[f] purpose that His own moral government might be merge[d] into the homes of families. We are still very far now fro[m] seeing the truths which nature is ready to show forth. Would that it might be the result of our time, with its keenness of scientific enquiry, to read these things in nature, and to render to Christ the things which are Christ's ; but in the meantime let us each try for his own part to do justice to that universal typology of the earth on which our Lord's parables repose. So may we also learn by the few specimens He has interpreted for us to spell out for ourselves a few more syllables in that Divine hieroglyph in which God speaks to us, that we may behold His glory in meat and clothes, in grass and tree, in every common thing.

Now it lies in the nature of a parable, if we understand aright, that it should exert a double action upon those who hear it, and this is the peculiar use of our Lord's parables. When the earthly parable is made a medium of showing forth spiritual truths, it will depend upon the spiritual condition of the listener himself whether he will be helped or hindered by it. It seems to me in this respect to be meant by Christ, "He that hath ears, let him hear," because this kind of speech needs a special kind of hearing. Let a man have only a fleshly mind and he will hear only the husk— a story about plants or men or sheep—and will have no mind for deeper lessons. He cares to listen to no more. But the divinely opened ear of religious faith and spiritual understanding perceives beneath the spoken words an unspoken idea, or he suspects a Divine meaning and is stirred to search for it, and thus he learns lessons of truth that are spoken to the ear of the spirit. Now once you have this inner ear, you hear that meaning of God better in the parable than if it had been spoken in a plainer form. The human interest given to the Divine truth brings it nearer to our bosoms, brings it, as it were, into our intellectual life.

The parable, therefore, is plainly by its very action upon men, an angel of judgment to one man and an angel of mercy to his neighbour. It cuts two ways, like a double-edged sword. When the soul is dead to truth, then the understanding is too dull to listen to the whispers of the spirit world, and the words of the parable spoken glide unheeded over the man—nay, they do more, they conceal the truth; because if the same thing had been plainly spoken you might have heard something; it would have given to the unspiritual man a *seeming* knowledge of the truth. But here there is nothing of this action for you. A poor little simple story suited to your earthly taste. You see the husk; to you is not given to know the inner life. But when the man has the eyes to see and the ears to hear, then he is led most graciously out of this courtyard of God's house into the holy place within, and the mysteries of the kingdom, which from the foundation of the world have been locked up, are opened and put forth into light, and the most royal principles of eternal truth are no longer disguised, and they stand forth as guests from heaven. The very veil wrapping up the truth stimulates the spiritual senses to seek to unveil; and nature for her part becomes the dearer when we trace the outline in her of the things of God.

This twofold aspect of parabolic teaching suited the purpose of our Lord. For some time He had been speaking openly to the people, and the result, as usual, had been to deaden or to quicken. A few only who wished to do the will of His Father were gathered round Him as earnest enquirers, who were open to the light and were growing in grace to receive it. And the time had come—it must come in the natural development of all spiritual movements—when especial attention was to be paid to these. The mass of the Pharisees represented by their spiritual leaders, had distinctly rejected Him by blaspheming against the Holy Ghost and ascribing His cures to demoniac agency. The time had come for what is called "a judicial blindness"—"By hearing ye shall hear and shall not understand; and seeing ye shall see and shall not perceive." This judgment is the hereditary seal of unbelief. It is repeated by John about the Jews of Judea and later by St. Paul. Five times spoken against the people, it is continued to this day.

But on the other hand not only twelve, but a considerable number besides had separated themselves from the idle crowd and from the wilfully blinded Pharisees, and this served as a test of their spiritual intelligence. They followed Him home, they clung to His skirts, they craved the opening of the parable. They knew there was more behind. Blessed were their eyes, for they saw so much of this that they longed to see and to hear more. Blessed were their ears—to those He really spoke that afternoon series of discourses. Here He virtually addresses Himself to the appreciative few in the hearing of the unappreciative crowd. As for these few, this veiled symbol was not meant to shut them out; it was meant, on the contrary, to shut them in. Dark to those who had not the seeing eye, to those on the illuminated side it shut them in the King's chamber.

Henceforth the Lord was to devote Himself on earth to the private instruction of the few, with them to go often apart, with a few of them even to be transfigured on far-off Carmel, to open up the arcana of suffering and sacrifice, to explain all things. For it is a fundamental law of the kingdom, which wraps up judgment and mercy in one, when whosoever hath of grace to him shall be given and he shall have more abundance; but whosoever hath not, from him shall be taken away even that he seemeth to have.

Now the numerous applications of this I cannot give at length just now. For example, how this world in which we live seems to be intended for a school of discipline, instinct throughout with spiritual lessons had man preserved his spiritual senses undulled, and which now speak to the ear and eye which God hath opened and which Christ hath taught. How we, sinful men with dull senses for spiritual things, are punished by walking blind and deaf in this beautiful world! Or how in like manner as the historical and symbolic types of revelation, through which you carry the earliest ideas of religion to your little child, has God taught the infancy of His Church by them. How these types become in our later years something like a blind idea to many of us. How many grown up men are in darkness of the precious truths these parables were destined to convey. The stories are there and please the old man as they did in his childhood, but they teach him not—seeing he perceives not. Year after year our mind grows indifferent to God's claim on us. There may come a time to us when plain statements of evangelical truth shall cease to convey any real sense of spiritual meaning to our minds at all, and the man, losing even what he had when he was a younger man, shall be reduced to a mere ring of empty words, the inner nature of the gospel becoming to him only a parable whose outer sense he seems to understand but whose inner power is hidden from his eyes.

But another application lies deeper, and this I must leave to your own reflection. With this I close—*Take ye heed how ye hear.*

V. The Lessons of Easter. MATT. xxviii. 5, 6. *"And the angel answered and said unto the women, Fear not ye: for I know that ye seek Jesus, which was crucified. He is not here: for He is risen, as He said. Come, see the place where the Lord lay."*

IT matters little, my brethren, what text we choose for our thoughts to-day, for the resurrection of our Blessed Lord from the dead—that great event which we to-day commemorate—includes all texts, transcends all texts. It is the full completion, the central evidence of the Christian creed; it is at once a fact which is the basis of our belief, and a revelation which is the corner-stone of our duty. In it are immediately involved the power of God, the deliverance of man, the restitution of the universe. Our faith in the forgiveness of sins, our hope in a glorious immortality, our love for a redeemed brotherhood; the redemption of the past, the ennoblement of the present, the exaltation of the future, are all involved in it. It enhances the dignity of life, it destroys the fear of death, it calms the vision of eternity. No wonder that the old Fathers of the Church call the day whereon we commemorate it the queen of festivals, the "Sunday of Rejoicing," pre-eminently and emphatically "the Lord's Day."

I trust that there is not one here present—not even the youngest, not even the most ignorant—who cannot reflect some dim gleam of its brightness, re-echo some faint music of its songs. Yet those will do so most who are truest and most faithful. It was to those holy and humble women, whose love for Christ had made them the last beside the Cross, the earliest at the Sepulchre, that the glorious tidings were first revealed; and similarly those who have felt most truly the significance of Lent will enter most heartily into the glory of Easter. But there is a natural joy in it for all. It comes with the sweetness of spring after the gloom of winter; it comes when the birds are re-awakening their song, and the trees are bursting into green leaf. Oh, may we never lose the simple joy which such sights inspire; may we all retain the simplicity of life that recognises a breath of hope and a voice of prophecy, when we mark the streaks of tender green that line the petals of the snowdrop, and see how, even from the hard clods and amid the bitter winds of March, the flowers are still able to lift their delicate loveliness, rich with fructifying gold. This is the season of the year—it is with these sweet gifts of returning spring that Easter comes to us; and it comes also after the humiliations of Lent with its lessons drawn from the darkest and most terrible warnings of Holy Writ; it comes after the deep pathetic narratives of the Cross and Passion, the Agony and Bloody Sweat, like a burst of morning splendour after the night.

Many eyes, my brethren, may look upon a precious stone, and may see the light of heaven reflected from it with flashes of different colour, but all lovely, all resplendent; even so each heart among us may catch a different and yet each a true sense of joy from the revelation of Easter. To one it comes as patience in the midst of failure; to another as consolation under bereavement; to another as the solution of all enigmas, and the end of infinite perplexity; to another as turning his whole thoughts from the vanity of earth to the sure and certain hope of heaven. And each of us has a right to each and every view of it ; but to-day I will try to bring but two of its aspects as briefly as I can before you—the sense which it inspires of faith under discouragement; the certainty which it establishes of victory over death.

I. Let us try to throw ourselves back in imagination to that first Easter morning. Fresh as we are from the records of Passion Week, we can realize something of what the disciples felt on that early dawn. What sorrow, my brethren, have we been witnessing; what infinite anguish of a Divine Deliverer! How have we seen Him, on whom the angels desire to look, reduced to tears and thirst and strong crying, and the suffering of anguish, and the death of infamy! Oh! what a scene—those three crosses upon Calvary, and Christ hanging on the cross; the Holy One numbered among transgressors; the darkness, the shame, the tumult, the horror! the Body stripped bare before the accursed multitude, with all the bruises of the Roman rods upon it ; the brow yet torn and bleeding from the bitter mockery of its thorny crown; the cruel taunts of priest and Sadducee which assailed His dying ears ; the loathly merriment of soldier and people which met His glazing eye. Oh! in that insane repulsion of absolute goodness— in that frenzied persecution of perfect love—there might well have seemed to be the final triumph of all that was falsest in the world's hypocrisy, and all that was most brutal in its hate. And imagine what a burden of unspeakable despair must have crushed the souls of the Virgin Mother, of the family of Bethany, of Mary Magdalene, of the beloved Disciple! "We knew," they would have whispered to each other in low, sad tones, "we knew His heavenly goodness, His holy power, His all-embracing love ; we trusted that this should have been He who should have redeemed Israel; but we have seen Him betrayed, buffeted, tortured, and, ah! this is the third day since we saw Him die by a malefactor's death. It is the hour of iniquity ; it is the power of darkness. Who can have any hope for love, or for truth, or for goodness any more? If He was hated, if He was defeated, if He died, surely God must have hidden Himself away in clouds and thick darkness, and for us there is nothing but desertion and despair." And then imagine the dawning sense of hope, the mighty revulsion of belief, the flood-tide of thrilling joy, the inspiring burst of rapturous conviction, the rising of the low chant into a "sevenfold chorus of hallelujahs and harping symphonies," when on that earliest Easter morning it was first whispered how, at His empty and angel-haunted sepulchre, the women had heard those blessed words, "He is not here: He is risen, as He said," and then that Mary had seen Him in the garden, and then that the Lord was risen, indeed, and had appeared unto Peter, until afterwards, in step by step of glorious revelation, He was known of them in breaking of bread, and they saw Him by the old familiar Lake, and they saw and heard Him, and their hands handled the Word of Life; and He said unto them, "Peace be unto you," and showed them His hands and His side. Ay, there in that Easter message, which is ours no than theirs, may we not see for ever that evil and cruelty and falseness and hate are rebels, and that they shall not win the day; that the serpent and the worm are not the universal conquerors; that sorrow may endure for a night, but joy cometh in the morning? Good men have died, and great men—ay, many a time—conquered it might seem, trampled under foot, in utter failure, in entire prostration, in immeasurable woe, and their work has been consumed to ashes, and their name has been debased, and the idolatrous priest, and the self-deceiving Pharisee, and the blind multitude have heaped insolence upon their end; but, for all that, here is our eternal pledge, even under gathering discouragements, of certain hope, even under present defeat, of future victory. Yes! to all the faithful, though they are not famous, to the weary vanguard in humanity's failing battle, to the forlorn hope in the combat with sin and pain, to the ungifted who yet are diligent, to the weak who yet are true, Easter comes as with the far-off sound of an archangel's trump. Your life, my brethren, lies before you; and in it many a trial, many a disappointment, many an appearance of failure, many a gallant struggle, it may be when the odds seem fearfully against you; nevertheless, choose but the right side, and you need never fear. Be this your pledge and watchword, and the motto on your flag of battle, even when its folds are rent and the hands of the standard-bearer begin to fail,—that every good deed is immortal; that every good cause must ultimately win; that others shall soar with wings where we walked with weary feet; that armies, if need be, shall spring out of our ashes, and Churches be ennobled by our blood :—

> Yes ! by all the martyrs and the dear dead Christ,
> By the long bright roll of those whom joy enticed,
> With her myriad blandishments, but could not win,
> Who would fight for victory, but would not sin.
> By these " our elder brothers who have gone before,
> And left their trail of light upon the shore,
> We can see the glory of a seeming shame,
> We can feel the triumph of an empty name!"

II. So, then, Easter teaches us faith under difficulties; and, further than this, it prophesies for us triumph over death. Again, let us try to think as they thought whose souls were dilated by the first Easter dawn. Before, they had seen the last insolent enemy obedient to the Saviour's word; they had heard His voice thrill into the dim infinitudes, and seen the kingdom of darkness give up, at His bidding, the young maiden of Cæsarea and the orphan boy of Nain, and surrender the body of Lazarus even from decay. But now, Christ was dead. Death—death the hopeless, death the final, death the impracticable—had conquered the Conqueror, and silenced the dread voice he had thrice obeyed. From the beginning of the world men had uplifted their praying hands, and women their streaming eyes, towards that dark portal through which, one after another, death had called away the souls of their beloved; but the ear of Death was dull, and from the infinite stillness of those numberless who filled the tomb no sound had come—not even one whispered answering sigh—not one faintest echo of everlasting farewells. Curtains of impenetrable mystery, gulfs of unfathomable darkness, had hid and sundered from the living those departed souls. And now, alas, for the perishing and miserable race! Death seemed to have won his final victory: and henceforth—(think of what this sorrow would have been, ye who have seen that ghostly messenger break with inexorable indifference into the circle that you loved—ye who have seen the old man bow his white hairs, or the light fade from the bright face of boy or girl, or some fair young child upon his dying bed :—

> Soft, silken primrose, fading timelessly)—

henceforth, it seemed as though the heart that has been once stilled has been stilled for ever, and the light that has been once quenched has been for ever quenched, and as though for ever around that voiceless sepulchre the sea of anguish breaks as ineffectually as the leaping and tormented billow about some lonely rock. Is it farewell, and farewell indeed for ever? And all the millions who now live upon the globe, shall they, too, die for ever, and this be the only end to their flush and bloom, to their skill and loveliness, to their majesty and power? and are those, too, dead for ever—the more in number, the countless millions of those vanished generations who once thought, and prayed, and hoped, and suffered, and loved? and is the record of humanity, indeed, but "one ever-extending pavement of gravestones, and ever-lengthening street of tombs and sepulchres;" and shall their dust be blown for ever about the desert, or sealed within the iron hills? Nay, Christ is risen; and, therefore, they too shall rise. They are not dead, but living, all these departed brothers who have been true children in the great family of God. Where, we know not, but in God's hand we know. Some lean on the bosom of their Saviour like John of old; some cast no shadow and leave no stain upon the golden streets; some stand upon the sea of glass, having the harps of God. All see the face of their Father, all have His name written on their foreheads, all have come out of great tribulation and washed white their robes in the Blood of the Lamb. And therefore, oh friend, oh father, oh brother, oh son—even, oh mother—though it is so hard, yet weep no more and sigh no more

> For the touch of a vanished hand
> And the sound of a voice that is still.

Be true, be pure, be faithful, and you too with them—if I may borrow those stately words—you too with them, "in supereminence of beatific vision, progressing the dateless and irrevoluble circles of eternity, shall clasp inseparable hands in joy and bliss in over-measure for ever." Are they dead? Nay, rather, we are the dead and they the living. They have cast off the sins of the painful body; we groan, being burdened in our house of clay. We wander in the desert; they have crossed the Jordan into the Holy Land.

We dream in the world's strange darkness; they are awake where God Himself is moon and sun. Our little boats are still tossing on the labouring sea; they are safe in the windless haven, moored to the everlasting rock!

But stop, my brethren! Have we a right to this language? May we not have forfeited these hopes? There is another death beside the natural death, another resurrection beside the resurrection of the flesh, and a hell and a heaven not only beyond, but on this side the grave. If any heart among us be tormented by its own meannesses, or cankered with its own sins; if in any heart among us there be the evil spirit of discontent, of hatred, of uncleanness, of avarice—if there be a self-disgust that works no penitence, or a self-conceit that scorns all effort at amendment—then, ah me! there is in that heart a rill of fire from the burning lake; but, thank God, on the other hand, if any of us have been striving, however feebly, after love, and purity, and peace—if any of us have been aiming, however interruptedly, to shake ourselves loose from the thick clay of our morbid vanities and base desires—if any of us have been determining, by God's grace, amid whatever failures, to rise upon the stepping-stones of our dead selves to better things—then there is in that heart a gleam of the blue of heaven and of the glory wherewith God enlightens it; there is in that heart a streak of the silvery dawn, that shall broaden and brighten into the boundless day. But let us not slide with fatal facility into appropriating to ourselves all the Christian promises, if we be living in the daily practice of all the anti-Christian sins. Yes, we shall all rise, but it may be to no joyful resurrection; or else what did St. Paul mean by describing it as his intense lifelong struggle "if by any means he might *attain* to the resurrection of the dead"? Ah, my brethren, if his life, even his life, was not sluggishly, torpidly, selfishly spent, in any sentimental conviction of his own inviolable security, can we afford to assume that—however idle we are, however selfish, however vile—we shall still be carried to heaven on angel wings? He toiled and agonized and fought, he mortified his corrupt affections, he bruised his body with blows and led it about as a slave, that so through the grave and gate of death he might pass to his joyful resurrection; and can we live anyhow—eating, drinking, sleeping, lying, slandering—and yet be saved? Read over the Collect for to-day, and note how the opening flight and burst of its exultation drops, as it were, and is hushed in the humble petition that "since God has put into our minds good desires, so by His continual help we may bring the same to good effect." Oh, let our sense of triumph end there too; let the spirit of our exultation descend, as it were, and stand with folded wings and heavenward eyes upon that humble but holy base. To the meanest, to the worst of us, God gives good desires. Oh, may we each and all cherish them tenderly as visitants from Him. The resurrection, if we view it rightly, is no sudden miracle, but a growing glory; not the reversal of our present existence, but the continuation of our spiritual life. But, if we are even now rising from death—from the death of sin, from the death of our evil hearts from the death of our uncharity, from the death of our selfishness—if, even now, we are beginning to feel and know that Christ is the Resurrection and the Life, then, indeed, we may kneel at yonder holy table with calm and happy hearts; then, indeed, with angels and archangels and all the company of heaven, we may laud and magnify God's glorious name, praising Him, in the full tide of Easter joys. For then we have a home in heaven, a hope in Christ; then we can look forward without horror, backward without despair; then the loosing of the silver cord, the breaking of the golden bowl, the shuffling off of this mortal coil, shall be but our preparation for the beatific visions of the Bridegroom's feast; then death shall be to us but a voice in heaven, saying, "Come up hither"—to regions of honour, and reality, and peace—to regions illimitably far above the follies and littleness of man—to regions where, after the storms and buffetings of a careworn and troubled life, we shall be safe and happy, and at rest for ever on the bosom of our Father and our God.

F. W. F.

VI. The Barren Fig Tree. MATT. xxi. 19. "*And when He saw a fig tree in the way, He came to it, and found nothing thereon, but leaves only, and said unto it, Let no fruit*

> *grow on thee henceforward for ever. And presently the fig tree withered away."*

THIS occurrence took place on the Monday before our Lord's crucifixion. After making His triumphal entry into Jerusalem on Palm Sunday, as we term it, He walked out in the evening of the day to sleep at the house of those well-loved friends, Lazarus and his sisters, in the quiet village of Bethany. Early on Monday morning He returned to Jerusalem, and on the road, probably, when they were near the city, He felt hungry. He saw one fig tree—such is the original expression—in the way. St. Mark adds, "afar off, and having leaves." It is clearly implied that there were other fig trees along the road, and that He fixed His attention on this one particular tree, which was distinguished from the others by having leaves at a time of year when the fig tree is bare, or only shows the first signs of what will become fruit by-and-by. In the fig tree, as you know, the fruit shows itself before the leaf, and therefore it might, perhaps, have been supposed that, beneath the leaves which made so fresh and attractive an appearance in the distance, there would be fruit, more or less nearly ripe. Our Lord came to the tree; He found nothing but leaves; and then, Lord of nature as He was, He uttered this word against the tree, "Let no fruit grow on thee henceforward for ever—no man eat fruit of thee hereafter for ever." And that some effect followed at once on our Lord's speaking, is plain from St. Matthew's report that presently the fig tree withered away. But it was only on the following morning, when they had once more walked out late to sleep at Bethany, and were again returning towards Jerusalem, that they saw the fig tree dried up from the roots.

We may feel, at the first glance, that this miracle is unlike our Lord's miracles generally,—that it raises some questions, at least, which cannot be well set aside. Let us consider them very briefly before we go to the lesson which the miracle is intended to enforce.

First of all, then, it may be asked whether this destruction of the tree does not seem to involve something like an act of injustice. Punishment implies moral responsibility, and moral responsibility is only possible in the case of a free agent. How could this tree do any act—how could it leave any duty undone—what made its destruction a moral necessity, or even a moral propriety? The tree had no will or responsibility of its own. It had leaves and not fruit, because He who gave it existence willed it to bear, in this unwonted manner, leaves and not fruit in the early spring. This fig tree, literally speaking, was just as destitute either of blame or of merit as were those lilies of the field, which our Lord held up to the admiration of his disciples, as being what they were without any effort of their own. Why, then, should the tree be treated as if it were a free agent who had been put upon his trial, and who had failed? Children, we are reminded, may vent their petty displeasure upon inanimate objects; but the master of the moral world might be expected to recognise—(so men have put it)—its true frontiers, and not to punish lower forms of life for faults which are only possible in higher existences. Nay, more than this, St. Mark incidentally observes that, when our Lord blasted the unfruitful fig tree, the time of figs was not yet. Many attempts have been made by scholars to give other meanings to these words in the original language; but there is, I apprehend, no reasonable doubt that they do mean that, at the end of March, or at the beginning of April, the season for the figs had not yet arrived. And if this be so, on what grounds of justice, we are asked, could the fig tree possibly be punished? In not bearing figs at that time, it was, surely, obeying the law of its kind. Could the Law-giver Himself blast it without some shadow of caprice—some suspicion of injustice?

Now, the supposed force of this objection is due to our treating a metaphorical expression as if it were the language of reality. When the Psalmist says that the seed of the ungodly shall be rooted out, everybody knows that he is using an expression which, literally, is only true of a vegetable, but which describes very vividly the utter destruction of a race of human beings. And conversely, we borrow words which apply, properly speaking, to human beings, and we use them when we are speaking of the animal or vegetable world; and so long as we remember that they are only metaphors, and do not properly apply to irrational or inanimate creatures, such a use of words may make our language and our thoughts more vivid, and no harm is done. Take this very word "justice." We speak of "doing justice" to a picture, when we mean justice to the artist who painted the picture. The picture itself cannot possibly be treated justly or unjustly, although we may form, as to our loss or to our gain, a true or a false estimate of its merits. Justice and injustice presuppose rights to be respected or to be violated, as the case may be, and rights, properly speaking, belong in a literal, as distinct from the metaphorical sense, only to a person.

In order to have rights, it is not enough to exist. Only a self-determining being who can produce, and can consciously possess what he produces, has rights in the complete sense of that word.

Thus, before and above all others, God has rights—rights absolute and unqualified over all His creatures, since all owe their existence to Him. And the mischief and the misery of human sin consist pre-eminently in this—that it involves a denial and a rejection of the rights of God. Man, too—every man—has such rights, because man, too, is a person. And one of the many mischiefs of slavery, for instance, is that it treats man, not as a person, but as a thing, and thus involves a denial of human rights in their most essential aspects.

But have the lower animals rights? Well, in one sense, they have. Just as they have a shadow of reason and of memory in their faculties of instinct and of association, so they have shadows of human rights. They have, at any rate, such a claim to our care and consideration, as is involved in the fact of their being God's creatures, endowed with feeling. But then, by God's appointment, these claims are subordinated, not, most certainly, to our passions or to our caprice, but to our necessities. To torture or destroy an animal out of curiosity, or spite, or pure wantonness, is to violate the law of the universe. To treat animals as intended to do human work, and to supply human food, is to observe that law; and against these last very enormous claims on the part of man, animals have no rights.

And, when we descend to the vegetable world, the case is even stronger. A tree is merely a thing. It has not a shadow of personality attaching to it; and when we talk of doing justice or injustice to a tree, we have to remember that, quite literally, these terms do not apply to anything that we can possibly do to it, and that to talk of "injustice" in blasting or cutting down a tree is good English if we are in the realms of poetry, but that it is nonsense if we are in those of moral truth. The tree is there to be made the most of by man. No moralist, so far as I know, has yet maintained that in using it to furnish our houses, or to brighten our hearths, we sin against any law of natural justice. Surely, then, if by its sudden destruction the tree can do more, much more, than minister to our bodily comfort,—if in its way it can be made to teach us a moral lesson of the first importance, there is no room for any question of injustice, unless we are to take leave of sober fact, and to bury ourselves altogether in poetry and metaphor.

Here, then, you will observe, it is necessary to dwell on the consideration that, as against our Lord, the tree had no rights,—that as St. Paul describes man in the hands of God, as clay in the hands of the potter, this description must apply with at least equal force to the lower creatures of God's hand; for even if our Lord had been only a man charged with a great and beneficent mission to mankind at large, and had destroyed a tree in order to advance one step in that mission, it would have been equally impossible to charge him with injustice, since, according to the true conception of the universe which ever subordinates what is merely material to what is moral, if a tree can be made by its destruction to illustrate a moral or spiritual truth, so far from being the object of injustice, it has distinguished honour put upon it; it does the noblest work that it can possibly do.

But if there is no injustice—if the tree had no rights— was there not in this act of our Lord a touch of severity which is, at least, unlike the characteristic mildness and beneficence of His action and bearing? There are, no doubt, my brethren, many who use this language who mean something more than it immediately implies. They wish to think that our Lord is benevolent in such sense as to have lost sight of justice—of all that is due to sin—of all that is due to the rights of God—of all the lessons that are necessary in order to enforce these solemn sides of truth. They would seem, sometimes, to have constructed in their imagination—in their literature—a kind of fancy Christ,

E

quite unlike the Christ of the gospels—a Christ warranted to bless all in this modern world, which the true Christ of the gospels must have condemned—must condemn. They have veiled His cross, it seems, from the eyes of men, for they have made it the symbol, not of an atonement for sin, but only of an act of heroism. They have respectfully removed the crown of thorns, and replaced it by a crown of roses. A Christ like this may not consistently speak a word at which a tree withers into death, and therefore the narrative has to be treated as a sort of foreign element in the text of the gospels—as a wholly anomalous and unaccountable incident which had better be passed over with a light step, as it will not bear examination.

And yet how untrue is this estimate of our Lord upon which the criticism proceeds. It is an estimate which would not really do honour to a mere man. What, brethren, is goodness? Goodness is benevolence, no doubt, among other things, but goodness is a great deal else than benevolence. Before all things, I apprehend goodness is truth, it is truth in conduct, and, as being truth, it is sometimes also justice, and, as being justice, it is sometimes also severity. One of the worst traits of the bad man in the Psalter is his moral indifference. "Neither doth he abhor anything that is evil." Easy good nature, which will not rouse itself at the cost of discomfort and even of giving pain to others, is not really goodness; it is indifference to that which goodness requires. And our Lord alike in His teaching and in His action shows Himself to be of an utterly different moral mould from this. As a Teacher, he tells men—classes of men—the sternest truths in the very plainest language. As compared with sin, He makes little account of pain. "Pluck out the right eye," He says—"cut off the right hand—sooner than sin." He reveals the sinner's doom more clearly than any one of His apostles. He does not leave it to them to proclaim the less popular side of the religion which He comes to teach. The last thing that could be said of Him with truth would be, that in Him all else gave way to a general benevolence.

But it may be asked, "Did not the tree feel?" I answer you, I do not know. Feeling, like life, is one of those mysteries of nature which lie closest to our existence here, and of the frontiers of which we know little or nothing.

Speaking broadly, feeling is an attribute of animal life; but we have all heard of plants which shrink from the touch, and it is barely possible that something analogous to feeling is to be found in plants of less sensitive organization.

Even if this be so—and here, let me repeat it, we are altogether in the region of conjecture—it is not, I submit, more cruel to destroy a plant in order to teach a great moral truth, than to destroy a plant in order to eat it. If by its destruction the plant does our soul a service, there is quite as good a reason for putting it to some sort of distress —if we must use the term—in the process of destroying it, as there is if it is wanted to support our bodies. Our Lord has a great and solemn lesson to teach His disciples; this lesson could best be taught by the destruction of this particular tree. Upon the whole, in the view of the needs of all His creatures, it was not severity; it was the truest mercy thus to destroy it.

But it has been suggested that our Lord was, in this matter, either deceiver or deceived, for St. Mark says that, "seeing a fig tree—one fig tree—afar off, having leaves, he came, if haply he might find anything thereon." St. Matthew implies as much. Did our Lord know that the tree had no figs on it? If not, how could He be what He claimed to be in relation to nature and to man? If He did know, upon what principle did He thus act so as to give the impression that He was really ignorant?

Christian faith, of course, cannot hesitate between these alternatives. Our Lord, as St. Augustine has put it, at least, was not less informed as to the general habits of the fig tree than an ordinary person. Despite the false promise of the leaves, He would have known that the time of figs was not yet, that it was too early to expect even the hasty fruit before the summer to which Isaiah makes reference. Whatever might be the case with others, He would not be misled by a premature and irregular show of leaf. He who could instruct His disciples on the preceding day how, in a village over against them, which neither He nor they had yet visited, they would find an ass tied and a colt with her —He surely had no need to walk up to the tree and lift the leaves in order to discover whether it had fruit or not.

But then this throws us on the other alternative. We

have to inquire why He acted as if the discovery had yet to be made,—why as if, on its being made, He spoke as one who felt a shade of disappointment, or of anger. And the answer is that this incident is, from first to last, an acted parable.

It would, perhaps, be truer to say that it is an acted prophecy.

In the East, action was and still is often a more vivid and effective way of communicating truth than language. When a prophet of Israel sat in sackcloth, with dust on his head, by the side of the road along which the royal chariot would pass, his action was a much more powerful rebuke to the monarch, for neglect of duty, than a sermon would have been, even though it had an introduction, three arguments and a conclusion. The East, as I have said, is traditionally the home of eloquent action; but in all countries and ages human action is a kind of human language, and it is often much more expressive than words which fall upon the ear.

In our intercourse with each other, and in our worship of God, action expresses thought and feeling in a condensed way, which often could only be put into very cumbrous and awkward language; and our Lord on this occasion was teaching—teaching in the main by action. He was acting a parable, and no objection can be urged against His action to which teaching by parable—that is to say, by putting forward an imaginary story as if it were literally true—is not always open. Just as when our Lord spoke of a husbandman, or of ten virgins, His hearers did not suppose Him to mean a literal husbandman, or literally ten virgins, so, when He walked up to the tree, they would have known that He was teaching them parabolically; and this action in walking up to it implied nothing whatever either as to His knowledge or His ignorance about its fruit. That tree, covered at this unwonted time with its pretentious crop of leaves, gave Him an opportunity of teaching a great and solemn lesson which those around Him needed to learn. He might have put His lesson, we may dare to say, into the shape of a parable:—"A certain man, seeking a fig tree in the way, far off, having leaves, came to it if haply he might find fruit thereon." But the spoken words would have arrested the attention of His disciples less visibly than the action under their very eyes; and our Lord who knew what was the real case of the tree, knew also how He could most persuasively instruct His followers.

What, then, was the lesson which on this occasion He desired to teach? Was it simply the shame and guilt, in every responsible creature of God's hand, of moral unfruitfulness? Did He cause the tree to wither because it was the symbol of nations and of men who do nothing for His glory and nothing for their fellows?

That He does punish such unfruitfulness is certain, but this is not the lesson which He would teach us here. The time of figs was not yet. To use figurative language, the tree did not sin by not producing figs at a time of the year when they could only have been produced in the open air by what we call a freak of nature, or, rather, in despite of her ordinary rules. This tree was a symbol of that which, in man, is a worse sin than a merely fruitless life. It had leaves, you will observe, though it had no fruit. That was the distinction of this particular tree among its fellows ranged along the road, with their bare, leafless, unpromising branches. They held out hopes of nothing beyond what met the eye. This tree, with its abundant leaves, gave promise of fruit that might be well nigh ripe, and thus it was a symbol of moral or of religious pretentiousness. Not simply as unfruitful, but because, being unfruitful, it was covered with leaves, it was a fitting symbol of that want of correspondence between profession and practice—between claims and reality—between the surface appearances of life and its real direction and purpose—which our Lord condemned so often and so sternly in the men of His time. And, as representing this, it was condemned too.

And thus the fig tree represented immediately, we cannot doubt, in our Lord's intention, the actual state of the Jewish people. The heathen nations, judged from a Divine point of view, were barren enough. Israel was barren also, but then Israel was also pretentious and false. Israel was the fig tree of the spoken parable which our Lord had pronounced just a year before. In that parable, you will remember, a man who had a fig tree planted in his vineyard, complains to the dresser of the vineyard, "Behold these three years I come seeking fruit on this tree, and find none. Cut it down. Why cumbereth it the ground?" And the dresser had pleaded for indulgence and delay.

"Lord, let it alone this year also, till I shall dig about it and dung it, and if it bear fruit, well: and if not, after that thou shalt cut it down." No Jew with his eye on the language of the prophets, particularly of Ezekiel, could have doubted that in this parable our Lord referred to the Jewish people; but what He then taught by words He now would teach, in its completeness, by action, for now the year for which the dresser of the vineyard had pleaded had just run out. Jesus had entered Jerusalem. He had seen how this precious year had been spent. His penetrating glance had surveyed all that was fair and unsubstantial—all that was hollow and pretentious—in the national and in the individual life of Judaism. Israel was covered with leaves. The letter of the law—the memories, the sepulchres, of the prophets—the ancient sacrifices—the accredited teachers—all were in high consideration. Israel was, to all appearances, profoundly religious. But the searching eye of our Lord found no fruit upon this tree beneath the leaves—no true soul-controlling belief even in the promises of the Messiah, of which they made so much —no true sense of their obligation and of their incapacity to please God. The Jew, as St. Paul afterwards urged, made his boast in the law. He was confident that he was himself a guide of the blind, a light of those that were in darkness, an instructor of the foolish, and a teacher of babes. But then, while proclaiming thus to the heathen nations around him his position and his prerogatives, he taught not himself. He, with the decalogue on his lips, could steal, could be an adulterer, could commit sacrilege. Even when this was not the case, so little was he alive to the exacting severity of the Divine law, that, "being ignorant of God's righteousness, he went about to establish his own righteousness, not submitting himself to the righteousness of God." During that year of patient appeal our Lord had stretched out His hands in entreaty all day long to a disobedient and gainsaying people. The tree by the roadside was a visible symbol of the moral condition of Israel as it presented itself to the eye of Jesus Christ, and there was no longer any reason for suspending the judgment which had been foretold in the Saviour's parable. "No man eat fruit of thee hereafter for ever." If humanity needed light, strength, peace, consolations, Israel could no longer give them. Israel was hereafter to be a blasted and withered tree on the wayside of history.

But the parable applies with equal force to nations or to Churches in Christendom, which make great pretensions and do little or nothing of real value to mankind. For a time the tree waves its leaves in the wind. It lives on, sustained by the traditional habits and reverence of ages. Men admire the symbol of so many blessings—of so much activity and life. There is nothing to raise a question as to the true state of the case, and the proverb is as true of nations, as of individuals, that they are often taken at their own estimate—that "so long as thou doest good unto thyself, men will speak well of thee." But, at His own time, Christ passes along the highway—passes to inquire and to judge some unforeseen calamity, some public anxiety, some shock to general confidence, lifts the leaves of that tree, and discovers its real fruitfulness. And thus history is full of withered fig trees. There are ancient dynasties—there are world-famed cities—there are national Churches—which have heard the condemning words of Christ, "No man eat fruit of thee hereafter for ever."

We may think, to us English, at any rate, these words do not apply. Surely it were better, as St. Paul told the Gentile converts who might deem themselves out of the reach of those dangers which had led to the rejection of Israel, surely it were better and wiser not to be highminded, but to fear.

And, lastly, to every individual Christian this parable is full of warning. The religious activity of the human soul may be divided, roughly, into leaves and fruit—into showy forms of religious activity and interest, on the one side, and the direct produce of religious conviction on the other. It is much easier, we all know, to grow leaves than to grow fruit; and many a man's life veils the absence of fruit by the abundance of leaves. This is always true. It is always easier, for instance, to take interest in and to discuss religious questions, than to submit the will entirely to religious principle. But it is especially true in days like ours—days of great activity—days of widespread unsettlement—days of religious revival—days, it may be (at any rate we are often so told) of transition towards some new phases in the life of the Christian Church. In days like these, every newspaper, every public place of converse, carries men's thoughts in one way or another to religious questions. And it is difficult to appreciate the extent of the change which has occurred in this respect, as far as this country is concerned within the last thirty or forty years. It has, no doubt, an encouraging side, for which we may thank God. This constant reference to religious matters brings the most important of all subjects before the minds of those who would otherwise forget it—brings it before them, whether they will or not. It reminds them, at any rate, although indirectly, that the unseen and all that belongs to it are of unspeakable importance to human beings. It is easy, and, unhappily, it is true, to say that much of such religious discussion and interest is, in itself, trivial and unsatisfactory enough. That may well be the case; and yet nothing connected with this vastest of all subjects is really unimportant, and trifles, as they appear, are often the keys to truths and principles which immediately underlie them. With whatever results, young persons now become acquainted, to a certain extent, with the controversies of the time, and converse on the tenets and observances which divide schools and Churches. But the danger, my brethren, is lest this interest, this knowledge, should be taken for more than it is worth. It is better than nothing—better than indifference, but it proves nothing as to the condition of the conscience—nothing as to the real tenor of the heart —nothing as to the deepest movements of the inmost life —nothing as to the soul's state before God, as to its prospects for eternity. An anxious question for all of us is whether the foliage, so to call it, of our Christian life is the covering of fruit beneath that is ripening for heaven, or whether it is only a thing of precocious and unnatural growth, which has drained away the true's best sap before its time and made good fruit almost impossible. To take an interest in religious questions, in religious society, in religious observances, is most right and important; but it is not necessarily the same thing as being the servant of Christ our Lord in whose soul His wonder-working grace is bringing forth the fruit of the Spirit—" love, joy, peace, longsuffering, gentleness, goodness, faith, meekness, temperance. These are the results for which our Lord will look, and no show of leaves, no fervour of language, no glow of feeling, no splendour of outward achievements for His cause and His kingdom, will compensate for their absence.

And for the production of such fruit, His grace is sufficient. Washed by His blood, illuminated by His word, fed and invigorated by His sacraments, the Christian soul is like a tree planted by the water side, that should bring forth its fruit in due season, and whose leaf also should not wither.

Pray, brethren, above all things that we may be real. Let us, when we have used strong religious language—let us ask ourselves whether we really mean every word of it. When men say kind and flattering things about us, let us ask ourselves how far, in God's sight, we deserve them. Let us be quite sure that it is far better that God should own the fruit of our lives by-and-by, than that men should pay compliments to the leaves here and now. When our Lord will visit us in death and in judgment, this we know not. We *do* know that when He comes, He will know and see all. We know that what He demands is fruit, and not merely leaves.

H. P. L.

VII. The Petition of the Moralist. MARK x. 17.
"Good Master, what shall I do that I may inherit eternal life?"

I FIRST call your attention to the petitioner here. I have described him as a moralist, but in this description I use the word in a wide sense. Morality has to do with this life, and the moralist is one who tries in particular to cultivate what is right between man and man, what is right belonging to this life, what is right arising out of his position and connections as a creature of time and an inhabitant of earth. In a wide sense of the word, this man was a moralist; at least, it was as such that he uttered this request.

I next proceed to point out that it was a great spiritual crisis when this request of his was addressed to Jesus Christ. Perhaps now may be a great crisis with some of you. Life is full, if we but knew it—we often do not until the crisis is over—life is full of critical moments. History is crowded with records of critical moments, on which history depends, when what is thought or not thought, said or not said, done or not done, may for weal or for woe affect all the future. War has such moments—so at least said Napoleon. There are critical times, sometimes narrowing into ten minutes, sometimes into one, in which what is said or done will decide the fate of the battles, and affect the balance of power, perhaps, all over the world. There are such times in politics; and was it not such a time in the history of Queen Esther, if she had stood for a moment irresolute before the festive door, if she had for a moment hesitated before her half-heroic, half-angelic resolve when she burst into that place which threatened to be the death of her, before she said, "If I perish, I perish," and went in to risk her own life, and to plead for the life of her people? And as to our own poor, frail, simple life, we know that there are critical moments when the mystical impulse of life says, "Shall I go, or not?" There are critical moments in physical life; but the most critical moment of all critical moments is a certain moment in spiritual life when the truth strikes as it never struck before, when the Spirit strives as it never did before in your history, and when all within you is a tumult working to a decision as to whether you will accept life or death.

It was such a moment in the history of this petitioner when he addressed this petition to Christ. He was wrought up to a point which he had never reached before. It was a great thing for a man like that—not like Nicodemus, by night—to come like a leper, saying, "Good Master, what shall I do that I may inherit eternal life?" It was a critical time: it could only come once in that man's history. He never saw Christ to speak to Him in this world after that. I am not speaking at random—you will see that Jesus was on His last journey to Jerusalem. He said, "Behold we go up to Jerusalem; and the Son of Man shall be delivered unto the chief priests and unto the scribes; and they shall condemn Him to death, and shall deliver Him to the Gentiles. And they shall mock Him, and shall scourge Him, and shall spit upon Him, and shall kill Him." That young man never saw his Saviour again in this life. Perhaps there may be a similar time in your soul's history which you may remember a million years hence. Not a night like the leaves of the trees in a forest, but a night the circumstances of which shall stand out for ever; a night in which you have to give your answer to the searching Spirit—an answer to Christ Himself, "Yes" or "No." If "Yes," in that word may be the germ of life; if "No," in that "No" may be the germ of death. May God help us, help me, help you. What if this *should* be the commonplace talk of man? Eternal life is not commonplace; the question of gaining eternal life is not commonplace.

In the third place, let us look at the petition. It is a petition in the form of a question—"Good Master, what shall I do that I may inherit eternal life?" This petition—allow me to call it so—has two things in it. It has two elements: first, what he wanted to have, and then what he wanted to know. He came to Jesus, wanting to have something. There are persons in this circle to-night who would have been ready to say, "What can you want?—you have everything." But though he had in all externality everything, there was one thing he wanted to have, and that thing was eternal life. He wanted that first. He had the great blessing and privilege of youth. There are some old men anxious about eternal life, but without, perhaps, the right feeling. They say, "If I were young again, I should not be so agonized as I am now." Oh, to be young again! There is nothing like youth; and, true, there is no privilege like youth. Youth! the very word has a fascination in it, when life is at its best with hope and poetry. Youth can run; youth can rest—no easy thing to rest; youth can rejoice. Youth! full of the freshness of life's morning. To think of youth with no stain on its glory! I do not wonder that persons who have not found the great secret think that if they had youth they would want nothing else. How long would you like to have that youth?—five years, ten years, twenty years? You are not permitted to have the youth spoken of here for a longer period in this life. That would not be enough for me; to have youth for a thousand years would not be enough. I like the idea of youth, but I want it in reality, and that is in *Eternity*. Speak about a million million years: what after that? Once a Hindoo who had left all his property to his priests, said to them, "What shall I be after I die?" "A bird." "What after that?" "A beast." "What after that?" They could not say. *After that!*

That is the awfulness of life! A million years of youth! What after that? When you come to think, if you have youth, you want *eternal* youth; for while you are speaking about youth, it flies. Youth in the strongest sense, too, is life. What causes a web of wrinkles upon a face is something that is not youth. Well, eternal life is eternal youth. I want that; I want it to work with. It is so fresh and emotional, that I am right in thus speaking about it.

But there is an awful shadow over it! *This youth must soon be gone*, and what then? And this thought pressed upon the young man's mind, and made him say, "Good Master, what shall I do that I may inherit eternal life?" The thing he wanted to have was eternal life, although he had great possessions. Some persons think if they had wealth, they would want nothing. The very word "wealth" is connected with the word "well" and the word "weal." Our Saxon ancestors thought that one of the things reckoned well for a man to have would be wealth. This man had wealth, but somehow he was not satisfied. If wealth is enough, it depends upon whether it is the right kind of wealth. This man was wealthy, but he could not carry his wealth with him across that mysterious thing called death. Death comes and shakes the power of the rich; they carry nothing out of the world. I want something out of the world. I want durable riches; I want bills that will be honoured in heaven; I want gold that will have celestial currency; I want things that will not fade away—in one word, I want eternal life.

One thing this young man wanted—to have eternal life. He had station, great social influence. Many persons prefer that to wealth. Many a man would be content to be poor if he could have power. Such men are ready to part with health, and sometimes with their bodies, and even to sell their souls, that they might have power in the world. Men *will* have power in the world. Well, if they have it as this man had, what then? The day comes when the king must die. We want something after this life. So this man went to Jesus, whom he believed to know all about eternal life; he went to Him in the attitude of worship, and said, "Good Master, what shall I do that I may inherit eternal life?"

The first element of the question indicated what he

wanted to have, and next what he wanted to know—what he could do to have this eternal life. And this question is very interesting for you. Look at the thing he wanted. He had already a good many things. This question, "What shall I do?" simply meant, "How can I make good my title?" It was simply a question of how he should get the title to eternal life. He said this, although he had got many things that seemed to help him. He had got a good creed about eternal life. It was the fashion among the Jews of that day to repudiate the old Hebrew creeds, and to accept the doctrines taught by the Greek philosophers. There had been, owing to commerce with classic thought, growing up a disposition to discard old Hebrew notions as narrow, to clothe Hebrew philosophy in a Greek dress. It was considered a clever thing to scout the idea of a life beyond the grave. As to the antiquated doctrine of eternal life, the companions of the young, the educated, would laugh at such a doctrine, or say to that man that he was following the faith of his grandmother. There was something very good in a man who could stand the shafts of scorn. Are you ready to do so for the creed of your father? There is that young man who said to you yesterday, "Where are you going to-morrow?" and when you said, "To church;" he exclaimed, "Is it possible!" I can understand that in such a case it is not easy for a young man to stand his ground. This man was, at any rate, right as to the main matter—eternal life and its reality —but he felt somehow that this was not enough, and do you not feel the same? A sound creed is a right thing to begin with, but not the right thing to stop at. You may have a sound creed about sowing seed, but you may not sow it at the right time. I am not certain as to whether this man had a definite opinion as to whether this sound creed was not enough; at any rate, it seemed to cross his mind that it was not enough to make a title to eternal life. This man wanted to know how to make good his title to eternal life. Jesus Christ tested him, and said, "Thou knowest the commandments," and then gave a summary of the commandments; and the young man said, "Master, all these things have I observed from my youth." If he had kept these commandments outwardly in reference to the body—had not committed adultery nor murder, nor robbery, nor borne false witness, nor defrauded, and had honoured his father and his mother—it shows a strong probability that the young man had had a good religious education according to the standard of the time. When I see a young man has maintained his outward integrity and morality, I always feel that he has had not only a true education, but a wise education—that his father and mother had not only screened him from evil things, but had warned him about them, and trained him in what was right.

There is a story about a poor old woman who never told her grandchild that there was such a thing as a well, lest she should fall into one! If there has been in the case of parents rather a screening from harm than a *teaching about* harm, as soon as the restraints of home are lifted, the young easily fall. These are things that teachers cannot teach, but which *must* be left for parents. What I would say on this point is, that this young man asked for a good title how to get eternal life, though he had what might have been called a good title. How many a worldling says, that if persons do what is right in matters of morality, God looks over their mistakes, their little sins. I am only now saying that this man wanted to know how he could make good his title to eternal life, although he had, as he thought, kept the commandments. Besides this, he wanted to know how to get this title. There was in his character a certain fascination and charm. He comes upon our minds with a sense of beauty: we love to hear the tremulous tones in which he speaks; we like to look upon his bright, eager face. We find, however, that humility, integrity, and charm are not enough to make a title to eternal life. If he wanted a title, so do you; if he put up that prayer, you also can.

There were two elements in his prayer: something he wanted to have—eternal life; something he wanted to know —how to get a true title to eternal life.

I advance to Christ's reply. It is summed up, "One thing thou lackest." He answers unspoken thoughts that are burning in the young man's mind, as to certain things he had done which might perhaps make a title to eternal life. This young man comes and brings his case before the sovereign counsel and sovereign judgment of the King,

He has a hope, and yet he has a fear; sometimes the one is high, sometimes the other. He hopes—I think you will detect this—that this good Teacher will say he has done enough. Perhaps he thinks he will have a compliment for his sensitiveness; but Jesus sees through the surfaces, and weighs in the balance the moralist or the ritualist, and this man He found short weight. He had many things, but says the Judge, "*One* thing thou lackest." Oh, brethren, here at times our souls are brought from sin. We are in earnest; how shall we apply these words of Christ to our own case? Does Christ say to any one of you, "One thing thou lackest"? At first sight it seems delightful for Him to say that we have all things but one. Does it not, however, depend upon what that one thing is? For a ship to have all things but one thing. What is that thing but a compass? Or a watch to have all things but one—the mainspring! Or for a house to want one thing, and that thing the foundation. Or a plant of fragrance and beauty having everything but one, and that the root. For a body to have everything but one thing, and that thing the soul: poor man to have everything but one thing! An inquirer after eternal life to have everything but one thing, but that one thing the thing needful, that one thing the true title—*that* the one thing lacking! That was the one thing which this man lacked. A man can be young and wealthy and influential, and have a sound belief, and have a true morality, and yet be lost; he can have a beautiful and winsome address, and be lost; he can have a house in the country and many servants, and be lost; he can come running to Christ, and be lost.

There are two conceivable ways in which a title to eternal life may be gained. I am speaking about a conceivable way—*perfect* obedience to the law. Now it seems that the first thing missing in this young man was a want of true understanding of the perfection of the law. The right standard of goodness, that is the very first thing which Christ indicates. The word "good" occurs in the three Evangelists. This young man wanted to know what *good* thing he could do. He called Jesus "Good Master." Christ was not going to accept that term "good" as a compliment. He addresses this term to Him as he would have done to any Rabbi. In the absolute sense, Christ is speaking about goodness when He says, "Why callest thou Me good? there is none good but One, that is, God." He now speaks in His man-nature. He wishes to call the man's attention to the ideal goodness—God without flaw. But the man would not see it,—he could only see surfaces, —so Jesus Christ tells him to sell all he had and follow Him. It was not a command to you; it was a command to him for a special purpose—a command from Him who saw that the weak point in that man was an excessive love of wealth. He wanted to make him see it too; but when the young man heard these words, he turned sadly away. If he had to give up one of two things, he would rather give up the future than the present. He gave up the eternal rather than the temporal; and would not the thought come to him, "I can get to heaven on the principle of perfection"?

There is the gospel way, and that is trusting in Christ; but the man preferred his wealth rather than the Saviour —trusted in his riches rather than in Christ, so that he lacked trust. I put it to you whether you have got the trust. Your title is in Jesus Christ, and the one thing you have to do is to get it by faith. If you had to do anything, what could you do? Go to the forest, select many trees, and with them build an ark of salvation? Could you build a bridge that could span the abyss from the house of Dives to the house of Lazarus? No; if the plan of salvation were left to you, you must give it up. But there is no need for it; Jesus Christ has done it.

So I come to the old Sunday-school story—"Believe on the Lord Jesus Christ." But I want to rescue Jesus Christ's gospel from a misconception. How easy it is to travesty gospel truths! Our true doctrine is, that we trust to the work of Jesus Christ for our title. But when we have an interest in Jesus Christ, what is the salvation that He gives? We have it described here—"life." Not merely safety, but life—eternal life, that follows the example of Jesus Christ's life; and this eternal life begins now, directly we believe. Heaven will be but the consummation of that which will begin in you now, if now for the first time you believe in the Lord Jesus.

C. S.

VIII. The Festival of Christmas. ST. LUKE ii. 15.

"*Let us now go even unto Bethlehem, and see this thing which is come to pass, which the Lord hath made known unto us.*"

THIS was the resolution of the shepherds on the original Christmas Day; may it be our own! "Come and see" is written upon the gospel; there is no secrecy and no concealment in it. It challenges inquiry; it invites search; it opens itself to handling. "That which we have looked upon," it says, "and our hands have handled, of the Word of life." Others may be timid for the gospel—the gospel is not timid for itself. "I spake openly to the world; . . . in secret have I said nothing:" it was the Saviour's own saying, it is the saying for ever of His gospel. Let us apply it to our great subject.

We have a fact before us: "Unto you is born a Saviour." It is a summary of Revelation.

It presupposes a ruin. They that are whole need not a physician, and they that are safe need not a preserver. It assumes that salvation must come from without. "Man cannot deliver his brother, nor make agreement with God for him, for it cost more to redeem their souls" (more than man can offer), "so that he must let that alone for ever." It declares, further, that the Deliverer, though He comes from without the creature, must enter into it by incorporation. There must be a birth to bring in the Saviour into the Cosmos which, as the work of His own hands, is external to Him. "Unto you is born a Saviour" —Incarnation makes Him such.

These are the three elements of the text and of the doctrine. It would be almost an impertinence to argue them. Who amongst us seriously doubts the first of them? What man of common intelligence can question his own sinfulness? He has had experience of it. He has done, many times—he has left undone, many times—not according to his own judgment of the thing that was right. He has resolved, many times, and it has come to nothing—he has condemned himself, many times, too late, and in vain for that which he wonders that he ever could have consented to. We may account differently for this state of things, but we cannot gainsay it.

Then, is all this misdoing and leaving undone to be treated as a mere misfortune—to be passed by, and passed over as leaving no permanent consequence, in the form of direct punishment, or in the form of incapacity for eventual happiness? If this seems to the man himself impossible; if his own conscience writes bitter things against him by reason of his own doing and leaving undone; can he make amends for it? Can he repair the past by effort or penance? Can he give himself back the lost time, or the lost opportunity, or the lost virtue, and stand before God in judgment as a self-saved man? If not this, must he not feel that, in all literalness of simplicity, God alone can save him, and that God alone can prescribe and reveal the way? Can he be sure that something may not need to be done in the way of reconciling mercy and justice—something in the nature of vicarious suffering—a bearing, in order to take away, the sins of the world? Can he say that there may be no necessity for a personal intervention of God Himself to atone before He can indwell? If there is to be anything of the nature of sacrifice on the part of God Himself—nay, if there is to be any contact whatever, even in the form of sympathy, between God and the creature—if there is to be any communication and communion, so much as of speech or of feeling, between the human and the Divine, there must be (we almost dare to say it) Incarnation; there must be that of which the Epistle to the Hebrews says, "Forasmuch then as the children are partakers of flesh and blood, He also Himself likewise took part of the same; that through death He might destroy him that had the power of death, and deliver them who through fear of death were all their lifetime subject to bondage." He must be born—such is the argument—on purpose that He might die. "Unto you is born a Saviour."

So simple, yet so profound, is the mystery of Christmas. It is this threefold cord, of sin, of helplessness, and of Divine intervention, which has given the festival its wonderful hold upon the heart and soul of mankind. It is not the saturnalia of the heathen mid-winter; it is the reasonable and spiritual festival of a humanity which knows itself, and to which God has spoken. If there were not a vast multitude of true Christians, able to interpret God to man, and man to himself,—able to say with a full heart,

"We know that the Son of God is come;" "that which we have seen and heard declare we unto you, that ye also may have fellowship with us"—there would be a vast difference in the whole tone and feeling of the celebration, even for those who do not enter into its highest and deepest significance. The Church keeps her Christmas as the birthday of her Lord; and the world, catching the reflection of her joy, bears the testimony of a common humanity to its beauty and its glory: may it be but true! The joy of Christmas commends itself, even to the world, as that which would be life to it, might they but believe. "Let us now go and view this thing which is come to pass," Christians say to-day one to another; and they would call their friends and their neighbours together—as they would on the discovery of a lost treasure—to rejoice with them, saying, in the yearning of a Christian love and a Christian philanthropy, even to them that are farthest off as yet from knowing, "Come and see!"

When we try to obey the summons, the first thing which we notice is, that Christmas day is the festival of redemption as a whole.

It presents to us, not so much one part or one element of the gospel, but rather the intervention of God in Christ to save sinners as a single and complete act, containing in itself all that was necessary to give it validity and to give it efficacy. St. Paul, in the last of his Epistles (the second to Timothy), so speaks of it. He speaks of the eternal purpose of God in Christ for the salvation of man as "made manifest," once for all, "by the appearing (Epiphany) of our Saviour Jesus Christ." That "appearing," that manifestation on the stage of time, had in it the whole train of action and suffering by which Christ wrought out our redemption; and that "appearing," that Advent, is the subject of our commemoration.

We might, indeed, say that each one of the great acts of the Redemption, rightly understood, has in it the virtue of the whole work. The Crucifixion, the Resurrection, the Ascension, each one looked back or looked forward to all the rest. Christ died as He that should rise, and rose as He that had died. But in an especial sense is this true of the Incarnation. Believe that, and all else is intelligible; we may almost say, all else is natural. "The mystery of godliness"—to use the word "mystery" for a moment in its popular rather than in its strictly Scriptural sense—"the mystery of godliness is, God was manifested in the flesh." This is what St. John makes the test of truth and error. "Every spirit which confesseth that Jesus Christ is come in the flesh is of God; and every spirit which confesseth not that Jesus Christ is come in the flesh is not of God; hereby know we the spirit of truth and the spirit of error." St. John, taught of God, foresaw that the real battle would always rage around the Christmas revelation : it is the key of the position as between faith and infidelity. Accept that, and all follows. Deny, or dilute, or explain away that, and neither atonement, nor intercession, nor judgment can retain one particle of virtue.

Let us not speak harshly or impatiently of those (and they are many) who find the real mystery of Christmas difficult or repellent to them, for indeed it passes understanding, and transcends (though it contradicts not) reason. Yet to excuse a man this faith, is to leave him still in darkness. Nay, it is to leave a hopeless discord and quarrel between two vast portions of revelation itself. Scripture is full of the humanity of Jesus. His hunger and thirst, His eating and drinking, His weariness and resting, His sighs and tears, His friendships and affections are written on every page of the Gospels—written in perfect simplicity in manifold variety; who runs may read them. The reality of His human nature is assumed throughout the record. That He was a man in flesh is true, if there be one particle of truth in Scripture. On the other hand, we find in the same record of Him, not only exercises of supernatural power, which might possibly be like in kind to those of other commissioned and empowered men; and not only words of superhuman wisdom, differing only perhaps in degree from those which holy men of God, moved by the Holy Ghost, have been enabled to utter before Him; but, which is far more remarkable, as being absolutely peculiar to Him—express claims of dignity and majesty, nay, even of unity with God Himself, such as would be presumptuous and blasphemous if they were not true, and which stand in striking and marvellous combination with the quiet and level humanity which is equally His characteristic. If we would do any justice to both these classes of statement, we must feel that, at one point out of sight, quite beyond the reach of our discovery, or of our definition, there was a junction in Him of the Divine and the Human, such as that which we faintly typify by the word Incarnation, such as that of which we commemorate the realization in our festival of the Holy Nativity.

We are not asked to understand this; and yet I say that, even as an inference, even as a hypothesis, even as a conjecture, it would be a relief from the utter confusion and chaos of the two classes of Scripture statement to which I have adverted. Without Incarnation, we must cut out either the one half, or else the other half, of our Gospels; or else we must retain the whole with that sort of puzzled look and paralyzed hold upon it which we must suspect to be the condition of thousands and tens of thousands even among our worshippers.

It would be a happy day for many if they might be brought, by God's blessing, to a decision upon this question of questions. If, in a case where it would be stupidity to doubt either the honesty or the information of the writers, a thoughtful man, struck by the contrariety, on which we have dwelt, of the Divine and the human in our Lord Jesus Christ, would try the doctrine of Christmas Day as to its satisfactoriness of reconciliation, and, while acknowledging the fact to be high above him, would yet receive it into his soul, for use, as one of God's mysteries, explaining everything but itself—explaining the Atonement, explaining the Resurrection, explaining the Ascension, explaining Pentecost, and the Advent, and the great Judgment—it is astonishing what light would spring up in that man upon all the concerns of his spiritual being; he would enter into the saying, as never before, that Christmas sets before us the work of God in Christ as a whole, and that to-day, in a more especial and comprehensive sense, we, His unworthy servants, are giving Him most humble and hearty thanks for the redemption of the world by our Lord Jesus Christ, for the means of grace, and for the hope of glory.

II. But the festival of Christmas, though its foundation lies so deep, has a thought for all natures. It is, in an especial sense, the festival of the brighter side of Christianity.

It is quite possible so to look upon this earth as to

discover nothing but gloom. God knows, better than we know, how deplorable is the havoc made by sin in the homes and lives and hearts of us men. We might easily draw such inferences from the spectacle daily before us as would paralyze effort and preclude cheerfulness. And it is quite possible so to represent religion as to make it a depressed and downcast thing, fit only for sick-rooms and death-beds; a perpetual Jonah-like proclamation, "Yet forty days, and Nineveh shall be overthrown."

But neither the one nor the other of these views takes in the whole landscape. There is a brighter side of human life, and God does not intend it to be scouted. Wonderful as it is to utter and to reflect upon, God Himself has made joy one element of our nature, has kept it so notwithstanding the entrance of sin and death, and has made cheerfulness (even amidst all the distressing facts and experiences of our being) an absolute condition of any vigorous or successful working. It is not intended that we should dwell in the dust and ashes even of a too true contemplation. God alone can see all things, and live. Except in so far as we can be useful, we had better turn our eyes away from ghastly and sickening spectacles. Except in so far as we require it for chastening and for sobering, we had better turn our backs resolutely even upon our own irreparable past, and fasten all our thoughts upon an available future. Certain it is that an admixture of joy is indispensable to all healthy and wholesome living; that it is not true that even a fallen world is all misery; that it is not true (else there would be an end at once to the development of all the stronger and hardier faculties) that it is wrong to use thankfully all that comes in our way of being and of making happy, were it only as a religious exercise of praise and thanksgiving.

Thus it is that the observance of Christmas as a season of joy and gladness is so right in itself and so honourable to the gospel. Although it is a commemoration which has in it all commemorations, some of them full of thoughts of sadness and suffering—full of recollections of sin, and its terrible offspring of fear and woe—yet, in itself, it has all the tenderness, all the hopefulness, with which men who have a heart in them contemplate infancy and childhood, the innocency of a new-born babe, and the endless capabilities of blessing which imagination foreshadows in the swaddling clothes and the cradle. God would have it so, that a birth should be a hope rather than a fear; and even He who knows the ambiguity of all human concerns, shall yet prognosticate good, and not evil, for the race which has yet to be run.

That which is true to human nature in reference to every birth and every beginning, has, of course, a tenfold appropriateness to the cradle of the Saviour. It would be a false, and certainly unscriptural, obtrusion of the thought that for many Christ (we fear) will have come in vain, to make this a reason for weeping over the sight which God has revealed to us in Bethlehem. Never let us so dishonour Christ as to doubt whether, on the whole, it has been good for humanity that He has been born. However difficult it may be for us to reconcile, or even to balance, the opposite results of His Epiphany upon those who believe and those who reject Him, of this we are certain, that His advent was proclaimed by Him who knew all, as "good tidings of great joy to all people," and that to represent it otherwise would be to charge God Himself foolishly, as well as to take out of the gospel all that has made it the power of God for salvation, and Jesus Christ, Himself the one Magnet of humanity, forming a new fellowship in the earth, and (as it is written) "gathering together at last all things in Himself."

Christmas is the festival of the bright side of the gospel —let us rejoice and be glad in it!

III. The last word is like this, for it describes Christmas as by common consent the festival of the family and of home.

It is in this light that Christendom views it; and anything which tends to strengthen that tie, the strongest and tenderest of all which connects humanity, must be for good, and must be of God.

It is a mistake to suppose that this use of Christmas depends upon the providential circumstances of the home; depends, for example, upon possibilities of meeting, or depends upon the continued life of its members. It is the spiritual gathering together which is the Christmas reality. They whose sons or whose brothers are serving their country or exercising an honest calling by land or sea, in

India or Australia, are reminded of the indestructible union over which the bodily severance has no power. They whose parents, or else whose children, are already in the invisible country, can still keep the feast with them, if not exactly in joy and gladness, yet in the strong and solid confidence of a safety far beyond any that an earthly home can offer, and a unity, not of earth but of heaven, to be realized, a little while hence, with those who are not lost but gone before. Christmas is the family festival still, though its tone must of necessity be affected by the circumstances, joyous or sorrowful, of its annual return.

"Let us now go even unto Bethlehem, and see this thing which is come to pass." The thing spoken of is the birth of the Saviour, Christ the Lord; the "sign" of it is "a babe wrapped in swaddling clothes, and lying in a manger," "because there is no room for Him in the inn." The commonness, the humility, the littleness is the sign—the thing signified is that which has changed the life of man, and opened the world beyond death to all who have faith to enter it. Thus it is always. God is seen, not in the great things of earth, not in the noble, not in the mighty. He is seen in the unconscious sleep of the helpless babe in the outdoor cradle. Thus He taught us how, coming to save, He made Himself one with the sin-ruined in their ruin; incorporated Himself not with the privileged few, but with the common many, that none might be able to say, "He overlooked me," that none might be able to say, "Thus far He descended, but not into the depths of humanity, not into the lower and lowest parts of the earth." "Ye know the grace of our Lord Jesus Christ, how, though He was rich, yet for our sakes He became poor;" yea, "He humbled Himself and became obedient," first to the likeness of men, then to the cottage home and the manger cradle, then, at last, "to death, even the death of the cross."

C. J. V.

IX. **The Story of Nain.** LUKE vii. 11–15. "*And it came to pass the day after, that He went into a city called Nain; and many of His disciples went with Him, and much people. Now when He came nigh to the gate of the city, behold,* *there was a dead man carried out, the only son of his mother, and she was a widow: and much people of the city was with her. And when the Lord saw her, He had compassion on her, and said unto her, Weep not. And He came and touched the bier; and they that bare him stood still. And He said, Young man, I say unto thee, Arise. And He that was dead sat up, and began to speak. And He delivered him to his mother."*

NOTHING can be more simple, quiet, and unassuming than the form and style of this story. The entire want of assumption and of high-colouring are strong, though indirect, proof of its truth. Truth is always unassuming, and yet, simple as it is, how pictorial it also is, and pictorial from the extremely natural way in which the little incidents are introduced, such as we cannot conceive to have been detailed by any one who had not witnessed the scene with his own eyes. The ring of truth is in such expressions as the touching of the bier, the man beginning to speak, and the delivery of the son to his mother by Christ. Add to this, to make it still more a picture, the scenery by which it was surrounded; set it in the frame that nature made then for it.

The village of Nain lay in the plain. To the north-east rose Mount Tabor, sweeping in a semi-circle and quite alone into the midst of the plain. To the north-west the great mass of Mount Carmel filled the sky. Further to the north rose the snowy peak of the great Hermon, and all around were corn and vines and olive and fig gardens, and the wind blowing freshly over Mount Tabor, as it always blows to this very day; exactly in front the village of Nain sparkling in the sunshine, standing among the trees and copses of the low and grassy slopes of little Hermon. A crowd, as usual, followed Christ along the road, and as He drew near to Nain, another crowd was at the gate. The open bier carried in front showed it was a funeral, and behind was the mother of an only son, "and she was a widow." The two crowds met and filled the road: and when Jesus saw the weeping woman, His human heart was touched. It is possible that backwards many years His memory may have travelled, and have recalled the sorrow of His own mother when, after three days of anxiety, she saw her first-born, her only Son, once more after being lost in the Temple courts of Jerusalem; and from that memory His compassion may have taken a deep or more comprehensive glance into the sorrow of this mother. He touched the bier; the bearers stood still: the simple word was spoken to her, then to him, and the man arose and spoke.

We will speak of some lessons we may draw from the story.

First, the words of His consolation were simple, as all consolation ought to be. In the midst of many, this weeping woman was quite alone. Others with her may have wept, but their tears were tears of sympathy; hers were tears of loneliness. Their sympathy could not sound the profound ocean of her sorrow—she was quite solitary, she stood alone in the desert of life. There had been one well of living water beside which she had rested, one solitary palm tree beneath the shadow of whose tenderness she had hoped to spend the evening of her years—her only son. Now the well was dried up and the palm tree withered, and it was grief intensified by the words of comfort from her friends—a grief, too, intensified by the crowd around her. The very multitude that surrounded her only reminded her all the more of her desolate home, and of one who was a multitude to her. It was then, in the midst of this impassioned grief, that she met Christ—met "the Man of sorrows and acquainted with grief." She saw upon His face the reality of His compassion, the full understanding of her grief. She felt no longer quite alone; another heart had touched hers with the invisible force of silent attraction which, belonging to all mankind, belonged in the greatest conceivable manner to the greatest and the highest man. The words of others had been many; Christ's were few; but the "Weep not" echoed in the woman's heart; there was in it infinite pity, mingled with a strange and cheering tone, which gains hope, and made her lift her head with delight. That is the consolation of Christ—short, deeply felt, impassioned, inward, silent sympathy, unobtrusive, voiceless, heard in the stillness of the heart, passing by all outward forms of feeling down to the centre of grief, and with a strange and entire comprehension of every individual heart that trusts it. Every form of human compassion is purely and nobly entered into; every phase of human feeling and thought are fully comprehended in all their detail. As he who has seen and obeyed the great principle, "Love thy neighbour as thyself," has comprehended in the one principle every conceivable phase of the duty of one man to another, so there is no such thing to those who cannot understand and feel His love and sympathy as real nobleness in life. You may have as unique a character as can be in this world—unique in feeling, or unique in thought: still there is a divinely-human consolation and comprehension in Him in whom all humanity was concentrated. Such should be, as far as we could make it, our way of consolation. Too much talking spoils comfort: better nothing given to a man whose heart is breaking with pain than the commonplaces which are additional wounds to real grief—well meant, indeed; but what chaff are they to a spirit dying of the awful hunger of sorrow! Give rather few words, like "Weep not"; but let them be crowded with the infinite of feeling; let them come out of intense compassion and love, comprehending the misery because you have forgotten yourself—that will console. Heart to heart is then felt. It is not in the words—it is in the spirit, the eyes, the tone, the pressure of the hand; and if the heart behind be true, then your consolation is felt as the comfort of Christ was felt by the woman.

And, again, Christ put this compassion of His at once into action. No sooner had the feelings of pity arisen within Him, than He came forward and touched the bier —did what He could to help the woman. That is a deep lesson to us, though a commonplace one. Wishing well to a person as a charity is worth absolutely nothing unless you do well also. It is like standing in a neglected and stony field, and mourning over its condition without ever attempting to plant anything; and yet that is what we are continually doing in everyday life; we are content to pity, and no more—to sit in our comfortable chair, indulge in weak and sentimental compassion, and never sacrifice a single pleasure or a single advantage to help practically the sick and the weary in this world. What a life all that is; and what an absurd self-deception it is to call ourselves Christians if we never, like Christ, come forward and touch the bier. These are the things which are the test of Christianity. We have a few shillings to spare. There is a little petty luxury we have long wished for, or fresh pleasure that we desire to taste, and our well-spared money will buy it. Well, shall we give it to ourselves, or help the sick and heal the wounded whose story has been brought to our doors? Shall we give up the pleasure and act like Christ, or pass by the bier and leave the widow to lament alone? Oh! go forward and touch the bier; put your pity into action. Your gifts will not be wasted. There are hundreds in this town carried out like a corpse to their burial,—poor souls, tortured by pain, sleepless at night, suffering as we have suffered, and shall suffer; at home many a widow mourning the loss of her sole support, many a wife before God, calling to Him to spare her husband's life, many a mother weeping bitter tears to Him, and asking Him to restore her child; and one piece of your gold, or one hour of your time sacrificed for Christ's sake, may often help, with God's blessing, to change sorrow into joy. You, too, may, like your Saviour, deliver the son of the mother. Remember then, that He who is to be your Judge has made such charity as this—or such want of charity—the test by which He will condemn or reward at the last; but He makes love to the sick love to Himself, and want of it to those who are sorrowful, neglect of Himself. "Inasmuch as ye did it unto one of the least of these My brethren, ye did it unto Me."

The third thing that comes out in the story is the consciousness of Divine power in the mind of Christ. No man who was a stranger would have intruded upon a mother's sacred grief. For Him it would have been an insult to stop the bier. We cannot conceive of Christ doing this simply for the notion of mere interference. But, on the other hand, He was not exactly in the position of a stranger: He was recognised as a great Prophet by many in Jerusalem: He was well-known over Galilee as one who helped the body, and when He touched the bier, wild hope, like a ray of stormy sunshine, must have gone through the heart of the mother. He must have known He was exciting that hope, and knew that the result of disappointing it would be to plunge her into deeper grief than before: and for both these reasons He would not have stopped the bier, unless He had been conscious of power to do what He did.

Contrast His consciousness of Divine power with His lonely, sad, and hidden life. A carpenter's son, "not where to lay His head," hunted by His foes, His friends unlearned and ignorant men, and yet feeling that within Himself He could master disease! And then add to this the marvellous restriction which He Himself laid upon this human power of His. Not once for the sake of ostentation, or to curry favour with people, did He use it; not once for Himself did He endeavour to step out of His humanity, and use these means to satisfy His own natural wants, to help His own natural infirmities; but always for lofty ends; always for profound, moral, and spiritual ends did He use that power He was conscious of possessing. That is the fourth thing we observe. Now I pass on to touch briefly upon the spiritual lessons to be drawn from the miracle.

The first is, that often in the midst of death we meet the true life. It is often when our dearest has died that we meet Christ at the nearest; often when death and danger come to us that we have the clearest knowledge of the life to come and of the rest to come, for then the world fades away, and we are thrown wholly upon God and upon heaven, just as by the law of compensation in this life one thing is weighed against another. Life is not all loss—outward loss, it is true—but inward gain, if we be true men. Friends go, and we see them no more; but the affections that have been trained by friendship deepen within the soul; the heart passes onward from the manifold affections of the earth; there is a perfect unity of love towards one who is father, and friend, and husband, and brother, all in one. Our best loved one dies, but our loneliness becomes peopled, as it never was before, by the infinite presence of God. The outward man decays; the inward man is renewed day by day. Our prosperity and wealth may be shattered at a blow; but the unsearchable riches of Christ are given to us if we be faithful. Death comes to entrance into that deep stillness whence no voices ever whispered even one secret, and yet he who follows Christ can calmly say, "This is life." These Christian contrasts are the deep blessing of the martyr. All is not lost when we follow, as the widow followed her son, the well-loved dead, and engage in the sad services of our Church. There are in it words of solemn faith and profound joy. In the awful calm in which we stand at the churchyard gate, there fall from the lips of Christ's minister Christ's own triumphant words, "I am the resurrection and the life," and though the dead rise not up and speak, yet we know for them, indeed, it is well; it is well that they should wait to meet us until we are rendered more fit to share in their immortal birth. For us, far better to remain, and think that as we lose friends here, our store gets so much greater in the world to come, and our meeting shall have delight a hundred hundred-fold. We wander, when winter is drawing on, through the melancholy trees, among the autumn's faded leaves, and yet in the midst of it our heart prophesies of spring, and of the light and the resurrection of life and beauty. And so should be the wandering here of the Christian man, passing slowly yet cheerfully onwards; watching life's faded leaves, it is true; but gathering from each death that happens around him, hopes of new spring and endless life and light. You have suffered, yet you have the right to rejoice. You have lost, yet in Christ you must have gain. Pass on, then, through life, with hearts braced for the trial, with spirits strong and calm, with faith and hope burning like twin stars within the sacred heaven of your soul, as is meet for those who, like the widow, have met, over the dead we love, the Lord of Life.

Lastly, there lies beneath this outward act of Christ, a spiritual meaning. Every miracle has a twofold object, to meet some physical want or distress, and so to manifest love in the redemption of the body, and so to point to Himself as the One alone who could relieve the higher wants of the spirit of man. Here, He who could raise one who seemed spiritually dead, was manifesting Himself as the spiritual resurrection, as the life of the spiritually dead. The meaning of this story is pointed by the words used in the context of the story of Lazarus. "I am the resurrection and the life," says Christ; "he that believeth on Me, though he were dead, yet shall he live: and whosoever liveth and believeth in Me shall never die." All those texts have a distinctly spiritual meaning. It is with us spiritually as it was with the widow's son. We begin life brightly enough; we, too, have our heaven of innocence before evil begins to work in us. Ere long we pass into the knowledge of evil, and innocence is lost for ever; sin darkens about us. We are not conscious of sin as sin, for we are not conscious of holiness; but the time comes when we awake to the sense of a holy law outside us. Our sinful state is irritated by the pure and piercing law of good into greater sinfulness, just as diseased lungs are penetrated by thin and pure air into greater disease. We are "dead in sin," as St. Paul puts it; and yet at another time, when the conflict with nature is stirred, we go on struggling with the law of sin in our members, weeping bitterly as we sit by the bed of a dead nature, until at last we utter the deepest and most wretched cry that comes out of our hearts, "O wretched man that I am! who shall deliver me from the body of this death?" Then upon the path of life comes by Christ the Saviour, and touches the bier, and that which was dead arises. He gives us not a law without us, which brings with it sin and death by irritating us still further; but a spirit of love within us, which brings with it righteousness and life. We are quickened together with Him, quickened by the love to God which He pours into our hearts; quickened by sharing in His Spirit; and when we share in the Spirit of the Saviour, and begin to love as He loved, then we rise into the same life of love which He possesses for ever. That which made our nature dead is banished and driven out because we love goodness, and it rises clean out of evil. Passions, intellect, will, appetites, senses—all are renewed and inspired by the Spirit of the living God—all have a new motive, and so are made new, not by being taken out of us and replaced by another will, another intellect, another heart; but by having so new, and fresh, and loving, and patient a motive given to us to live justly, that we are all changed and renewed, and we become new men alive in Christ Jesus.

Nor will His work cease at this. As the same vital forces produce first leaves, and then the bud, and then the blossom, and then the fruit, the crown of all in the plant, so the same Divine Spirit of Christ, which raised us here from the death of sin, shall also quicken our mortal bodies by His Spirit that dwelleth in us. That is the last meaning of the story. It is a glorious witness to the resurrection of the body. The fruit shall follow upon the blossom; we shall meet our Saviour once again, and hear His voice, arise, and enter, body, soul and spirit, into the perfect resurrection.

S. B.

X. Casting out Devils.

LUKE viii. 35. *"Then they went to see what was done; and came to Jesus, and found the man, out of whom the devils were departed, seated at the feet of Jesus, clothed, and in his right mind."*

IT is, I think, John Foster who somewhere says that Christ's miracles were "the great belt round the farthest sun." It is quite true for us who believe in the historical character of our Lord's miracles. But they were something more than that: they were a great part of the sun in themselves. Out of them is this thought, that on the lower level of material and physical nature we may learn great lessons as to what He was, and His power to do in the spiritual world. Now that is not a mere bit of pulpit use of words, but in this case, as in so many others, extremes meet; and to the people who do not believe in the historical character of the gospel, we say a miracle is, first of all, a fact—if you like, operation—and then it is a symbol.

They say, "Oh, no; because it is a symbol, it is not a fact—it is merely a throwing into a legendary form of spiritual ideas." I will accept the interpretation. And first of all, taking these stories in their plain, simple literality, as being things that did verily happen on this green earth of ours, and thereby manifestations of a present God, I take them to be also patterns, types, pictures, symbols, prophecies—anything you like—perennial powers which are constantly sent out from Jesus Christ over all the deformities and weaknesses of this blind, paralysed, thirsty, dying world of ours. And when He said, "Go and tell John what things ye have seen and heard; how the sick are healed, the blind see, the lepers are cleansed, the dead are raised up, and the poor have the gospel preached unto them," He stated in the last clause the deepest meaning and highest blessedness of all the forms and manifestations of His power.

And so the words have not only a bearing upon that story with which they are immediately connected, but as throwing out in a picturesque and powerfully true form, the blessed truths referred to. But first of all, to begin with, of the way in which we look at these New Testament miracles as connected with their historical veracity. So one or two points about the narrative. I do not deal with the style of the disease, or of the cure. The thing I want to fix upon is that picture, so beautiful in the suffused calm as it were, side by side with the dreadful story which has preceded it of the paroxysm of madness and misery from which the man was delivered. The things I want to emphasize in this connection are two. "They found the man, out of whom the devils were departed, *sitting* at the feet of Jesus, clothed, and in his right mind." Turn to Mark; he leaves out these words, "at the feet of Jesus," and so, you see, puts the mere attitude of *sitting* actually there as being the prominent thing which struck the men as they went out. As it stands in Luke's Gospel, the main emphasis is thrown upon the thought, "at the feet of Jesus." And you will see that the thing meant is, that there were three characteristics about the man when they came out, which were noticeable: first, sitting; second, clothed; third, sane, controlling himself. And the explanation of all three follows in the clause which stands independently, "at the feet of Jesus." That is to say, the picture of our narrative is this: here is the man as they knew him, with the paroxysms of his possession upon him, rolling among the mountains and tombs day and night, in the terrible restlessness of his malady, incapable of controlling for a moment the muscular working of his disturbed frame, the indications of his tortured and torn mind. Look at the change. He whom they had known constantly on the move, incapable of a moment's cessation, restless, ceaseless, mad—at once the tension has collapsed, and there he is seated quietly, with no more agitation and disturbance, the limbs that formerly had rejected the chains, clothed: in his tranquillity some returning consciousness of the decencies of life had marked the influence of the mind; able to hold his hand on the bridle and control himself. *Compos mentis*, as the phrase is, master of himself—no longer hurled hither and thither by the lion power which had had hold of him, but lord of his own faculties. And so sitting, clothed, sane, restful, decent, master of his own being, and all because of his closeness to that Lord. He laid himself along there at the feet of Christ, the attitude of the disciple, with love, with humility, with thankfulness, with the instinct strong within him that said,—

"Here at Thy feet 'tis good to be,
Thy voice to hear, Thy presence see."

The nervous fear of the return of the ancient evil was still strong within him, and he did not venture to go away from the side of Him in whom was peace and healing. And so, when the Master was about to go away, his prayer, in singular contrast with the prayer of the onlookers—that He would depart out of their coasts—was, that He should suffer him to be with Him, for he dreaded to be alone, lest the old devildom should surge upon his spirit once more. But Christ says to him, "Go to thy home, and tell what things God has done for thee." The man, with the freshest, most uncertain, most tremulous possession of the new position, of the new light, need not be afraid; no man need be afraid of going where Christ sends him.

So much for it as a picture, as a bit of historical fact.

These two points are, I think, often slurred over—of the restfulness and the explanation of "at the feet of Jesus."

Another point about this incident, taken as being a pattern specimen of the transforming power of Christianity on a wide scale in the world's history. I don't spend much time over that. First of all, transformations like that; then down to the externals and the material part of it.

Transformations like that are the common trophies, the every-day results of the spread through the world of the gospel of Jesus Christ. Account for it as you like, it is no part of my present business; but here is the fact to be dealt with by all honest men, that the old story of the man, the outcast, devil-ridden, mad under the possession, being brought back by a touch, by the power of Christ's love, into quiet, into sanity, into decency; that that is only a picturesque way of saying what the poorest preaching of His great name is doing over all the world. You tell us that Christianity in its missionary aspect has failed. Very well, admitted that the quantity of results is not what might have been expected, what I say is, that the fact of one single soul taken out of the dirt and slough and demoniacal abyss of heathendom; some rampant, raving, savage taken, clothed, brought within the limits of civilization, taught decency, taught propriety, delivered from the gross and the sensual—though with many infirmities—and set upon a path of, at least, incipient purity; that this is a fact that cannot be accounted for by the people who say Christianity has failed. I want to know what else does that. Go to those dark islands of the Southern Pacific, where seventy or eighty years ago you had the lowest depths of savagedom. Look at them now. Travellers make merry with the strange hybrid of an English Christianity grafted upon a Sandwich Islander,—and I do not know that the men who have gone to do the preaching have always gone the wisest way about it—the main central thing is, that here comparatively ignorant men, people with no knowledge of the genesis of idolatry, and no power of dealing with philosophy, have gone there and said, "Jesus Christ loves me, and He came to die for me." And somehow or other that has got into men's minds, and it has made them, instead of rampant demoniacs, to be in restful tranquillity, clothed with many a material good, in their right minds, at the feet of Jesus. Young man! is there anything else, do you think, will do that? And until something else will do it, I want you to consider whether that is not the power of God and the wisdom of God. So they said long ago; so we, I think, may very quietly say now. Let them do the same with their enchantments, and then we will begin to discuss how they have managed it.

We say, Christ crucified, the germ of all social, moral, and political, and intellectual advancement, and who hath won men that will fight with heathendom and savagery and devildom over all the world! And so, to the other points for a minute or two. For instance, one of them is this, that here then, with this picture of the man, "sitting, clothed, and in his right mind, at the feet of Jesus," interpreted by the facts which we see round about us—and these things are being wrought out in many a back slum, and all round about us—these may tell us the true method of dealing with all social and political and moral problems. Christianity *does* conduce to the material well-being. It was worth while to tell that the man was *clothed*. That point came in worth noting, even in the midst of the better thought, that he was restful—the influence of the mind. And at the feet of Jesus. We Christian teachers have, I think, been seriously to blame in not sufficiently depicting that side of Christian truth.

And then another set of Christian teachers have sprung up all round about us, and say, "Oh, you people who are always talking about conversion, and the fantastic experience of individual lives, you have forgotten the main characteristic of Christianity, that is a *social* force intended to lift whole masses of men." Yes, I believe that too. And still further, what some of you will think very narrow, that there is very little prospect of permanence and going far with any kind of reformation or amelioration of the conditions of humanity which does not flow from the power of the gospel of Jesus Christ. If Christianity is nothing more than a means of saving a man's own miserable soul, in shutting up for him a future hell, then it is not worth preaching, I was going to say!

If Christianity is nothing more than a social agent—a means of keeping down the police and the poor-rates—then it is still less worth preaching. "What God hath joined, let no man put asunder!"

And I say this, the power of the gospel to lift masses of men in their material and social well-being is a result of the power of the gospel to deal with the far deeper disease of the sores and sins of single souls. The individual first, and the mass afterwards. First of all, peace and forgiveness through our Lord Jesus Christ, and then all the beauties and graces of life after that; but first of all he has to get the power of the devil crushed out of him, and the Master will do that. We may either take this picture as being not only a pattern on a large scale of Christian perfection in the world, but also, my dear friend, it may be, and ought to be, to you and me, a prophecy full of blessedness as to what Christ will do for you and me, for each of us by himself. And here is the message it seems to proclaim. First of all, am I speaking to any man or woman that is ready to say, "Oh! I have tried so often, that it is no use trying any more; I am shut out by the obstinacy of my nature, by my many failures, by my long service and slavery to sin. And the old proverb, that 'It is never too late to mend,' is but very poor, cold comfort." But He has a message for you. There are no outcasts beyond the sweep of Christ's large mercy, beyond the leverage of Christ's great love; and you, brother and friend, and all of you, the very poorest wretch on the face of the earth, we may all light up eyes of hope and say, "I too have a place in Christ's love, and for me too was that blood shed, and it has not been shed in vain." I ask you to take the picture, and for a moment or two take the two verses in contrast: "There met Him out of the city a certain man, which had devils long time, and ware no clothes, neither abode in any house, but in the tombs. For oftentimes it (the unclean spirit) had caught him: and he was kept bound with chains and in fetters; and he brake the bands, and was driven of the devil into the wilderness." That is what he was. Are you worse than that? Are you more hopeless than that? Are any of us much better than that? Are not you like that? Come, that is a more testing question, is not it? Are not you *like* that? Conscience, answer! Memory, answer! Well, what then? Then here is the other, "And they found him sitting at the feet of Jesus, clothed, and in his right mind." Lesson the first.

Lesson the second. Here is what God sends me to offer to every man and woman in this place to-night: rest for distraction; peace; tranquillity; quiet of heart, of conscience, of memory, of soul, of hope. Rest! self-command; power of ruling your own animal nature. And that is something, young man,—the power of ruling your own passions, your own purposes, your own thoughts. Emancipation from the madness of sins, from the delirium of dissipation, from the insanity of a life hid up by the things that are seen and temporal. I tell you, the only reasonable man in the world is the Christian man; and religion is nothing more than the superlative of common sense! And so the madman is the man that says, "Tush! I do not think of a God; and as for the 'beyond,' we will jump at it." Dear brother, rest, strength, righteousness, wisdom— all that can clothe your spirit with radiance and beauty, and loveliness and peace—I bring to you "at the feet of Jesus." Take Him for your Helper, and the ejected demon will not come back. Go away from Him and he will, and "the last of that man shall be worse than the first." Keep near Him, love Him, hold firm by His hand, bring your heart, and your thoughts, and your will, and your purposes all under His control, and turn to Him and say: "Lord, I am weak; cast Thou Thy strength about me. My heart is empty; fill Thou it." And He will give you, in His own good time, liberty from many a struggle and much difficulty, the victory from all your sins, will make such poor characters as you and I may know ourselves to be, images of His own body, radiant with His own lustre, and perfect with His own completeness. Keep near to Christ, and Christ will lift those that have found safety and healing at His feet, will lift them up to be partakers of His crown and His throne.

XI. The Lost Coin. LUKE xv. 8. "*Light a candle, and sweep the house, and seek diligently.*"

THREE parables stand together in this chapter. The occasion of all is one and the same—the murmuring of scribes and Pharisees against the Saviour who would eat with sinners. And the general drift of all is the same—the feeling of God towards repentant sinners illustrated by man's feeling towards a possession lost and found. Thus far there is unity—there is even identity—in the three. But no two parables of our Lord are really identical, however like may be the incidents of one to those of another. And so it is here. There is a climax natural and real in the three losses in this chapter. In the first parable, the owner of a hundred sheep loses one of them. In the second, the owner of ten pieces of silver loses one of them. In the third, the father of two sons loses one of them. Now, the second lost thing, though it is the less valuable, is to the owner more so. The third is a loss different in kind, and appealing yet more forcibly to the understanding and heart of mankind. There is a climax also in the thing signified. The sheep has strayed in its ignorance from the flock and the pasture. The son exiles himself of self-will and rebelliousness from the home and from the father. Between these two extremes of mere simplicity and utter wilfulness lies the insensate unconsciousness of the lost coin. If the first figure is the type of the erring soul, the second is the type of a soul ignorant of its death, utterly unconcerned with the thought of sin and ungodliness, and needing a special ministry of loving-kindness suitable to that particular condition. On the other hand, this soul itself is already, in the figure of a parable, a coin. It is not a mere fragment of brass or silver unappropriated. It has already an image and a superscription. It may be covered with dust; it may be stained with weather; it may be half defaced with much handling; it may be hidden under heaps of rubbish; but it has not returned, and it cannot return, into the uncoined state. The impress of a Royal Owner is upon it; and His treasury, however far distant, is its origin and, therefore, its home. Meet emblem, my brethren, of man's soul in its lowest, its most lost, estate. "I am God's coin," said one of old. "From His treasury-house I have wandered. Have mercy on me!" Made in God's image, after God's likeness, we cannot unmake, though we may undo, ourselves. We cannot cease to be God's property, though we may put ourselves to very base uses. We cannot be re-issued from another mint, though we may cease to circulate as God's coin. The very figure is a sermon. There is that in us all which testifies whose we are; and we do no honour to God when, in a misplaced humility, we speak of ourselves as not yet His. The finally lost spirit has effaced the superscription. When that is accomplished, there is no recovery and no return; but while the day of grace lasts, the image is there, and God, who speaks to us from heaven, speaks to us as His own. It is a mighty secret of love and redemption. We are God's, and therefore He seeks. We are God's, and therefore we can be found.

Some, in their anxiety to find types everywhere, have busied themselves in interpreting the figure of this woman. We will not follow them in saying positively that she has a name, though some of her characteristics might, I grant, be found in God's Church. I would rather see in this feature of the parable how God takes to Himself, and makes part of His Divine nature, the essential graces and virtues not of man only, but of woman—speaks of Himself now and then, in places that I could point to, as not the Father only, but (with reverence be it spoken) the Mother also, of His creatures, as though pleading with us in tones which must penetrate the heart of all who have ever known the love of woman—of mother or sister, or wife or daughter—and bidding us not only to feel His tenderness, but also to reciprocate and to hand it on.

Thus at every turn we see a distinctiveness in this parable, something peculiar and unique in its imagery; and so it is not less with those brief clauses of it which I have made my text. The woman who has lost one of her ten pieces cannot acquiesce in and rest in her loss. Little in itself, to her it is vital. She waits not for the light of day, but, discovering her loss at night, by night she sets herself to repair it. She lights the lamp, sweeps the house, and seeks diligently till she finds it.

It is a parable, beloved brethren, of the love of God. God represents Himself as missing one soul. Little is that soul in itself to the great God. Myriads of such spirits, washed and sanctified, already people the blessed home where God is. But God would show to us that each one is precious. Each one was separately created: each one has a place designed for it in the universal temple: each one not filling that place leaves a blank. The eye of love misses it, and therefore the hand of love seeks it. We would not speak where the Divine Interpreter is silent: we would speak but timidly, and with peradventure. If Christ, the Divine Interpreter, had here spoken as He speaks in the key to the sower and to the tares, might He not, perhaps, have said this: "The coin is the soul, and the candle is the word, and the house is the man, and the sweeping is God's discipline, and the diligent search is the meaning of this lifetime, and the finding is the everlasting salvation. And as the woman in the parable calls together her friends and her neighbours to rejoice with her in the finding, so does the love of God share its joy with an innumerable company of angels, often as one sinner is brought to repentance, often as one lost life is reclaimed to sorrow and prayer, and faith and amendment." No loss, in God's judgment, is comparable to the loss of a soul. A soul may be lost—is commonly lost—life still continuing. Doubtless in the sight of God there are some soulless lives present here this evening. Whosoever cares not for God, lives not to God, asks only how he can please himself—get the most of earth's goods, its wealth or pleasure or honour—avoids trouble and pain, shirks duty, would sin and not suffer, would do wrong and hide it, would pass for the thing he is not, or be endured, accepted, honoured, being the thing he is—that is, a soulless man; that is, one of those coins which have God's image and superscription upon them, but have got hidden in the dust and mire and refuse of this world and are as much lost to all the real purposes of their being as the shilling that has dropped between the chinks of your floor, or behind the wainscoting of your wall.

Now, know that, though you may care little about your lost soul, God cares for it much. God has lit His candle—the candle of Divine revelation—and He is throwing its illumination upon you. We wonder why you have come here if you do not intend to be shone upon. Here in this place the secrets of hearts are revealed, and soulless men are shown their destitution. Oh, be sure, conscious or unconscious, you came here to-night to be shone upon. There is that in you which cries out for God—which will not rest—which you cannot persuade to rest—out of God's light; and you are here because you feel that. Yes, many a man feels without knowing what he wants. The Divine Master interprets. You want God's love and the love of God. The one is the echo, the reflection, of the other. And God's love has lit her candle, and will throw its light full upon you. God is going to look for your soul. Hinder not, thwart not, the search. But love herself might kindle the light, and yet the lost cannot be found; for indeed, brethren, that soul which is the coin, when lost as we have described, keeps itself well out of sight,—is thoroughly overlaid, overgrown, overwhelmed, with weeds and thorns, with papers and books, with long indulged habits and easily besetting sins; and no mere lighting up, no, not if the candle is that of God's word earnestly preached and keenly applied, will suffice to discover it. That is the object—to discover the lost soul. Therefore the parable goes on to speak of a sweeping. I know it is a homely figure,—too homely, perhaps, for some tastes,—beneath the dignity, some might say, of this pulpit, only that here Christ has gone before—has written it in His book, and given it to me for my text.

And how wonderful, however homely, is this figure. The love of God first lights up in the world this lamp of revelation, telling man what man could not know, for no man hath ascended up to heaven to read there, in the light of that world, the things that were, and that are, and that shall be. First this, and remembering that this light will never fall of itself upon the lost coin, the very loss of which lies in its being out of sight of the man himself. Then, secondly, the love of God sweeps—sweeps, I say, the house, which is the man. Oh, this—the stirrings of the life which Providence works—is not this the real meaning of that disappointment, that sickness, that bereavement, which seemed to you so casual, or so wanton, or so cruel? The love of God had failed in its illumination. You might have let it suceeed, but you did not. You suffered the dust of earth to lie thick upon you,—perhaps the amiable dust of kindly sentiment, of satisfied affection; or, perhaps, the ugly dust of eager grasping, of predominant self, of overmastering passion; and so, evading the illumination, you necessitated the sweeping. It was the love of God still. I pray you lose not that thought. Only it was a love which, in order to succeed, must now sweep, when, if you would have had it so, its bright shining would have been enough. And then there comes into the very life's life a stir and an agitation which cannot be disregarded, though it is easy to misinterpret it. Now begin all manner of questionings, from which previously you were free. To your astonishment, truths once self-evident become now incredible. While you cared not for God, you took God for granted. Now you want Him, and you cannot believe. You thought, before, that at any moment God could be found if you happened to want Him. To question God's being, or His attributes, or His word, or His omnipresence, would in those days have been monstrous to you; but now you want Him, and you cannot find. The besom of the Divine discipline is busy, and its first effect is to raise the dust which it would remove. All is confusion, all is added doubt and added conflict. Your very sins seem more powerful. While you were let alone, you could fancy yourself independent; you only sinned because you chose to sin. Now you find that sin is your master, and you are its slave. An alien usurper holds the key of the being, and you are not your own. Yet in truth, strange as it may be to say it, the condition is more helpful. You are passing now from death unto life, *passing*, not *passed*. The love of God is at work, and will seek diligently till she find.

Marvellous word! Record at once of difficulty and perseverance. How much is required ere the finding be accomplished! To find the lost soul is not easy. The whole work of sanctification is wrapped up in it. Every thought has to be brought into captivity; every motive has to be elevated; every habit uncoined and re-nicked. Objects indifferent once, or distasteful, are to be made the aim of the life; and that holiness which, to fallen man, is repugnant, must be cultivated for a purpose to fallen man repulsive— that he may at last see God. This is the meaning of that diligent search by which love at last shall find; for without success, love cannot live. It is not enough for love to have done its duty in trying to find. Love cannot sleep till its object be accomplished. No toil is too great, may she but attain.

Surely, brethren, we read here the explanation of much that is so perplexing in our life's history. Why is it that God will not let me alone? God knows that I do not want Him. Again and again I have prayed the Gadarene prayer, "Depart from me, O Christ! Torment me not before the time. Grudge me not this brief truce. Is not eternity long enough, which is before me?" No, we will not frame into words these dreadful blasphemies, though they are the secret prayers of many. We will but interpret.

This seeking is unto finding. Love will not stay till she finds. Help her, brethren, every one, in her gracious, her wonderful work. Let her find. Help the joy of angels. Let the heavenly feast be cheered by the tidings of another finding. Kick not against the goad. It drives till you will let it lead. Then all is peace. Love and you are at one. Then, as a prophet has written, there is "quietness and assurance for ever."

What remains but that, in a brief word or two, we treat the text as I first read it—as a precept. "Light a candle; sweep the house; and seek diligently" till you find. Your soul is the lost thing. The love of God is seeking, but you have the power of frustrating that search. The mystery of the free will is one of two enigmas; the mystery of Divine grace is the other. How can they co-exist? Perhaps Heaven will tell us the secret. We know not, but at present we see this—that the neglect of either half of the truth is the loss of the whole. Enough—that shall suffice for us in the present—both parts are true. Meanwhile, be we workers together with God. Let the free will help the grace. Light a candle. God has lit it in the word: light it in the soul. Take the lamp, which is God's word, and let it shine. Take the bushel off it, and let it shine for thee. This is a different thing from hearing sermons; this is a different thing from reading the Bible patiently, tolerantly, or even attentively. This implies a resolution on your part that the Bible, that the gospel, shall mean something for you. This implies that you will not live and die with a mere sound buzzing in your ears—no, not if it be a pleasant sound like that of which Ezekiel wrote of old; but that you must and will have not a sound but a voice, an articulate voice, come to you out of that book. However little it says, even if four-fifths or nine-tenths or ninety-nine-hundredths of it be at present unintelligible to you, and unreal, yet the little it does say shall be a voice and not a sound—a voice of information, a voice of direction, a voice of counsel, and a voice of comfort. I will keep to its plainest parts till I have them by heart and by soul. I will never hear one sermon without learning from it, and doing something after it. Thus shall I light God's candle within, and make it shine through the chambers of my imagery. Then I will sweep the house.

Remember, what you are looking for is your soul. You see your mind plainly enough—you see your heart—you see your life, so far as these things have to do with this world, with its business, its studies, and its affections. But the soul is still out of sight. That one silver piece, so inestimably precious, if not in itself, yet to God and to the man, is still covered up, overlaid, hidden. Then I must sweep for it. It is a true parable still. I must look well into my inmost life. I must ascertain which way my life looks at present,—whether downward or upward,—whether around or beyond,—whether to self, that ugly, deformed, obscene idol, or to God and my brother. I must investigate thought and speech; I must search out habit and temper and spirit; I must see where that innermost being is, and how occupied, which alone can converse with, live for, and at last live with, God. Oh, I dare not die, and therefore I will not live, with all this unsettled. I must seek diligently till I find. I must not search languidly, search for a day or an hour, and cease. I must find this hidden, this buried, this lost thing inside me; and, if nothing else would stir me to this, let the thought of the love, let the thought of the joy, here disclosed, arouse me to it, and animate and quicken. Think of the revelation of that world here made to us; spirits unfallen, spirits that left not their first estate, spirits to whom sin is intelligible and the spectacle of sin must be hideous, stooping from the heavenly places to watch and to sympathize with His finding of the sinner; angels beholding the face of God as the angels of Christ's little ones; angels desiring to look into God's human dealing, and finding in His Church a disclosure altogether new of His unsearchable wisdom; God Himself occupied, not alone, not chiefly, with the upholding of systems, each atom of which is indispensable to the revolutions of the universe—occupied rather with this, the setting right a disarranged soul, the bringing harmony out of that human discord, the eventual bringing home of that stray exile, self-exiled, and yet not forgotten. Oh, if this be heaven, if this be God, how, *how* shall I escape if I neglect so great salvation?

C. J. V.

XII. "Where are the Nine?" LUKE xvii. 17. "*And Jesus answering said, Were there not ten cleansed? but where are the nine?*"

IN order to do justice to the act of mercy which is recorded of our Lord here, and to the subsequent conduct of the lepers, it is necessary, my brethren, to remind ourselves of the physical, of the religious, and of the social misery which leprosy involved. The leprosy of the Bible belonged to the class of skin diseases which are especially provoked by the dry, hot atmosphere of Egypt and the East acting upon a large, exposed surface of the human body. These diseases are aggravated, as of old in Egypt, when large numbers of men work together in kilns, or among dry and powdery substances, or when they are neglectful of personal cleanliness. The leprosy of the Bible is not, it would seem, the disease which goes by that name in modern Europe, and which is still not uncommon in Spain and in Norway. The two diseases may have been always distinct; but, on the other hand, it is well known that, in the course of years, a disease will exhaust its type, disappear, and then reappear in a modified form.

The leprosy of the Bible is what is now known as the Mosaic or white leprosy. Its symptoms are enumerated in the 15th of Leviticus. It was the leprosy of Miriam, of Naaman, of Gehazi, of King Uzziah. It was little better than a living death. Beginning on the surface of the body, it poisoned all the springs of life. One by one, the limbs of the sufferer decayed and fell away. The leper, in Scripture language, was "as one dead, of whom the flesh is half consumed when he cometh forth from his mother's womb." This loathsome appearance, which must have inspired the patient and all around him with a sense of extreme humiliation and disgust, was aggravated, it is needless to say, by very considerable suffering. And, to crown all, no cure was possible, except by Divine interposition. No skill of man in that age could cope with this foul disease. "Am I a god?" exclaimed the king of Israel, on receiving the Syrian ambassadors on behalf of Naaman—"Am I a god, that this man doth send unto me to recover a man of his leprosy?"

And leprosy was not merely physical misery. It had in Jewish eyes, and on Divine authority, a religious significance. It was viewed, not so much as a punishment of sin, but as a symbol of the expression of sin's presence and triumph. Beyond other, or alone among, diseases, leprosy was the chosen symbol of moral defilement. It was a visible manifestation of sin. The spiritual eye of a wilful or degenerate race was too dull to discover the stain and wound which moral evil leaves upon a spiritual being; but a loathsome disease might inflict this lesson in moral truth upon man's sluggish or reluctant senses. From physical evil which man did see, he might learn something about moral evil which he did not see. And this leprosy was the outward sign of an inward curse. It was, so to put it, a sacrament of moral death; and, accordingly, the leper was bidden by the ancient law to bear about on him the emblems of the dead. His garments were rent, as if in mourning for his dead self. His head was bare, as was the wont of those who held converse with the dead. His lip was covered. He could only be legally cleansed with the cedar wood, the hyssop, and the scarlet, as those who had been defiled by contact with a corpse.

To this physical and religious misery there was added

another—a social one. The leper was banished from the companionship which might have soothed, if it could not cure, his pain. He was put out of the camp, or city, or village, which had been his home, even when the disease was not yet proved, and when the suspected mark might turn out to be purely innocent. A seclusion of seven days, and, under certain circumstances, of seven days more, from the communion of the confederate people, was sternly prescribed by the ancient law; and, when leprosy had been proved, influence and station, however exalted, could do nothing to avert or to mitigate the sentence. Miriam, the sister of the great lawgiver himself, was thrust without the camp. Uzziah, king though he was, must dwell in a separate house till the day of his death. And this was in part, no doubt, a sanitary precaution. Whether based upon popular apprehensions, or on an accurate estimate of the contagious nature of the disease, I do not now inquire; but it was much more due to the religious estimate of leprosy which was current in ancient Israel. The leper was a living emblem of that sin which no mere human healer can cure or expel—of that sin which excludes from the camp or city of God—that everlasting city into which, as we know, "there shall in no wise enter anything that defileth."

It was in our Lord's last journey towards Jerusalem, on the frontier of Galilee and Samaria, that He saw, on the road towards a village which is not named, ten lepers. They might not come near the gates, as being tainted with the fatal disease—as lying under the ban of God. They kept together in a band, endeavouring, no doubt, to find in each other's company some solace for their sufferings, for their sense of humiliation and disgust, for their exclusion—their forced exclusion—from the civil and religious life of their countrymen.

Misfortune makes strange associates, and of these lepers one was a Samaritan. Illness, too, will make men think of God who have never thought of Him before; and as our Lord passed along the way, He drew the attention of these poor outcasts to Him. Conscious of their misery, they stood afar off, and yet, even if nothing came of it, they must appeal to Him. They might—it was possible—they might have heard that one of the distinctive features of

His work among men was that the lepers were cleansed. They might have heard that He had commissioned His representatives not merely to heal the sick, but specifically to cleanse the lepers. They had, no doubt, an indistinct idea that He was, in some sense, the Healer of mankind; and so, as He passed, they lifted up their voices in agony, and said, "Jesus, Master, have mercy on us."

This prayer was, in itself, an act of faith; and, as such, our Lord at once tested it. There they were, all the ten, covered with leprosy, but He bade them do that which already implied that they were perfectly cleansed. They were to take a long journey, which would have been a waste of labour unless they could believe that He could make it worth their while to take it. "Go," He said, "show yourselves to the priests." To go to the priests for inspection, unless they were healed, would only have led to a repetition of their sentence as proved lepers; and, therefore, after His sermon on the mount, our Lord had first healed a single leper, and then had sent him to undergo the prescribed inspection. Here it must have perplexed them sorely. Here He does nothing for them at the moment. He bids them go in their uncleanliness, as if they were already cleansed. Could they trust Him? That was the question. Could they trust Him sufficiently to make the venture—to obey when obedience, for the moment, seemed irrational, in firm persuasion that obedience would be justified by the event? Yes, they took Him at His word. They set out for Jerusalem, a distant journey along an unwelcome road: but, lo, as they went, and, as it would seem, before they could have gone far, a change was already upon them. They looked around, each one at the other—each at himself. They saw that an unseen power was there, cleansing them—they knew not how—of the foul disease, restoring to them the freshness and purity of their childish years. "As they went, they were cleansed." It was in the act of obedience that they obtained the blessing. It was by assuming that our Lord could not fail, that they found Him faithful.

They were all of them cleansed—all the ten; but, like Naaman, the Syrian leper, returning with his blessing for the man of God, one of them thought that something was due to the Author of so signal a deliverance. He left the others to pursue their onward course. He left them to claim, at the hands of the priests, their restoration to the civil and religious life of Israel. He left them: he could not do otherwise. He left them. He turned back, and with a loud voice glorified God, and then he threw himself at the feet of his Deliverer, to thank Him for this act of mercy and of power. And our Lord blessed him once more in another and a higher way. A greater possession far than that even of freedom from leprosy was assured to this poor Samaritan in the parting words, "Thy faith hath made thee whole." But ere He did this, our Lord uttered the exclamation, "Were there not ten cleansed? but where are the nine? There are not found that returned to give glory to God, save this stranger."

My brethren, He who knew what was in man, and who had already tasted so much of human ingratitude, could not have been surprised at the conduct of the nine lepers. But He calls attention to it as having, like His own merciful act itself, a typical value. The averages of gratitude and ingratitude among men do not vary much from age to age; and what here took place on a small scale would reappear, he knew full well, again and again, in the history of Christendom and of the world. Of Christians, it is probably true at this moment—literally true—that about ten per cent. are grateful to God for His mercies in nature and in grace, and ninety per cent. are more or less conspicuously wanting in anything that can be properly termed gratitude. And if this, or anything like it, be the true state of the case, it is a fact which certainly deserves attentive consideration; for want of gratitude towards Jesus Christ on the part of a Christian seems, at first sight, quite inexplicable, for gratitude is a natural virtue. Man is capable of gratitude, even in some of its highest forms, without the grace of Christ at all. Plato could thank the gods that he was a man first, then a Greek, then an Athenian; last, that he had been born in the age of Socrates. Seneca could write to his benefactor— "I know that I cannot adequately thank you, but I shall not cease to say that I cannot." Not merely civilized, but barbarous, human nature is capable of the courtesies and of the self-sacrifice of true gratitude. Nay; there have been remarkable traces of it among the lower creatures. Every one has heard of the lion who refused to

H

touch a Christian when the latter was exposed to the beasts in the amphitheatre, because he recognised the friend who had once tended his wound in the cavern of the desert. And for us Christians, how overwhelming are the motives to gratitude! The number, the magnificence, the practical value of the blessings which we receive from God, through Jesus Christ our Lord, conspire, with our sense of His love and His generosity, to make gratitude, one would think, strictly inevitable. And yet, as if anticipating what would be the real state of the case, Scripture insists, with great copiousness and fervour, upon what might have been, we should have thought, taken for granted. "When ye have eaten and are full," says Moses, "ye shall bless the Lord your God." "What shall I render to the Lord," says David, "for all the benefits that He hath done unto me? I will receive the cup of salvation, and will call upon the name of the Lord." "In everything give thanks," says St. Paul, "for this is the will of God in Christ Jesus concerning you." "Whatsoever ye Colossians do in word or deed, do all in the name of the Lord Jesus, giving thanks to God and the Father by Him." "Be careful, you Philippians, for nothing; but in everything, by prayer and supplication, with thanksgiving, let your requests be made known unto God." "Let the peace of God dwell in your hearts, and be ye thankful." "I exhort, therefore, that first of all," he writes to Timothy, "supplications, prayers, intercessions, and giving of thanks, be made for all men." These are but a few of the passages which might be quoted, and their number shows how much, in the mind and judgment of the Holy Spirit, such precepts would be needed in the days to come. Whether they are needed or not, my brethren, is a question for your consciences and for mine—a question on which it does not seem necessary to enter at very great length.

Of the unthankfulness which so seriously depresses and blights our whole modern Christian life, one reason, in many cases, is that we do not see our great Benefactor. I do not forget that some of us may feel true gratitude to those human friends who have been kind to us in past years. and who are now out of sight. But take men in the mass, and it is quite otherwise. Little by little, as the years pass, too many of us forget the benefits that we owe to the dead. The pressure, the importunity, of the present and of the seen makes us overlook the great debt of thought and love which we owe to the past and the unseen. There is a cynical proverb—one of those proverbs in which our poor human nature passes such stern judgment upon itself—" Out of sight, out of mind."

In the miracle before us, you will remember, the lepers were still uncleansed when they left our Lord that, in obedience to His command, they might show themselves to the priests. When the miracle was wrought upon them, the Worker was out of sight. He would have walked on towards the village; and they, avoiding the village in obedience to the law, were pursuing their way towards Jerusalem. Yes, at that moment of awe and blessing they did not see Him. No shadowy form hovered around them to remind them that He was present in power to bless and heal them. No word like the "I will: be thou clean," which had healed the leper at Capernaum two years before, now fell upon their ears. No hand was raised over them in felt benediction; and yet, minute by minute, the foul disease upon them was disappearing—when, or how, they could not exactly tell—and at last they saw—they could not doubt it—they saw that they were healed, but the Healer Himself they did not see. As now in His Church, so then He was out of sight, even when His action was most felt and energetic. His words still lingered in their ears; but it was not impossible, amid the distractions of a new scene, to forget their import; and thus, out of the ten men, nine actually did forget it.

Now what is this but a sample of what passes in our daily life? Numbers know what it is to have recovered from illness, perhaps very serious illness. God, by His providence, has directed us to use means which might assist —which could not insure—recovery. We have recovered, and now we proceed to account for our recovery. "It was a good constitution," we say, "that carried us through;" or, "It was a skilful change of treatment just at the crisis of the illness;" or, "It was a change in the weather;" or, "It was a change of air." Now, if this were not intended to be a complete account of the matter—if it was remembered that weather, clime, medical skill, strength of constitution, are all instruments in the hands of a supreme Agent, and that, ever mindful of His agency, we are merely describing the particular instrument which He has selected to carry out His purpose, then no harm would be done, but do we not too often stop short at the secondary or immediate cause of our recovery, and altogether forget the first cause? We see the secondary cause: the first, or real, cause we do not see, and we are so largely the slaves of sense that the horizon of our view becomes the measure of our gratitude. Alas! brethren, how do we thus turn God's loving generosity against Himself. Unlike those vulgar benefactors who insist upon being recognised while they dispense their bounties, God, generally speaking, hides His hand. He acts through laws which seem to operate spontaneously. He acts through agents who are, at the moment, perfectly free and self-determining. He conceals Himself behind the vast processes of nature, behind the slow movements of history, behind the clouds of heaven, till, at last, we conceive of the world, of the universe, as going on without Him— without Him, its sole Author, its absolute Lord. His generous self-concealment is taken for a forced inactivity, and, of those who still believe Him to have been the Author of all that is not Himself, too many think of Him as men now-a-days think of those old builders of schools and colleges, who have left their great foundations to later ages, and are powerless to exert any control over their handiwork. Thus God's very generosity only provokes our thanklessness. He keeps out of sight, and we take it for granted that He would show Himself if He could—that His agency is only invisible, because it is shadowy or unreal. Oh, singular perversity of our fallen nature, which is thus bound down and enslaved in its captivity to sense that we forget God our Saviour, chiefly because He is too loving to overwhelm us at once with the sense of what we owe to Him!

And a second cause of unthankfulness is our imperfect appreciation of God's gifts. No doubt, while the nine lepers were covered with their foul disease, placed under a social and religious ban, excluded from the society of their countrymen, they would have thought that no blessing in life could possibly compare with that of being cured of leprosy. But what did they think after the cure had been wrought? Too probably, something like this—that health was no such peculiar blessing, after all, since health, when they looked around, was shared by multitudes. In being free from leprosy, they were, after all, only like the great majority of their countrymen. Why should they become enthusiastic over a condition of things which was not the exception, but the rule? And is not this the temper of many Christians now-a-days? We are not—I admit it— we are not incapable of gratitude. We can rouse ourselves to acknowledge signal and extraordinary blessings. The one survivor from a wreck, or in a railway catastrophe, can still say, "Thank God!" with unaffected sincerity. But why should he thank God for benefits which he shares with all the world?—for existence, for preservation, for life, for food, for strength, for the use of reason, for friends, for home, and the like? He does not say that he ought not to be thankful for these things: he secretly thinks to himself that his gratitude will be somehow vulgarized, if it is lavished upon these every-day gifts. Had God given less, or had He given what He gives less indiscriminately, He would, it appears, have been thanked more warmly and more frequently than He is.

And this same feeling is sometimes applied even to the blessings of grace and redemption. All our lives we have heard of God's "inestimable love in the redemption of the world through our Lord Jesus Christ," of "the means of grace," and of "the hope of glory" beyond this world. We think so little of it, it may be, because this blessing is in its scope so vast and so inclusive. If the eternal Son of God had redeemed us and none others,—if, instead of willing all men to be saved and to come to the knowledge of the truth, He had made a very select few—ourselves among the rest—objects of His exceptional love, then, we think, it had been otherwise; but when His love is as diffused as the rays of the sun in heaven—when He opens His arms upon the cross to all the families of mankind, and bids any who will to drink of the water of life freely, men ask, "Why should we individually dissolve into ecstasies of gratitude in acknowledgment of blessings which are the portion, confessedly, of countless multitudes?"

This estimate of a blessing which takes little account of it, unless it be a rarity, like hot-house fruit or flowers in mid-winter, or in the early spring, is not—believe me, brethren—is not really due to a high ideal of excellence which will see the great only in the unwonted. Its true source is that dulness, that harshness, of spiritual perception which health and prosperity too often inflict upon the soul. We cannot see clearly through the thick film which has thus been formed over the spiritual eye. If we did, how impossible it would be to forget that God could not, without being untrue to His own glorious perfections, mete out His love and sympathy in the narrow measure which, it seems, would earn our gratitude. If we did see, we should own, with full and thankful hearts, that love is love, blessings are blessings, salvation is salvation, whether we share them with the many or with the few. The deliverance of the lepers was not the less signal because the health to which they were restored was the portion of the great majority of their countrymen ; nor was their gratitude less due because, in another form, it was due from thousands of Israelites.

And a third reason in many minds against cultivating and expressing thankfulness to God—(men do not mention it)—is the utilitarian one. Men do not see—if they said out what they think—do not see the good of thankfulness. The value of prayer, of course, in Christian eyes is plain enough. Christians believe that certain blessings are to be obtained from God by the instrumentality of prayer ; and not to pray is to forfeit the blessings which prayer obtains. "But thankfulness," men say to themselves—"what does it win for us that is not already ours without it ? Man already enjoys that for which he gives thanks, and God surely does not want our thanks as if they were a sort of equivalent for His bounty. He blesses us out of the joy of doing so ; and whether we thank Him or not must be of small concern to such a being as He is." Certainly, my brethren, God does not expect to be repaid for His benevolence by any equivalent in the way of thanksgiving that you or I can possibly offer Him. And yet He will have us thank Him, not for His own sake, but for ours. He, enthroned in His uncreated perfections, He loses—can lose—nothing, though we, to our loss, should forget Him altogether. But we cannot be wanting to the great duty of thankfulness without being untrue to the very fundamental law of our existence,—without the worst results upon ourselves. For what is thankfulness, such as God demands? What is it but that which is at the bottom of all real human excellence —the frank acknowledgment of truth? Just as prayer is the recognition of our dependence upon God amid the darkness and uncertainties of the future, so thankfulness is the recognition of our indebtedness to God for the blessings of the past. And to acknowledge truth like this is always moral strength: to refuse to acknowledge truth like this is always moral weakness. Accordingly, the worst excesses of the heathen world are traced by St. Paul up to the ingratitude of the Gentile nations for the light of nature and of conscience. "When they knew God, they glorified Him not as God, neither were thankful, but became vain in their imaginations, and their foolish heart was darkened." And, in the same strain, all the later apostasy and misery of Israel is referred, in the prophetic song of Moses, to the original vice of forgetting what God had done for that favoured people. "God had found Israel," says the lawgiver, "in a desert and in the waste howling wilderness. He led him about; He instructed him; He kept him as the apple of His eye. As an eagle stirreth up her nest, fluttereth over her young, spreadeth abroad her wings, taketh them, beareth them on her wings, so the Lord alone did lead him, and there was no strange god with him. He made him ride on the high places of the earth, that he might eat the increase of the fields; and He make him to suck honey out of the rock, and oil out of the flinty rock." But, then, after all, looking across the centuries, Moses thus addresses the degenerate race: "Of the Rock that begat thee thou art unmindful, and hast forgotten God that formed thee." And then he utters, in the Divine name, the prophetical sentence, "And he said, I will hide my face from them. I will heap mischiefs upon them; I will spend mine arrows upon them." And then he adds, in yearning love, "Oh, that they were wise, that they understood this, that they would consider their latter end!"

And this law is not the less true of individual Christians and of Christendom. Nations, Churches, men, who forget their one great Benefactor, are in a sure way to ruin, temporally and eternally. God cannot be forgotten with impunity. Thankfulness, like the rivers which flow into the ocean, and which are again replenished from it—thankfulness is the source of new blessings to the soul. Only in thankful hearts is the Christian life securely maintained, and to that life it contributes three important results.

It first of all stimulates us most powerfully to active well-doing. A man will do, out of gratitude, more—much more—than he will do out of fear or out of hope of reward. Thankfulness for redemption was the motive power of a life like that of St. Paul, as it has been the motive power of all the greatest and most fruitful lives that have been lived in Christendom. "He died for all, that they which live should not henceforth live unto themselves, but unto Him that died for them and rose again"—this is the motto of all such lives. Gratitude, like love, lives not in words, but in deed and in truth. Often those who feel most what has been done for them say least about it; but they *do* most. Gratitude can work; gratitude can suffer; gratitude can persevere; but one thing gratitude—for the inestimable love of God in the redemption of the world by our Lord Jesus Christ—one thing gratitude cannot do: it cannot bring itself to feel that it has done enough. It cannot in this world lie down with a sense that it has really paid off its debt to the Redeemer.

And, again, gratitude makes worship, especially public worship, real, serious, reverent. Praise is the very soul of the Church's worship, and praise is the voice of thankfulness. The first object, we are told twice every day, which makes us Christians assemble and meet together, is that they may render thanks for the great benefits which they have received at the hands of God. And these thanks are expressed in the greater number of the psalms, in the hymns, in the canticles, in the *Te Deum* beyond, perhaps, other hymns—(who but the thankful can possibly understand such a psalm as that?)—above all, in the holy sacrament, on that very account named by the first Christians the eucharist, wherein, to use the words of our Prayer-Book, we entirely desire God's Fatherly goodness mercifully to accept this our sacrifice of praise and thanksgiving. It has been said that our public worship would be much less unworthy of Him to whom it is addressed if, before beginning, each Christian would think exactly what he most needs to obtain by prayer at the hands of God. It may be said, with at least equal truth, that this improvement, so much to be desired, would be secured if we all of us had more of the spirit of the one leper in the Gospel, and less of the spirit of the nine,—if each act of worship could be a conscious turning back on the road of life, to fall at the Redeemer's feet and give Him thanks for the incalculable blessings of pardon and of grace which those who know anything about him—anything about themselves—know that He, and He alone, has won for them.

And, lastly, thankfulness here on earth is the best possible preparation for the spirit and for the life of heaven. Heaven is the home of thankful souls. The occupations of heaven would be misery to those who feel not gratitude. "Blessing, and honour, and wisdom, and thanksgiving, and power, and glory, and might, be unto our God for ever and ever." "Worthy is the Lamb that was slain to receive power, and wisdom, and riches, and strength, and honour, and glory, and blessing." How shall we sing those songs, or any of the songs of the redeemed, hereafter, if here and now we do not learn their spirit? If the habits which are being formed by us in this life will be carried by each of us into the eternal world, how earnestly should we pray God to give us that "due sense of all His mercies, that our hearts may be unfeignedly thankful, and that we show forth His praise, not only with our lips, but in our lives, by giving ourselves to His service," to whom, the Father, the Son, and the Holy Ghost, be ascribed all honour, power, might, majesty, and dominion, henceforth and for ever!

H. P. L.

XIII. The Prodigal Son. Luke xvi. 11–32.

THE passage opens with the gathering of one of those remarkable throngs that assembled to hear the Saviour wherever He went, and that increased in the later months of His life until they became so unwieldy as to be positively dangerous. "Then drew near unto Him all the publicans and sinners for to hear Him." It is not a mere matter of fine criticism that emphasizes such words as, "Then drew near unto Him": they are words which carry, in connection with many other elements, the impression which is produced upon the minds of all who study the personal habits of our Saviour. There is abundant evidence that He never stood afar off, as if in merely official relations; that He never made such a separation of Himself from His people as is implied by audience and speaker according to ordinary modern usages. He went with the throng. We have little hints which show that when He wrought His miracles, they were wrought in the way of affection and personal attention. If a blind man was to be healed, He took him by the hand, and led him out of the town, and then healed him. He would go near to persons, and put His hands upon them, and pronounce the sanative benediction.

So there gathered about Him, wherever He went, those who were attracted by the singular power which He had, and of which sympathy was largely the secret. There gathered about Him a large class of people; and not only did they stand and look afar off, held back by a certain awe, but they came where He was. They came, even unbidden, into the dining halls. They came into His very presence. They wept upon His feet. They touched Him. They indulged in various familiarities toward Him. And when it is said, "Then drew near unto Him all the publicans and sinners for to hear Him," we are to imagine that He stood in a throng of these worst men—as they were esteemed by the genuine Jew.

The publicans were hated because they were foreign officers. Usually they were Jews; but what business had a Jew to be collecting taxes from his own people to put into the treasury of imperious, haughty Rome? He turned against his own kind, and became the instrument of a foreign despot. Aside from any extortion that they might practise, the ignominy of serving an enemy toward whom the Jews cherished the utmost bitterness and hatred rendered the publicans, the tax-gatherers, the most despicable of men to the patriotic feeling of the Jewish nation. The sinners were men and women of an abandoned character; men and women that had lost moral restraint, and had gone to the very extreme in vice—the outcasts, the undone, the wrecks of society. Here was a goodly audience gathered about Him of these publicans and these sinners; and you may well suppose that the orthodox Jews felt the utmost horror of it. "The Pharisees and Scribes murmured." That is, they whispered, muttered. You know that sometimes good men are apt to do that when things do not go to satisfy them. There is a great deal of talking behind the back, and a great deal of criticism and whispering going on, about persons who are not, according to their views, sound, and right, and safe. So was it with these men who had spent their whole lives in being good, and were so proud about being good that they had not got past the body, and had not had time to attend to the inward man, the soul—these men, who were so exceedinly scrupulous, who knew the truth, who had found it out—who knew to a line just what the Church was, and just what Church should be; and who had complied with the requirements, who had fulfilled the law, they thought, in every jot and tittle. If anybody did not know what the flavour of piety was, they could tell them. If anybody wanted to know anything about God and the eternal government, they were the ones to inform them. They were the favourites of God. They had the law, they had kept the law, and they knew what it consisted in. When they went after our Saviour, and looked upon His methods of teaching, and listened to His discourses, they went as critics; and seeing about Him this great unwashed throng, this great crowd of men vomited out of the waste places of Jerusalem, or of the Galilean cities, that surrounded Him, they said: "This Man receiveth sinners, and eateth with them."

Now, they could have got along with Him very well, probably, if He had kept a good distance off, in pontifical robes, or with an air more impressive than any pontifical robes, and had laid down the law to those wicked men out there; but He made Himself as one of them, and they came close up to Him, and He made them His fellows; He received them not simply into His presence, but into His company. They sat at the table with Him; and in that oriental country, to eat bread with one was to recognise him as a friend. He not only talked to them, but He ate with them; and that was thought to be as bad as to commune with them at the same table, He belonging to one sect and they to another.

Then it was that our Saviour uttered this exquisite parable of the Prodigal Son; and we will follow the course of the Prodigal Son, for the sake of bringing out, afterwards, several points that may well occupy our attention.

The point that He makes, and what may be considered as the text, is: "I say unto you, there is joy in the presence of the angels of God over one sinner that repenteth."

In another place, the same thing is said in another way: "Likewise joy shall be in heaven over one sinner that repenteth, more than over ninety and nine just persons which need no repentance."

This is the text—Divine sympathy with broken down, sinful men, and Divine joy in their recuperation; the sympathy of God and the helpfulness of God to all that have sinned, and are making even the feeblest strife to regain themselves. God is on the side of every sinner that desires to cease sinning. "A certain man had two sons: and the younger of them said to his father, Father, give me the portion of goods that falleth to me. And he divided unto them his living. And not many days after, the younger son gathered all together, and took his journey into a far country."

It is a striking fact that the first step that was taken amiss and downward (the first impulse probably anteceded this, but the first actual downward) step was the one of no longer desiring to abide under the parental roof. The bonds of affection were slackening. The wish to be his own master was growing in him. A vague and wild curiosity to know what was in the world was stimulating him. He could not bear the routine of morality in his father's house. He could not endure the restraint of his father's eye and voice. Therefore he determined to take his possessions and go and see the world. There have been thousands since his day who have wrecked and ruined themselves because they wanted to see what was going on among men. So he took his property and went forth from his father's house, and came to a far-off country, where he could not be sent for nor interfered with. He had wild liberty. He had absolute confidence in himself. He felt perfectly certain that he knew enough to take care of himself. "Let those remain tied to their mothers' apron strings who want to," said he; "I am a grown man, and I know a thing or two." No doubt if any counsel had been offered him, he would have thrown it off indignantly. He was going to a far country where nobody could oversee him. He sought liberty, but it was the liberty of the lower nature. It was not the liberty of the moral sense, striving to disengage itself from the thrall of superstition. It was not the liberty of a noble nature, seeking other channels for sympathy and beneficence. It was not the liberty of a generous soul who, seeing the truth, is resolved to break through old accustomed ways, and give up the world, though it should cost him his name or his life. It was not the liberty of the upper man. It was the liberty of the lower man. It was that kind of liberty which is called *licence;* and he soon became licentious—for it is said, "He took his journey into a far country, and there wasted his substance with riotous living." He poured out freely his means upon the cup. He indulged in the wildest and merriest dances. He was full of gaiety, because he was full of youthful spirits. He denied himself nothing that his eye saw, that his ear heard, or that his heart coveted; and his passions became his counsellors. "When he had spent all [and it did not take him a great while to do it], there arose a mighty famine in that land; and he began to be in want." Of course now there was nothing for him to do but to ask assistance from those neighbourly fellows who had met him so often, and enjoyed his hospitality. The moment he made his necessities known to them, of course they would succour him. Not so. When he sought their aid, they were nowhere to be found. Those who had shown him so much friendship, admired him, walked with him, coquetted with him, gone into every excess with him—they, surely, by their loving sympathy, would bear up a fellow-sinner. No, they had other friends now. They could not attend to him. All his companions were gone. There was none who cared for him.

There is many and many a young man who is walking on the same track in the world. To-day he has friends enough. Just as long as his pocket holds out, his company will be sought; but when his pocket gives out, he will be abandoned. No selfishness is so hideous as the selfishness which prevails among the passionate who, having enjoyed all the wild delirium of pleasure with each other, heartlessly abandon one another in the hour of extremity. "When he had spent all, there arose a mighty famine in that land; and he began to be in want. And [since he could do nothing else] he went and joined himself to a citizen of that country; and he sent him into his fields to feed swine."

He went into the saloon to begin with, and he went into the pig-pen to end with. It was not a long reach from the glory, the dazzle, the pride, the vanity, the lust and the licence of his youth, to the humiliation and the shame, the degradation and the want, of a swine-herd. There is no recall of him, no yearning after him. But there are a great many men that spend their substance and their youth and their health in riotous living who have a heart left. There are many bad men who have much in them that is good—who have a sense of honour lingering in them; who have aspirations, and who have yearnings for things high and noble. There is many a man who has philosophy with which to reason on his own mistakes, and who longs to reascend the path by which he descended so swiftly.

So was it with this young man, who had spent all, and began to be in want; and who went and joined himself to a citizen who sent him into the fields to feed swine. He went, and for aught that we can see, he did his work faithfully. He began to be sensible at last; for when a man has gone down by false steps of self-abuse, it is something if he accepts his situation, and sets up, in the low depth to which he has sunk, some foundations for renewed life.

Well, you will observe how this young man is spoken of, as if he had been insane. It is said, "When he came to himself." He had not really been himself. Every man has an equator, and all below that line is animal, while all above that line is himself. The upper manhood, the higher nature, is not the animal in you. It is that which allies you to the angelic, to God, to the invisible and eternal world. There is many and many a man who lives in his lower nature, and who is, as it were, insane, but whose sins, whose remorse, and the misery which comes from these, begin to bring him to his higher and better nature. He has proved the lower nature, and found its falsity, its oppression, and its danger; and through the suffering which comes from the wild indulgence of his lower nature—that which he is to leave with the dust when he dies—the door is open to that which is higher. "He came to himself." As a man that has been insane is, by some cooling draught or potion, brought to sanity and reason again, and is softened, and made rational, so this young man was brought to himself.

Blessed are they who, after following temptation and solicitation, and reaping misery, learn by that misery what is the royalty of their better nature, and are ashamed of sin and of sinning. Such was his extremity of suffering, that he "would fain have filled his belly with the husks that the swine did eat; and no man gave unto him." He was alone; he was uncared for and unprovided for. Those sweet and edible pods which were fed to the swine he would have chewed for his own sustenance.

Well, he had time for one thing—he had time, amidst his grunting charge, amidst the chanking swine, to think; he had time to suffer; he had time to be sorry. There are a great many men who have not time to be virtuous, who have not time to be religious, who have not time to do a great many things; but there is no man who does not find time, by-and-by, to be very sorry, very sad, in his adversity. So did this young man, "when he came to himself;" and I do not know that there is anything in this world more touching than that vision of home which rises, in their extremity, upon the wicked, either to torment them, or to lure them, by the hope and promise of sympathy and succour.

I have stood by the side of those that were sick, and I could bear to witness their pain; I could harden myself, as a surgeon would, to perform all the offices that were needful for their restoration; but when, in the midst of their trouble, when perhaps unconscious of what they were saying, they would call out, "Father! father!" or "Mother! mother!" it was more than I could bear. The going back of those who have gone through a career of licence and wickedness to the visions of childhood, its sweet innocence, the security of home, and the joy and pleasure of household fellowship—I think there is nothing that touches a sensitive person more than this.

And so the Prodigal Son, when he was reduced, through indulgence, to extreme distress, and when no man would show him any charity or any succour, began to bethink himself of his own father's house; and he said, "How many hired servants of my father's have bread enough and to spare, and I perish with hunger! I will arise and go to my father, and I will say unto him, Father, I have sinned against Heaven, and before thee."

Now, that is honest; that is manly. He did not say, "I will arise and go to my father, and I will state the circumstances." Oh, no. If there is anything in this world that is the devil of the casuist, it is "circumstances"; but he was not so bad as that. Having sinned, he had courage to look upon his sin and call it sin, and know that it was sin, and take it in all its magnitude. He attempted no acquittal, no palliation, no excuse, no piteous fear, addressed to the compassion of his old father. "I will arise and go to my father, and will say unto him, Father, I have sinned against Heaven, and before thee, and am no more worthy to be called thy son."

Here begins to spring out the exquisite delicacy and sensibility of a heart that is returning to a wholesome repentance, to nobility and to truth. He is already partly reformed whose soul begins to move to higher instincts. "I am no more worthy to be called thy son; make me as one of thy hired servants." Beautiful that is in its simplicity and humility. He knew how to go down, and, blessed be God, he knew how to go up too; but there are a great many men who know how to go down, but do not know how to go up.

Well, how fared it with him? "And he arose, and came to his father. But when he was yet a great way off, his father saw him."

Men see a great way with telescopes; eagles and vultures see a vast distance; but I take it that there is no eye that is so unerring, and that sees so far and so sure, as a parent's eye looking for a lost child. "When he was yet a great way off, his father saw him." And he saw all that was good in him; for fatherhood in its purest form is the truest expression, as it is the sign and symbol of the Godhead. "When he was a great way off, his father saw him, and had compassion, and ran, and fell on his neck, and kissed him." He waited for no word. He put him upon no conditions. There was no preparation. His father did to this son that returned just that which God does, and to all eternity will do, to every erring or struggling spirit that uprising, goes to Him—he gave him something of Himself, He gave him acceptance; he gave him sympathy and kindness. It is the nature of God, it is the nature of every true father, to do it.

The beauteous child, flattered and deceived, in an evil moment flees and wanders, and goes from bad to worse; and the mother's heart is sore through years, hearing from her and yet not being able to recover her; but at twilight, on some evening, as the mother sits and sees things darkling, there comes a form, ill-clad, with feeble step and sunken cheek, through the open gate. The mother knows her, and with open arms rushes to embrace the child that has come back. No word is spoken. Both hearts are pouring out a sacred tide. She bears her child to the house. "Mother, I have come home to die." "My child, live." Ought not the mother to say, "The public sentiment of this neighbourhood requires that I should call out from you some token that you have repented?" Ought she not to put her on some condition? Would it not be a violation of public sentiment to take her back without words? Nay; is there anything that cleanses away the sin of a child so fast as the loving heart of a parent? Men seem to think that there must be some preparation through which a man shall come to God. Yes, the everlasting nature of God Himself. That is the preparation. It is the heart and soul of Divine love that quickens to remorse the hearts of men that go wrong; that brings light to their darkness; that sees them afar off; that draws them by the cords of love; and that takes them then with a heart overflowing with forgiveness, not because they have done this, that, or the other thing, but because God is infinite in sympathy and in love; because God's nature, the moment your soul is open to it, pours a stream of cleansing redemption into it. God forgives from what He is, and not from what you have been.

The young man had come, you know, with a good orthodox confession; and he was going to pour it into his father's ear; but he found himself embraced, and wept over, and kissed. He struggled through, and said, "Father, I have sinned against Heaven, and in thy sight, and am no more worthy to be called thy son." He could not get out the other part—"make me as one of thy hired servants." He was smothered in his father's embrace, and he could not get it out.

What was the father's reply? He did not hear what the son said; it all, as it were, went to the wind; and he called to his servants, in fatherly gladness: "Bring forth the best robe, and put it on him, and put a ring on his hand [that scrawny hand which had just come from the husks and the swine], and shoes on his feet; and bring hither the fatted calf, and kill it; and let us eat and be merry." And the reason was: "For this my son was dead, and is live again."

That was reason enough for you and me, and for every noble man and woman, because God has lent us a little of His own feeling. There is no other argument.

Our Father in heaven is purer and better than earthly fathers; and if an earthly father knows how to bear and forbear, and wait to be gracious, and, with a generosity of love, to forgive those who have gone wrong, how much more shall God forgive, and cherish, and build up to eternal life, every one that comes to Him, or that desires to come to Him.

Well, this is a beautiful picture; but still, we must finish the whole scene. There was one other son. We have now, next, one of these perfect folks who censured Christ for eating with sinners; one of these pharisaic precisionists; one of these men who thanked God that they never stumbled; one of these men that knew what was right, and always did it. The story is in this language: "This my son was dead, and is alive again; he was lost, and is found. And they began to be merry." The old house shook. The lights glanced through the windows. The music was wafted into the field, where this exceedingly good elder brother was. "Now, his elder son was in the field; and as he came and drew nigh to the house [he could not imagine what they were about there], he heard music and dancing [it seems to have been a long time since there had been anything of that sort in the old house]; and he called one of the servants, and he asked what these things meant. And he said unto him, Thy brother is come; and thy father hath killed the fatted calf, because he hath received him safe and sound. And he was angry, and he would not go in : therefore came his father out, and entreated him. And he answering said to his father, Lo, these many years do I serve thee, neither transgressed I at any time thy commandment; and yet thou never gavest me a kid that I might make merry with my friends; but as soon as this thy son was come, which hath devoured thy living with harlots, thou hast killed for him the fatted calf."

Well, now, I would rather be the repenting prodigal son than the elder brother. Was not he a mean sneak? and was it not designed that these two brothers should stand over against each other and teach the world? The contrast between a man who by strong and impetuous inclination is led to sin, as the publicans sinned, as the sinners sinned, as the harlots and courtesans of Galilee or Jerusalem sinned—between a man who is carried away by his overpowering passions, but who, when he sees the final results of his wicked course, rebounds, and goes back, and frankly, honestly, acknowledges his sin—between such a man and one like this elder brother? Is not that character painted so that it seems a great deal more admirable than that of this precise fellow who never sinned at all, to his own thinking? He never got drunk—no, he was too stingy to get drunk. He never could afford wine. He spent nothing on courtesans. He was too cold, too unsympathizing. He did not give a loose rein to passion. It was the very pride of his life that he never did wrong. He was one of these locked-up, tied-up Pharisees, who are so afraid of going wrong that they do not go anyhow—who are so afraid of doing wrong that they do not do anything. He was self-contained, self-worshipping, and exceedingly proper. He was going toward heaven stiff, stingy, lean, mean, selfish. He was going to heaven like a mummy. And when his brother went away, he probably damned him in his heart right orthodoxly; when he heard how he was going on afar off in foreign lands, no doubt he had a very great horror of sin, in other folks; and when he heard that he had come back again, doubtless he said, "The beast of burden back on my father's hands! Now he will be dividing his substance with him, and I shall have less. Besides all that, look at the difference between us. I never ran away, and he did. I never fell into any impetuosities, and he did. I never squandered anything upon harlots, and he did. In all my life I have never done anything that was improper. I am made like a clock, having a stroke at every hour, being regularly wound up, and keeping time; but that fellow has been through all sorts of circumgyratory courses of evil. My father has made for him a royal feast, but he never made a feast for me. He never gave me even a kid, but he has given him a calf"—and he was so mad!

Where was that brother's heart? Where was his love of the cradle? Where were his childhood memories? Where were those ties of kinship and blood relationship that should have stirred every man to gladness who had a spark of manliness in him, on hearing that the prodigal had come home? Where was that impulse that should have led him to rush into the house and greet his returned brother, and say, "Let me help you"? He would not go in. He stood off, and grumbled. The salvation of his brother from destruction, his restoration to honour and love, the repairing of the breach in the household—all these things fell on him without producing any more impression than they would produce upon a stone. And yet he offered his sacrifices and rattled through his prayers every day, and kept, he thought, a pretty correct account in his bank up above. O Pharisee! Cold, unsympathizing moralist! How can one help despising such a man? You despise him when I am describing him. There is not a man, woman, or child, who does not feel, as I do, that this kind of dry morality is hateful. You feel that a man without any heart, without any pulse, without any warmth in his blood, hardly belongs to the human family.

And yet, many of you will walk in the street, and when you see some poor, drunken, filthy, ragged fellow, who has fallen step by step all the way down, and is trying to reform, I am afraid you will pass him by without a thought of sympathy—without one yearning. Yea, I do not know but you will thank God that you are not as other men are. Perhaps you will say, "I might have fallen into such wickedness, but I was strong, and so was saved from it."

When we see these flaunting mistresses of the street, there is much that shocks our delicacy; yet I never look upon them but, inside of me, there are not tears which move as from a fountain. When I see them, I see the mother; I see the childhood; I see the girlhood; I see the sad days of neglect and abandonment; I see the dying; I see the cheap funeral, with no mourners; and not only do I see the things that are visible, but I see the inner and spiritual reality. Do you see these things? Does your heart go out toward strict people, and orthodox people, and Church people, and your set of people in your denomination? and do you look upon those who are outside of your denomination, upon those who are not Church people, upon worldly people, upon people who have made mistakes in life, who have stumbled and gone to the ground, degraded and ruined, from a high point—do you look upon these with coldness, and even with bitter contempt? Then you are the elder brother.

If there be any meaning in this parable, it is that if a man stands where he probably thinks he is proper and right and virtuous, and has no compassion for his fellow-men who are in distress or want, even though it is by reason of their own folly, then he is the elder brother. Such a man is more despicable than he who has sinned more grossly, and yet seeks to repent. That is the meaning of our Saviour when He said, on another occasion, to these proud Jewish religionists:—"Verily I say unto you, that the publicans and the harlots go into the kingdom of God before you." It is as if He had said to them, "Their chances are better than yours." Hardness of heart, the want of charity for others, lack of sympathy and genuine beneficence—this is a crying sin; and against no class in Judæa did our Saviour hurl such anathemas as against cultured people, whose consciences were educated, but who were hard-hearted toward their fellow-men, and whose piety was without sympathy.

Dissipation through the basilar passions is not less bad than you think; it is worse than you think; but the dissipation of the upper nature, by which all that is Divine in a man is turned to coldness and selfishness, is a worse dissipation than the other.

In closing, I will add a few points. In the first place, let me say that according to this narrative it is never too late to mend. Perhaps there some persons who have strayed in here who have been thinking to themselves,

"What did he pick out that subject for? I wonder if he knew that I was coming. He has described my case exactly. I have been running away from my parents, from my instructors, from my own self. I have slipped and slipped; I have lost my name and position; I am hovering between life and death; and it is strange that he should have selected such a subject as that." No, it is not any more strange than that God should think of you, and by His providence should draw you where you hear such themes discussed. And I have a personal message for you. I have to say to you, to-night, you are a great deal worse than you think you are; you are a great deal worse than you yourself can measure or understand; and yet there is mercy in the heart of God for you. It is not too late for you to mend. It is not too late for you to turn round and go back to your Father and say, " I have sinned against Heaven, and in Thy sight!"

I have to say, secondly, to all such persons, and to all who are struggling to amend their mistakes, and to rise to a true life, that the heart of God is in its full tide of sympathy, and that those who need His help will receive it. "The bruised reed shall He not break, and the smoking flax shall He not quench, till He shall bring forth judgment unto victory."

Do you remember that remarkable scene which took place when our Master, a month or two before the crucifixion, was for the last time going from Galilee to Jerusalem? As He came to a Samaritan village, the people refused to give Him shelter, or food, or drink. The disciples had been sent forward to prepare for His stay there over night; and John, whose name is now synonymous with the most perfect gentleness and love, but who had a fiery temper, said, with James, "Lord, wilt Thou that we command fire to come down from heaven and consume them?" And the Master rebuked them, and said, "Ye know not what manner of spirit ye are of; for the Son of man is not come to destroy men's lives, but to save them." Jesus Christ came into the world to save sinners. Jesus Christ came to teach this grand revelation of the universe: that in spite of all the dark appearances of things, regnant in the centre of all power, in the midst of all that wisdom, whence issues that which controls all laws, there is a Heart that is full of compassion. The law of the universe is to restore, to recuperate; and the heart of God is on the side of every man who needs Divine love, Divine pity, and Divine mercy. You have not the power in yourself to do everything. You can do something; but, after all, the great work, the transforming work, the blessed work that is done in us, is the pouring out into our souls of the nature and inspiration of the love of God manifested to us through Jesus Christ.

Not only is God's heart on the side of the poor and needy: it is on the side of those who have stumbled by reason of strong drink, by reason of dishonesty, or by reason of headstrong passions and lusts. If you have gone through every one of the grades of defilement, and you find yourself at last among the swine, the heart of God is still on your side. It is on the side of the off-scouring and the most wretched of creation. Are you without a friend and without a benefactor? God is your Friend, and God is your Benefactor. "Yes," you say, "He would be if I would repent; but I do not feel like repenting." God is your Benefactor, repenting or not repenting. Repentance does not change Him; it changes you. When the son was yet a great way off, and before one word had entered into the father's ear, the father ran to meet him; and if you have in your soul one single movement toward hope; if there begins to be in your soul a letting go of things that are past; if there begins to be in your soul one aspiration, one yearning; if you say, "If I could only try; I have tried once, and failed, and it is of no use for me to try again; but yet I cannot give it up, and I would be glad to try again," those thoughts in you are the fruit of the Spirit. They are the result of the moving of the Spirit upon your understanding, and conscience, and heart.

Now, I beseech of you, grieve not the Spirit of God; for what is He? He describes Himself as one whose tenderness and gentleness are such that the bruised reed He will not break, and the smoking flax He will not quench, till He brings forth judgment unto victory. That is, He is so gentle in His dealings with men whose integrity, whose standing, is liable to be cast down as is the tallest reed that is the least able to stand against the wind —He is so gentle in His dealings with them, that He will not overthrow them. So gentle is He in His dealings with men, that in no way will He make it hard for them to stand or to recover themselves.

You know, when the flame is first lit on a candle how faint it is, and how reluctant it is to burn; so that the least breath of air, caused by the movement of your body, blows it out; and if there is in your soul the beginning of a desire for a better life, no larger, no brighter, than just the tip of the flame kindled on the wick of a candle, so gently does God deal with this merest speck of light of another and better life, that He will not quench it till He brings you through all the stages of reformation.

You have gone wrong, all of you. There is not one here who cannot lay his hand on his heart, and say, "I am a great sinner, and it is the grace and forbearance of God that give me life and mercy." There is not a single one of you that cannot say, "Lord, I have sinned, and I am not worthy to be called Thy son;" and yet you have the assurance that God's heart forgives, that God's love strengthens, and that God's wisdom will guide you till you are brought through various states of development to that condition in which you may be transferred to the heavenly land, and begin again, with ampler power and a better guidance, to reap nobler fruits and an eternal blessedness.

H. W. B.

XIV. Christ Washing the Disciples' Feet.

JOHN xiii. 12-15. *So after He had washed their feet, and had taken His garments, and was set down again, He saith unto them, Know ye what I have done to you? Ye call Me Master and Lord: and ye say well; for so I am. If I then, your Lord and Master, have washed your feet, ye ought also to wash one another's feet. For I have given you an example that ye should do as I have done."*

THIS touching incident—Christ's washing the disciples' feet—is fully related by this one Evangelist only; but it seems to me to be implied in the narrative of one other, that is, Luke. He tells us that at that table there arose a strife which disciples should be greatest; and it is at least possible that the occasion of that strife was the coming of the period at the table when the basin and the towel should be carried round, and that one after another refused the office as if it might prejudice their claims in the coming kingdom. And so, when it came to Peter, he said to John, and John said to another one, "You take it," and Christ said, "Here, give it to Me, and I will take it."

And so, if we connect the strife who should be greatest, with the strife who should not take the basin and the towel, then the words which the Evangelist Luke records receive a very profound addition to their meaning. "I am among you as he that hath power. Look at Me as I stand here, girt with the rough towel of servitude; and having done this menial office, I am amongst you as he that serves. The servant is not greater than his master, neither he that is sent than he that sent him. I have given you an example." And so these verses bring before us this great work of humiliation and of service. I want to get on to the various phases of this example. First of all we get—thrown into very remarkable prominence—the great and wonderful fact of that Master serving.

"Ye call Me Master and Lord;" and look then at the grand self-consciousness, the lifting up of Himself and His authority, as it were—" and ye say well; for so I am." "If I then, your Lord and Master, have washed your feet, ye ought also to wash one another's feet," etc. That is to say, He brings into the closest connection, as needing to be embraced in one act of thought, the two opposite poles of His dignity and His lowliness; as if He had said—"You cannot understand My servitude, unless you comprehend My masterhood. You cannot understand My authority, unless you have seen My humiliation and service." And that is one instance of a general law which runs through the New Testament, viz. that wheresoever you find a special emphasis and stress laid upon the lowly and the human side of Christ's character and nature, there you will find, in the closest juxtaposition, something about the corresponding idea—the dignity, the greatness, and the divinity. Like those double stars astronomers tell us of, revolving round one common centre, one of them opaque, one of them glowing, the black one and the golden one bound together by the power of their mutual centre. And so the glory and the lowliness, the majesty and the meekness, are indissolubly connected in the character of Christ. And so, if you take up the Gospel story, you will find many illustrations of that idea which I have not time to take. Here is just two or three of them. There He is, sitting in the stern of that fishing boat, the demonstration of that humanity in the weakness of our frail and fleshly need of rest; but He wakes to say, "Peace, be still," and immediately there is a great calm. There He is at the grave of Lazarus, with the tears of human sorrow on His cheeks; but before they are dry, He says, "Lazarus, come forth," and the sheeted dead comes forth, obedient to that quickening word. And so you get into near prominence the lowliness and the weakness, the humanity—there, side by side, you get something that manifests the divinity in the humanity, and the flashing glory of the manifest God shining through the obscure medium of this fleshly, limited life of ours. And that double star, as I said, is here in our text: "Ye call Me Master and Lord: and ye say well; for so I am." Christ—and this is a remark of some importance—Christ never rejected any adoration, any submission, as being above His deserts and beyond the realities of the case. Any amount of love, reverence, submission—and I venture a step further—adoration and worship which men chose to bring, He took, not because He was greedy of praise, or wanted to have His vanity tickled; not like small men, that He desired to swallow or to receive the incense of popular adulation; but because in the depths, He knew that He would come to be the hope and the supreme love of mankind. And so, whatever of praise and honour and servitude, the most rapturous expressions, He never says—"Stand off: I myself am also a man. Worship God: I am of thy fellow-servants." But He says, "Ye say well; for so I am."

And then, side by side, you get this—the bringing together of the lofty hope and the little service. You find in the grand, solemn words of the Evangelist, the strange paradox: "And Jesus, knowing that the Father had put all things into His hands, and that He was come from God and went to God"; the consciousness of absolute sovereignty, dominion, personal authority, and the consciousness of coming from God and going to God, leads—to what?—to this: He then threw off His garment and took the towel and girded himself. You, Peter, won't do it; you, John, won't do it. Ye stand upon your little points of dignity; and I here, because I know that all things are in My hands, look, I serve.

If we are to understand the sweetness, the greatness, the mystery, and the miracle of Christ's lightest act in human form, we must carry to the consideration of it the thought that here we have the manifest divinity to whom —according to the great words of the Apostle Paul—it is voluntary humiliation to be born, and the mystery and crown of willingness and submission that He should die: "Being found in fashion as a man, He became obedient unto death." He took upon Him the form of a servant, and in that taking of humanity manifested His lowliness, and therefore manifested His glory. I do not pause to ask or to answer the question, on what theory of Christ's nature there can be humiliation in His birth, in His manhood, and voluntary self-submission in His death: I only point you to the fact that if you want to know the depths of His lowliness, you must measure it by the height of His glory: "I, your Lord and Master, have washed your feet."

And then, still further, there is another great lesson that comes out of these words, viz. the highest purpose of this miracle of submission. It is not only as a lesson of humility, and of what true dignity is, that He takes the basin and washes His disciples' feet; but there is something in it still more than that: the common act of domestic good, the common, secular, domestic act of washing the feet of the guests, is lifted up into lofty regions and charged with a great message to the world, and is made by Him the symbol and the figure of the great means by which we partake of His life. So the common act of washing the guests' feet, too, symbols the highest and chiefest glory whereby the Master became the servant, and the Lord of all became the least of all. What did He come for? What did He wear our flesh for? Why did He suffer our sorrows, enter into our joys, bear our burdens, be limited by our relationships, do our work, die our death? What was all that for? The highest purpose is to make men clean; that is, better than all other, and moral purity is more than intellectual purity. It was not worth Christ's while to come from heaven and die to make you and me pure, good, free from defilement, and make us possessors of His own morality. "My mission is to wash you from your moral defilement and stains."

And then, let me remind you that this great miracle of lowliness, with its lofty purpose of purifying, is, in simple reality, the standing law, and the perpetual law of Christ's work. It was beautiful that there in that upper chamber he should rise from the table and gird Himself with the towel, and take the basin, and wash their feet. It is not less wonderful nor less dear, that at the table in the kingdom, where He sits exalted, He should still be ready to wash your feet and mine. It is true yet, "I am amongst you as he that serves"; it is true yet that the active presence and energy of Jesus Christ is granted to us, in order that through that energy and presence felt by us, we should be made pure and clean. And whatever there was of wonder in the humiliation on earth, it does not seem to me that there is less in the lowliness of the exalted Christ, who, on His throne, is yet with us; and crowned with the crowns of the world, is also still girt with the towel and bearing the basin. For, to-day Jesus Christ will cleanse us, and to-day His gentle hand will be laid, if you like—with no disgust, with no repugnance—on the foulest of our filth, the blackest of our dirt, and the whitest of our leprosy; and He will cleanse us, if we will, from our foulest stains. "If I wash thee not, thou hast no part with Me." Christ's purpose in all that He does for us, and in us, and on us, is to make us pure and clean. Has He effected that purpose with you, or do you pluck away your feet from His gentle hand and say, "Thou shalt never wash my feet"? Or do some of you say, "Oh, I don't think there is any need of their being washed—they are clean enough"; or do you simply turn away from Him, and care not to subject yourselves to His gentle touch? Do you, dear friend, take that solemn word, "If I wash thee not, thou hast no part with Me"? Admiration, acceptance under His message, nominal profession, devout emotion, all the rest of it, is all nought, and you have got nothing to do with Christ unless you have got this to do with Him, that He is making you, day by day, purer and better men and women.

Still further, there is the thought of the inexhaustible

significance, and the hidden depths, of His work upon us. "Know ye what I have done to you?" Not they. "What I do thou knowest not now, but thou shalt know hereafter."

And so He says to us all, "Know ye what I have done to you?" We know it in a fashion, in a measure; we know a little if we love and ponder on the height from which He has come, and of the depths into which He has descended. But we have no test to fathom the one, nor ladder to get to the height of the other. And so we know not all that He has done for us. If He has given us a germ and a seed, it is only yet in its infancy. And like some man coming from a tropical country, who has got two or three slips of some feeble aromatic plant in a little flower-pot, and a very small modicum of water, and he tends and takes care of it on the voyage; but he does not know what it will be like in the greenhouse at home when it sends out the heavy fragrance and the long spikes.

And so, finally, all this great miracle of mercy is a law for your lives. I have given you an example, the general thought of Christ as an example specialized here—"that ye should do as I have done to you." First learn the true use and meaning of all that you have of character and condition of superiority. Some of you pride yourselves on your intelligence, some on certain gifts of character, upon pecuniary resources, upon rank, upon dignity. Well, one law applies to them all. If you are better than your neighbour, it is that you may help him, that you may put your hand down to the poor struggling fellow-man and give him a lift. And if you have got money, it is your stewardship, and the Great Steward will see that your account is strictly rendered. And so—as my text puts it —the meaning of all superiority is, to stoop, and the purpose of all that you possess is service. The true purpose of all service, or at least the main purpose, is to help men to be good, or, as my text puts it, to help wash their feet,—a dry, dirty business that fastidious people don't like. Ay, but there is no other way to get men better than that. You cannot make better by any other means than by putting out your own hands and laying them upon the unclean portions of these evils which surround you. It is not to be done with your skirts gathered, and with your smelling bottle in your hand. Loyal submission and humility, a brave acceptance of the lowest task, putting your sensibilities in your pocket, and trying rather to make these poor creatures feel that you pity them and would fain help them, than that they should not come "between the wind and your nobility."

Still further, let us learn the true measure of our service. "As I have done to you." That is a new theme now, and Christ's measure is our measure; and until we have stooped as low as He did, we have not exhausted the power of the pattern, nor fulfilled the measure of our obligation. And so, brother, let us gather ourselves up into this one thing, "as I have done to you." Well, then, you cannot imitate Christ's example unless Christ is something much more than an example to you. You must first of all have a consciousness of His cleansing in yourselves before you can imitate Him; or, to put it in more general terms, Christ's cross must be the crown of my own hope of heaven, of forgiveness, of purifying, before Christ's life can be a pattern for my life. You must begin with trusting in that great sacrifice altogether for yourselves, and then, and then only, you can make it the law of your lives. First of all we have got to go to Him and say, "Lord, not my feet only, but also my hands and my head." And then, with compassion taught from Him, and with a gentleness of touch that He has breathed into our nature as well as into our rough fingers, we can come and say to others, "Jesus Christ has made me clean." Begin with Christ as something much more than an example.

> "Lord, as to Thy dear Cross we cling,
>   And pray to be forgiven,
> So let Thy life our pattern be,
>   And fit our souls for Heaven."

XV. The Ascension of Christ. ACTS i. 9. DAN. vii. 13, 14.

"*And when He had spoken these things, while they beheld, He was taken up, and a cloud received Him out of their sight.*"

"*I saw in the night visions, and, behold, one like the Son of Man came with the clouds of heaven, and came to the Ancient of days, and they brought him near before Him. And there was given Him dominion, and glory, and a kingdom, that all people, nations, and languages, should serve Him: His dominion is an everlasting dominion, which shall not pass away, and His kingdom that which shall not be destroyed.*"

THE book of the Acts of the Apostles gives the earthly side, what the Apostles saw; the wonderful end of that forty days, the renewed communication between them and their blessed Master through those days from time to time by a law unknown and undiscoverable to them. He was with them, and He vanished from them. He stood amongst them, and He left them alone. Now the invisible, colourless air revealed suddenly, while the door was locked, the beloved form and features to their astonished gaze; and again, at once, with all of them gathered round Him, with the intenseness of loving attention He vanished from amongst them, and they saw Him no more. The forty days had come to an end. The "little while and ye shall see Me" had run itself out. The time had come of which more and more clearly He had spoken to them when He had said, "I shall go to the Father," and as though foretelling them of the mighty close, He gathered them upon the mountain height, apart from the possibility of fraud, apart from all possibility of error; the bare hill and valley and the sky above them was all upon which their eye could rest. No conceivable misapprehension possible; no sudden storm scattering their attention, and then passing away to leave them alone; but the calm air of that Judean country, upon the bright hill with the light, clear, still and liquid, with the air breathing softly from the neighbouring sea, with that gathered circle listening as perhaps they had never listened before to the word of blessing as He spoke it, and to the syllables of prophecy as He dropped them, every attention of body and mind concentrated upon Him, and He close beside them. The mystery was accomplished. He rose from amongst them, and as they speechlessly gazed, they saw Him ascend into the sky above, until the mantling cloud hid Him from their sight. "He was taken up, and a cloud received Him out of their sight."

And still, my brethren, the cloud hangs; still it intercepts the gaze of those who upon this earth are looking up to Him. Still the cloud-canopy is drawn. Twice only has it opened its veil to show to eyes upon earth what is going on in heaven; once for the support of dying Stephen, the first of martyrs; once for the conversion of St. Paul the Apostle, the persecutor of the disciples. Excepting these times, the cloud has remained drawn; the earth has seen Him no more. Still the scene is that of waiting expection, adoration, and desire—still the gaze of the apostles beholding Him as He was taken up, whilst a cloud received Him into heaven.

But what of the other cloud, my brethren? Go back to the voice of prophecy, and read the triumphant notes. The apostles write in the book of Acts the earthly side; Daniel, the prophet, saw years before, in that Chaldean land, what was on the other side of that cloud. "I saw in the night visions, and, behold, one like the Son of Man came with the clouds of heaven." There is the cloud again, the other side of it. We ourselves see in the heaven over us the mantling cloud in all its frowning blackness looking down upon the earth, as though it did but shut the light out; but as we look at its upper side, we see the heavenly glory streaming into it like the dew into the fleece, and every fold transfigured into liquid fire. And so it was with Daniel. He saw the side of the cloud that received Jesus out of their sight. "One like the Son of Man came with the clouds of heaven, and came to the Ancient of days, and they brought him near before Him. And there was given Him dominion and glory, and a kingdom, that all people, nations, and languages, should serve Him; His dominion is an everlasting dominion, which shall not pass away, and His kingdom which shall not be destroyed."

Well then, brethren, here we have the other side. He ascended to His native heaven; He went back again to the throne of glory. He was again with the Ancient of days.

He was indeed again with the Father, but, mind you, not as when in His infinite compassion He came forth out of that glory to redeem man. He ascends—the man Christ Jesus. The humanity which He had knit into a union, indissoluble with the Godhead, in the person of Himself as the Eternal Son, the humanity mounts now to that throne of glory. That never-to-be-dissolved union, God and man, man and God! He ascends to the Ancient of days, and as man, He takes the mediatorial throne. Mark you, it is *that*,—it is not the throne of the everlasting Godhead. Even though the mystery of the eternity was not yet revealed to Daniel, see how here, as everywhere in the older dispensations, the whole is interwoven in the very imagery of the prophecy—the bringing the Son of Man to the Ancient of days, the eternal Father, the co-eternal Spirit, and He, the everlasting Son, blending together in the Ascension into the innermost circle of the uncreated light; the giving to Him everlasting dominion; and the giving to Him the mediatorial kingdom, the kingdom, mark ye, of all the earth, of all tribes and languages and places, for whom He had shed His blood, to be His for ever and ever, because that mediatorial kingdom passes into the everlasting kingdom when our Lord shall be all in all. Here then is the glorious side of that cloud which received Him out of their sight. Mark, my brethren, the points for Ascension Day. First, that our very nature—true human nature, not something mingled between human nature and the Deity, but true human nature in the person of the man Christ Jesus—is at the right hand of the majesty of the eternal Father. Remember, the only one perfect man who had ever lived upon this earth! Adam had not reached the perfection which was to be got by maturity before he had fallen from it by sin. And every child of Adam receiving his stained nature is thereby incomplete and imperfect. The one man whose nature was the perfection which existed from eternity in the mind of God was Christ Jesus. He lived in the full perfection of the nature which you and I are wearing now in its torn, ruined, and imperfect condition. He ascended then to the right hand of God and sitteth there, then till now, at the right hand of God in the uncreated glory of the Father. That is the great cardinal idea of Ascension Day.

And now, mark some of the consequences God reveals to us as having followed from it. In the first place, this was the bearing of the blood of the Atonement into the Holy of Holies. All the elaborate imagery of the old law fulfilled; the Mission of the High Priest upon the great Day of Atonement accomplished—he who then went once only in the year within the veil with the blood of the great sin-offering that he might make atonement for the sins of the people, and for his own—that now accomplished by Him who went into the Holy place not made with hands, but into the heaven of heavens, that He might once for all appear before the Eternal Father with the blood of the sacrifice once offered by Him to make full atonement for sinful humanity. And then, thirdly, this,—that as upon the great Day of Atonement the high priest not only made intercession, but then offered up the prayers of the whole people of Israel who were praying without, so that each man with his own burden, each woman with her own grief, in the congregation of the faithful people without, making their own secret prayer, Hannah-like, in the bitterness of their own soul to Him who was between the Cherubims, knew that at that very moment the high priest was sprinkling the hidden Mercy Seat with the blood of the Atonement, making intercession for them, and that each prayer of theirs, which was breathed without, went straight up to Him who was between the cherubims, because the high priest was in this way offering the accepted sacrifice for himself and for the people. There is the figure of that which you and I so need—which you and I may, if we will, so blessedly possess. He is within that veil. He ever liveth to make intercession for us. He pleads before the Eternal Father, the blood once shed upon the Cross. No repeating, as men have idly dreamed; no prolonging, as men have curiously imagined, of the one sacrifice—the sacrifice once offered on Calvary in its perfection—neither needing nor permitting repetition or prolongation, but offered once for all for the sins of man. That sacrifice was completed by the great High Priest in the very presence of the Eternal Father for each one, offering this day the bitterness of his own spirit before the Father. And as that prayer was taken up by the high priest, and there in the accepted place, in the Holy of Holies, before the great altar, was offered up for him who was praying it without, so the feeble prayer of this earth—the prayer which in all our feebleness we have been offering or shall offer up to-day—*that* shall be taken by the pierced hand, and from the throne of mediation, with His own prevailing intercession, be offered up for us to the Eternal God our Father.

God specially provided that the great High Priest should be one taken from amongst his brethren, and studious care was taken in every respect to equalize him with his brethren, even provision being made that he should always know the joys and sorrows of married life—a wonderful provision if you think of it, but the meaning of it being this, that he should be one amongst his brethren who was capable of knowing, by that intimate acquaintance of community of experience, everything which every Jewish brother could feel—that too has been fulfilled for us in our ascended High Priest. He was made in all things like unto His brethren, sin only excepted. That He, having been tempted, should know how to succour them that are tempted. And, remember, you must give to "tempted" not the meaning only we commonly give to it, the having been tried by temptations of the Evil One, but having been tried, having had every nerve tried, having had every fibre of that perfect humanity, every single thrilling string of it, stretched to the utmost, and made to vibrate to the extreme power of its vibration, that there should be in Him, having been tried to the utmost, the power of responding to every single sorrow of every human heart which He came to redeem. Just as you have heard some harp, standing silent in the room, when a musical instrument playing in another part of it has touched some note or string of that harp, begin, as it seems automaton-like, to vibrate at the same note, because it answered so perfectly to the note that was struck upon the other instrument. Oh! that the heart of Jesus on that throne of light might vibrate to every single note of trial, difficulty, and bereavement filling every human heart; so that in the midst of the manifold difficulties of life, we might know that in things temporal, in the trial and trouble of our own heart, in the strife with sin, in the pangs of guilt, in all the agony of that deeper and more inward life (which is in every one of us, even though it may lie yet unwakened to the sense of its own being, like some deep nerve in the body of any one of us, which slumbers now, but which something may wake up into such an agony of feeling that it may gather in itself the whole of our being), that in the midst of every trial when it comes, we may find in Him this perfect sympathy, for in Him is the perfection of humanity joined to the Almighty Majesty of Godhead.

These are the points, my brethren, for our attention, and the practical issue of them, I think, is most plain. First, unspeakable consolation for each one of us that will lay hold of Him. When we look back upon the sins of a life— sins of boyhood, sins of youth, and sins of manhood—and the heart begins to lie down—then to look up and see on the other side the cloud, the throne of mediation, and the Perfect Man pleading for us, yea! for thee, offering the blood shed for thee, and so saying again to thy soul, "Is not this sufficient to reassure thee?" Is not this enough to make thee forgive thyself when the everlasting Father hath forgiven thee for the offering?"

And these two things must never be parted—perfect forgiveness, and God's strength to strive against sin—and then you can never exalt either too much. But if you take alone the pardon, when God has welded together the pardon and the strength, you may come into the deadly deceitfulness of living in sin, and then thinking that because you have certain feelings you are a forgiven man. It is a new life God gives you, and the life of peace is the life of strength and the life of calm—nay, of exulting comfort —and it is the life of obedience too. And art thou tempted so that thou thinkest thou cannot resist? At this very moment, is there a heart, as there well may be, that is saying: "I know it is enough for most people, but my case is so peculiar. I was led into sin in early life, and it has become part of me. I have striven against it, and strive in vain. I cannot help it, I cannot help it. I hope death will deliver me from it"? Look up to the other side of that cloud, and see the Man Christ Jesus, the Virgin-born, the Son of Mary, with thy nature ready from that throne of power to give thee His own might, and in that might of His to overcome thine enemy, and to strengthen, Samson-like, thy weakness. No, brethren, take the two together.

And then go on with the subject further, for the Merciful One has compassion on us. He knows it is not enough for us to have a bright hope for the future only. Your Heavenly Father knows ye have need of these things. Think of the peace this will give us in the troubles of this life if we will but use it. It is like the storms of April. There is a bright sky and the clouds gone, and we array ourselves to go forth into the brightness; and we say, "The storms are past. Look how bright it is!" and even as we say it, there gathers over us a yet darker canopy, and there falls upon us a heavier shower. And so it is in this life. We cannot tell whence it comes, when it goes, what may be its shape, what ruin it may work! It may leave us with a heart broken and with a home void, with love robbed of all its glory, so far as this world goes, and only a burden to be borne meekly in a blessed companionship with the unseen for the rest of life. Ay! it may be so to-morrow with any of us. And oh! think of what the joy is for any such as we are, to be able to look through that cloud and see the Perfect Man's heart beating with our heart in our anguish, and to lean our burden upon it. When we have said, and it may be in truth, "It is my all that He has taken from me;" said it so that life can never again be the same thing; yet to be able to lean that broken heart upon His perfect love, not in the distance that is between the Creator and the created, but in the nearness that may be between the Man of Sorrows and the sorrowing man.

Well then, if these truths are what this day is to teach us, let us make them ours. Let us look up—let us look, as having seen, not only the side of the cloud which the apostles saw, but that too which was given in the night visions to the seraphic eye of Daniel. Let us look up and see Him there. Oh that each heart would indeed mount up, and with Him continually dwell! What a glory does it add to this life, even to know how, if you walk with the companion of your heart's love, out abroad into the world of God, that every flower is brighter, and every scent sweeter, and every song of the birds more musical, and every waving of the leaves more lovely, because your heart is walking in such blessed companionship! And can we walk with the blessed Son of Man—can we go abroad into life's joys or life's sorrows, into beauty or into darkness, and not have life ennobled for us if we are walking in the blessed companionship which is allowed for us with the ascended Lord? Oh! brethren, this is the lesson of Ascension Day, and it should go with us every day and every hour of our life, that like as we believe Him to have ascended, so we in heart and mind may thither ascend with Him.

S. W.

XVI. Paul and Festus—A Contrast. ACTS xxvi. 25.

"I am not mad, most noble Festus, but speak forth the words of truth and soberness."

IT was no even-handed contest in which the Apostle found himself engaged when he appeared in this audience-chamber at Cæsarea—the place, the season, the persons, and the surroundings of the scene might well have appalled a man of less conspicuous courage and feebler convictions. It was the occasion of a great state ceremonial—a Dhurbar, we might almost call it—when the Imperial Viceroy, the representative of the laws and majesty of Rome, newly arrived in his province, received the welcome and the homage of the most powerful native prince. King Agrippa, we are told, had come to Cæsarea to salute Festus. We happen to know from other sources that he had reasons of his own for wishing to conciliate the favour of the new governor. Just at this time he had a quarrel with the Jews, and he was anxious to secure the powerful support of Festus. He had recently added to the palace of the Herods, we are told, a lofty dining hall, from which his guests could look down upon the inner temple. The priests and guardians of the sacred precincts resented this act, because it was indecent and contrary to all precedent, that their most sacred rites should thus be exposed to the profane gaze of mere idle revellers. They therefore built up a high wall, and shut out the king's view. Agrippa, on his part, resented this indignity, and endeavoured to get the restriction removed. He applied to Festus for aid, and Festus warmly espoused his cause. All this we have on the authority of the Jewish historian Josephus. I mention the fact here for two reasons. In the first place, it illustrates the historical accuracy of the sacred narrative. Where we are able to test incidents in the Acts by contemporary history, we cannot fail to be struck with the coincidences that are manifest and which afford the highest guarantee of historical credibility. The officious welcome given by Agrippa to Festus on his arrival, the cordial relations existing between the Jewish king and the Roman governor, as here related, receive a flood of light from this account of the Jewish historian. The narrative of St. Luke and that of Josephus fit together as separate pieces of an historical whole. But another thought is suggested by the incident, suggested by what is said and what is left unsaid by the great Jewish historian of the day. His account illustrates the false estimate of the relative proportions of events which men inevitably take who are mixed up in them. The aggressive insolence of Agrippa was the one topic of general interest at the time. It was eagerly discussed, we cannot doubt, among high and low, among the priests and the people, at every public concourse, and in every domestic circle. It alone has obtained a place in the record of Josephus. When the rumour got abroad, that the king had hastened to Cæsarea with a splendid retinue to welcome the new governor on his arrival, all voices would be eager to tell, and all ears open to hear, how Festus had received his visitor, and what line he was likely to take on the great question of the day. But this interview with Paul—who cared for it, who talked about it? It was a wholly unimportant episode in a conjuncture of the highest public moment. The historian says nothing about it, and why should he? The name of Paul is not once mentioned throughout his narrative. Yet time has wholly reversed the verdict of contemporary history. Of the magnificent palace of the Herods, or the goodly buildings of the temple, not one stone is left standing upon another. For eighteen centuries they have been a desolation and a ruin. The aggressiveness of Agrippa and the policy of Festus have alike passed away, leaving not a trace behind; but the words of St. Paul are living and germinating and fructifying still. Still his outspoken reply to the blunt taunt of the Roman governor appeals to the latest generations as a most powerful witness to the gospel —"I am not mad, most noble Festus, but speak forth the words of truth and soberness." Still his pathetic rejoinder to the flippant sarcasm of the Jewish king stands out as a model of Christian courtesy and largeness of heart—"I would to God that not only thou, but also all that hear me this day, were both almost and altogether, such as I am, except these bonds." The quarrel of Agrippa has vanished out of sight, the pleading of Paul is the inheritance of all ages.

Never, possibly, had the Apostle found himself before a more uncongenial audience. The imperial governor, the native sovereign, their splendid retinue—Roman officials, Jewish priests, soldiers and civilians, courtiers and holiday makers, some coldly indifferent, others bitterly hostile, but all alike devoid of sympathy for him. But the text directs us to one person above all the rest in this unfriendly concourse. The attitude of Festus towards St. Paul more especially demands our attention. Festus was not a man whose opinion could be lightly disregarded. We have not here to do with the sceptical, worldly, cynical Pilate, or a cruel, reckless profligate like Felix. The governor before whom Paul stands is a far higher type of character than those. He is eminently just; transparently sincere and outspoken; a prompt and vigorous ruler. He is the very man to whom in the common affairs of life we should entrust our case with confidence. Nothing could be more upright than his treatment of the prisoner from first to last. His predecessor had cruelly detained St. Paul in bonds for two whole years, but Festus brings on the case at once. The Jews ask him to send Paul to Jerusalem for judgment, but he refuses to take this unprecedented step. Next they press him to give judgment against the prisoner, and he boldly refuses—"It is not the manner of the Romans," he says bluntly, almost rudely, "it is not the manner of the Romans to condemn any man without a fair trial." Accordingly the prisoner is confronted with his accusers. The governor hears their complaints; they are many and serious, but he judges them to be altogether vexatious or irrelevant; they do not come under the cognizance of the Roman law, and he is ready to release the prisoner. But the prisoner appeals to Cæsar, and so the case is taken out of his hands. But even then he is not satisfied—he wishes, at all events, to understand the rights of the case: "It seemeth unreasonable to me," he says, "to send the prisoner, and not withal to signify the crimes laid against him." The whole narrative thus sets Festus before us as a man of strict integrity, a man worthy of the highest respect in the ordinary business of life. This is the bright side of his character. But he has no ideas and no aspirations beyond. His view is strictly limited to the affairs of this world. When the future and the unseen are mentioned, he is lost in confusion; he is as helpless in dealing with such topics of thought, as one who is blind in discriminating the hues of the rainbow. He is blunt, even to contempt, when he refers to "one Jesus which was dead," and whom Paul yet affirmed to be alive. This was decisive to his mind. Could any sane man maintain an absurdity like this! He listens for a time with patience while Paul pleads his cause, but at length he can no longer restrain himself. He is confirmed now in his first surmise. He rudely interrupts the prisoner, shouting rather than speaking, "Thou art mad, Paul!" What is this but the incoherent rambling of a maniac? All this talk about sin and repentance, and forgiveness and salvation, what is this but the very phantom of a diseased brain? What is this story of the apparition on the way to Damascus with the light and the loud voice, notwithstanding all these many circumstantial details which invest it with the air of sober history—"Thou art mad, Paul!" All this has just nothing in common with the solid experiences, the stern matter-of-fact duties of the Roman magistrate and Roman citizen, in short, with the acknowledged realities of human life—"Thou art mad, Paul!" Yes, *it was madness*, sheer madness, to commit social suicide as this Paul had done, for indeed his conduct deserved no other name. He had given up a high and honourable position among his fellow-countrymen; he was learned after the manner of their learning, he was orthodox after their standard of orthodoxy; he stood well with the chiefs of his nation; he was on the high road to preferment, and yet he suddenly gave up all—for what? To become an outcast, a wanderer on earth; to be hated by the Jews and scorned by the Greeks; to drag out a miserable career of penury, of suffering, of toil and of danger;

to carry his life in his hand from hour to hour, to be shipwrecked, imprisoned, scourged, stoned and left for dead; to be spurned by all men as the very filth and offscouring of society, the scum of the world. Who has put the case more strongly than himself? Ay! he knew—no one could know better—that he was mad, irretrievably mad as the world counts madness. "We are fools," he says of himself, "we are fools for Christ's sake." "Thou art mad, Paul!"

But it was not only Paul's practical conduct that betrayed his hopeless insanity—his religious creed also was nothing better than the raving of a maniac. Whoever heard before of one claiming the allegiance and the worship —yes, the worship—of the whole world for a crucified malefactor, this Jesus, this dead man whom Paul affirmed to be alive? There was no difference of opinion here between Jew and Greek. On most questions affecting religion the one spoke a language quite unintelligible to the other; but here there was absolute unanimity of sentiment: Festus and Agrippa, the Roman soldier and the Hebrew priest, alike must join in condemning these ravings, this doctrine of Christ crucified—nay, Christ risen again; it was a scandal to the Jews, and it was folly to the Greeks. Here again no one knew better than the Apostle himself how his teaching was regarded by the learning, the intelligence, and the sagacity of his age. He knew it, he repeated it, he gloried in it, he invited all men to become mad as he was mad. This very madness, he maintained, was the indispensable condition of all higher knowledge. "If any man thinketh to be wise in this world, let him become a fool that he may be wise."

So, then, two wholly irreconcilable views of life confronted each other in Festus and Paul. Paul was sincere. Had he not given the amplest proof of this? Festus also was sincere. His whole conduct breathes the air of sincerity. And yet between the two there is a yawning and impassable gulf. If Festus is right, Paul is mad, irretrievably mad. If Paul is right, Festus is blind, stone blind. It is not my purpose now to treat this scene in its bearing on Christian evidences. From this point of view it would suggest not a few important reflections. I may point, for instance, to the calmness and sobriety of the Apostle's statement, to the perfect assurance with which he details the history of his conversion and the grounds of his belief, to the manly and courteous simplicity with which he replies to the rebuke of Festus, and the sarcasm of Agrippa. Certainly nothing is more unlike the raving of the maniac than the whole tone and manner of St. Paul on this occasion. Or, I might turn away from the scene itself to its results. I might remind you that the civilized world itself, after long wavering and much halting, did ultimately prefer the madness of Paul to the sanity of Festus. I might ask you to reflect how enormous has been the gain to mankind from this preference, and how irretrievable would have been the loss if it had taken Festus as its teacher, and condemned Paul as a lunatic. I might point out to you how Christianity rescued a helpless world which was hastening to its ruin, seething, as it were, in its own corruption; how it endowed society, thus rescued from premature decay, with fresh vigour and youth by infusing into it new aspirations and hopes; and how this reinvigorating influence contained in itself the potentiality of all that is noblest and best in modern civilization and modern life.

All these considerations, and others besides these, I might well urge upon your attention. But I have no design of dwelling on the evidences of Christianity now. I am speaking now as a Christian to Christians. It is a practical and not an intellectual conviction, which I would wish to enforce upon you. I would impress upon you, as I would impress upon myself, the magnitude of the alternative. No ingenuity and no indifference can bridge over the gulf which separates the view of human life, taken by Festus, from the view of it by St. Paul—the view taken by the upright and reasonable man of the world, who lives only in the present, and the view taken by the Christian, whose whole soul is dominated with the presence of God, with the consciousness of sin, and with the conviction of eternity.

God forbid that we should set ourselves up as judges of others. God forbid that, possessing as we believe we possess, a wider vision and a clearer light, we should speak meanly, or think wrongly, of the upright loyalty of the honest citizen, the respectable father of a family, in whom, nevertheless, the religious motive is scarcely perceptible, if perceptible at all. Honesty, truth, uprightness, whatever in human life is lovely and of good report, is consciously or unconsciously the very reflection of the perfect attributes of God Himself. We wrong God when we wrong such men as these. But still the fact remains. Here are two antagonistic views of human life and human destiny. Men may strive to patch up a hollow compromise between them, but no truce can be real, because no meeting point is visible. It is the alternative of sanity and madness, of light and darkness, of life and death. If you have decided that the Christian's view is sanity, his light is life, this it must not, it cannot, be inoperative in you. It will pervade your whole life; it will influence the thoughts and actions of every day and every hour; it may not, indeed, change the forms of the outward business of life —except in a very few cases there is no reason why it should—but it will infuse into them a wholly different spirit; it will breathe the breath of heaven into the work of earth.

All this, I say, stands to reason. It cannot be a matter of indifference whether you are responsible in your actions only to the judgments of human society, with its caprices, its prejudices, its misunderstandings, its narrowness, its blindness, or to an all-seeing eye, who overlooks nothing, misinterprets nothing, misjudges nothing, who scans motives, discerns tendencies not less than overt acts. It cannot be a matter of indifference whether wrong-doing is simply a violation of order, attended with inconvenient consequences, simply a breach of some social compact which your fellow-men are bound to resent in self-defence, or whether it is sin, that is, a rebellious defiance of an all-righteous, all-holy God, an act of base ingratitude towards a loving Father in heaven. It cannot be a matter of indifference whether He who appeared in our flesh and walked upon our earth more than eighteen centuries ago was—and I shudder to apply the term even as a bare hypothesis—a lunatic—a lunatic, I say, because there is no escape from the dilemma—and that all His words, all His works, all His aims, all His aspirations, all His promises, His whole life and His whole teaching were, on the alternative hypothesis, built upon a mere delusion, or whether

He was indeed the only begotten Son of God, whom the Father in His infinite mercy sent down to live our life and die our death, that He might rescue us from the prison house of sin. It cannot be a matter of indifference whether this life is our entire life, whether intelligence, conscience, conscious personality, all that we call ourselves, shall vanish at the touch of death, evaporating into gases and dissolving into dust, whether, therefore, it is the true and sole aim of the wise man to play out his little part here as decently, as respectably, as successfully as he can, or whether there is an eternal hereafter before which the triumphs of the present are just nothing at all.

This, then, I say, this is the tremendous alternative. Did I exaggerate when I called it a contrast between light and darkness? There is no halting between two opinions here; no passing to and fro at convenience, for the chasm is broad, and it is fathomless too. Accept, therefore, the alternative which you have chosen; accept it with all its consequences, think over it, master it, live it. Men will taunt you with your inconsistency: they will do so justly, but be not discouraged by this. Let the taunt nerve you to greater efforts. It will stimulate your action: it will not shake your creed. The inconsistency must necessarily be greater as the ideal is higher. Festus, no doubt, was a much more consistent man than St. Paul. The standard of Festus was the ordinary standard of honourable and upright men, and it would seem he did not fall far short of it. The standard of St. Paul was absolute self-negation, and he is constantly bewailing his shortcomings, his feebleness, his worthlessness, his nothingness. The mere voluptuary is far more consistent than either. His aim is sensual pleasure, and he devotes himself to it heart and soul. Indeed, it is difficult for sense-bound men like ourselves to project ourselves into the eternal and the infinite. It is difficult amidst the surroundings of earth to live as citizens of heaven; but this is the far-off goal towards which you must ever be striving. The seal of immortality is stamped upon you. Do not forget this. Endure to be called madman when you stand before the judgment-seat of Festus. That is inevitable; only, remember meanwhile that you are the sons of God; you are the redeemed of

Christ; you are the temples of the Spirit; you are the heirs of eternity.

J. B. L.

XVII. The Life of St. Paul.

1. Paul's Early Life and Conversion.

St. Paul's is a name which occupies so commanding a place in the New Testament, and therefore in the teaching of the Church of Christ, that it is difficult to dissociate him from the method and tone of an ordinary sermon. Nor would I, on any account whatever, be supposed to imply that the real historical Paul of Tarsus is a different being from the apostle who has so high a place in the heart of every Christian, or that a more intimate acquaintance with the reality must, in this—as in some cases undoubtedly it must—strip his aureole from the head of the object of our childish reverence. It is because with St. Paul the very reverse is so eminently the case that we do well, I submit, to look at the Apostle's life from a slightly different point of view from that in which it or parts of it are commonly presented to us, and to attempt to weigh within very restricted limits some parts of its moral and historical significance.

Every noble life, every conspicuous career, implies a period of preparation and development more or less traceable. This is one of the reasons which make biographies always so popular a branch of literature. They enable us not merely to recognise excellence, but to trace it, or to attempt to trace it, to its source. Few men have their lives written at all who have not done something noteworthy; and the interesting question for all of us is how they came to do it,—what were the circumstances without, what the impulses, what the lines of thought within, that led them on step by step until they reached the point of triumph or of excellence? Some of us, perhaps, have been reading lately a book which, in more ways than one, will have recalled, across however great an interval, the memory of St. Paul—I mean Miss Yonge's life of that devoted missionary, Bishop Patteson. A great deal of that book is only what might be found in very ordinary lives—in the lives of some among ourselves. But then everything—even the most trivial details of home and school and college and friendships and correspondence—is more or less interesting, because everything is from the first regarded as leading up to a life-work of singular devotion, crowned by a singularly noble death. In all such cases the catastrophe or the victory reflects a splendour not their own upon all the trivial details that may have preceded it.

Now, here it would be logically natural to say what the apostle of the Gentiles was in himself to Christendom and to humanity, but there are obvious reasons for addressing ourselves to our work historically; and I must therefore assume you to be more or less familiar with much on which I shall hereafter insist somewhat at length, while I shall ask this question: How did St. Paul come to be what he was at the beginning of his apostolical or missionary life?

There are, as a rule, three elements—I might almost say three periods—to be distinguished in the preparatory life of every man who achieves much, or anything considerable. There is the raw material of personal character, developed, moulded, invigorated by education or whatever takes its place,—in short, the man's original outfit. There is secondly, some new influence or influences which give, or may give, a decisive turn to hopes and aims—which raise, or may raise, the whole level of life to a higher atmosphere. And, lastly, there is, as a rule, a period in which the two earlier elements are fused and consolidated—a period of reflection when the true work of life is already more or less clearly in view,—when the intellect is being cleared,—when the will is being braced until the decisive moment arrives for undertaking it. I do not say that these periods can always be made out with chronological precision, or that they always preserve, so to speak, their due perspectives; but in their elements they will always be found to exist wherever a man's life embodies anything that is morally remarkable; and therefore let us see how they apply to the case before us, the case of Saul of Tarsus.

Education, I have already implied, is the work partly of teachers,—partly, in some cases mainly, of circumstances. We shall best appreciate what it must have done for St. Paul if we briefly remind ourselves of the history of his early years—of his life up to the date of the death of St. Stephen.

It is very difficult to fix the year of his birth. We know that he was a young man when Stephen was martyred. He would probably have been born in the later years of Herod, or early in the short reign of Archelaus, when, under the sway of the Emperor Augustus, the Roman world was at peace, and when the wickedness of the imperial despotism had not yet fully developed itself. The pirates who had infested the Eastern Mediterranean had been sternly suppressed. The Jewish people was still enjoying everywhere ample toleration under the Roman rule, and a Jewish family like St. Paul's, settled at Tarsus in Cilicia, would have been in sufficiently comfortable circumstances. For Tarsus was a free city of the empire; that is to say, it was governed by its own magistrates, and was exempted from the annoyance of a Roman garrison; but it was not a colony like Philippi in Macedonia, and the freedom of Rome, which St. Paul says he had at his birth, would probably have been earned by some services rendered by his father during the civil wars to some one of the contending parties in the State. It is at least probable, from the expression "a Hebrew of the Hebrews," which he applies to himself, that his parents were originally emigrants from Palestine. We know that they were of the tribe of Benjamin, and that they were strict members of the Pharisee sect. Probably his father was engaged in the Mediterranean trade. To his mother, it is a remarkable circumstance, there is not one reference in his writings. He had a sister whose son lived in later years at Jerusalem, and who would have been his playmate at Tarsus. The Talmud says that a father's duty towards his boy is to circumcise him, to teach him the law, and to teach him a trade. We know from the Epistle to the Philippians that the first of these precepts was accurately complied with on the eighth day after the child's birth. The second would probably have been obeyed by sending the boy not to one of the Greek schools in which Tarsus abounded, but to a Jewish school attached to one of the synagogues, where, after the age of five, he would have learnt the Hebrew Scriptures,—at ten, those floating maxims of the great Jewish doctors which were afterwards collected in the

Mishna, so as, at thirteen, to become what was called a Subject of the Precept, after a ceremony which was a kind of shadow of Christian confirmation. The third requirement was complied with by setting him to make tents out of the hair-cloth supplied by the goats which abounded on the slopes of the neighbouring mountains of the Taurus, and which was a chief article in the trade of the port,— tents which to this day, according to Beaufort, are used largely by the peasantry of south-eastern Asia Minor during the harvest time.

At or soon after thirteen, the little Saul would have been sent from home, probably in a trading vessel bound from the port of Tarsus for Cæsarea, on his way to Jerusalem. Already, as a boy, the holy city must have possessed for him an interest surpassing any which could be raised by any other place on earth. Every great festival would have been followed by the return of one or more of his countrymen to Tarsus, full of the inspiration of the sacred sights, full of the splendour of the new temple—of the fame, of the learning, of the great doctors of the law. Especially he would have heard much of the two rival schools of Hillel and Shammai, of which the former exalted tradition above the letter of the law, while the latter preferred the law to tradition when they clashed. Of these the school of Hillel was much the more influential, and when St. Paul was a boy and a young man, its one great ornament was Gamaliel. Gamaliel, we are told in the Acts of the Apostles, was "had in reputation of all the people." He was evidently one of those men whose candour, wisdom, and consistent elevation of character would have secured him influence in any society, or in any age of the world. He was named by his countrymen "The Beauty of the Law;" and the Talmud declares that since his death the glory of the law has ceased from Israel.

It was at the feet of Gamaliel, St. Paul tells us, he was brought up; and this expression, "at the feet of Gamaliel," exactly recalls to us the manner in which the Rabbinical Assemblies of the Wise, as they were termed, were held. The teacher sat on a raised platform—the pupils on low seats, or on the floor beneath. At these meetings some passage of the Hebrew law was taken as a thesis; it was then paraphrased in the current Syro-Chaldaic dialect;

various explanations, aphorisms, opinions, were quoted; the teacher said what he had to say; and then he was cross-questioned by his hearers. And although, especially in the school of Hillel, there must have been a large mass of legendary and even absurd matter in these lectures and conferences, such as we may still read in great abundance in the Talmud, there must also have been much of the highest doctrinal and moral value—integral elements of the first Divine revelation—"read, marked, learnt, and inwardly digested," during those long and earnest discussions. This, at any rate, was the educational process by which Paul of Tarsus was "taught according to the perfect manner of the law of the fathers." There, side by side with Onkelos, also a pupil of Gamaliel, and subsequently the famous author of the Targum which bears his name, he would have learnt all that the highest minds of his day had to say about the creed of his fathers; and if, looking back from the riper experience of his later life, he would himself have said that in those years a veil was still upon his heart, the profound spiritual blindness would not have interfered with the intellectual value of this part of his education. The culture of the mind, we all know, is one thing; the real growth of the soul is another. A modern university abounds in men of the highest mental culture, who make, and would wish to make, no sort of claim to being religious men. Their intellectual vigour is not, therefore, stunted or impaired. Paul, indeed, was religious, though in a mistaken way, and his first creed, with all its shortcomings, was the main instrumentality of his mental education.

At this period of St. Paul's life, we are, to a certain extent, in the region of conjecture; but it is, upon the whole, scarcely doubtful that he would have returned to Tarsus in the prime of manhood, before he reappeared in Jerusalem as a member of the synagogue which was connected with, or maintained by, the Jews in Cilicia. This visit would have completed his acquaintance with the language, and, to a certain limited extent, with the literature, of Greece. The commercial and educated classes in Tarsus, like similar classes everywhere on the seaboard of the Levant, would then certainly have spoken Greek, just as now they speak Italian; and, as a little boy, Paul, whenever he got out of the narrow circle of his family and of the persons whom he met on the Sabbath day at the synagogue,—whenever he played or entered into conversation on the wharves which lined the banks of the Cydnus, would have had to speak Greek too. His later use of the language, although never quite detached from Jewish idioms and forms of thought, is, upon the whole, that of a man who had used it from childhood ; and his use of the Greek poets, of metaphors which a Greek would understand—in some places, of distinctly Greek modes of argument—in not a few places, of abstract terms on which Greek thought had conferred their meaning and their power, shows that his early education, if mainly Rabbinical, was by no means exclusively so. It would seem to be at least probable that (to omit any other conjectures of the sort) he had read portions of the Republic of Plato. Of the three classes of metaphors which are commonly used by him in his later writings—the architectural, the agricultural, and the theatrical—the boyish memories of Tarsus probably supplied the material. He had then gazed with a curiosity which does not repeat itself, we all know, in later life, upon temples, some of them in the process of construction—temples which he had never entered ; and they supplied his language about the edification of the Christian Church, and about the pillars which supported it. He had watched the cultivation of the rich meadow land at the base of the Taurus. Was he not thinking of this when he afterwards wrote, "I have planted; Apollos watered; God gave the increase"? Above all, he had heard much of the Greek games: he may have witnessed some local sports which imitated the world-famed originals —games which he describes with such vivid appreciation when writing to the Corinthians. If we except one expression in the Colossians, which seems to refer to the destruction of the piratical strongholds in Cilicia by the Roman forces some years before he wrote, his military metaphors, like the famous passage at the close of the Epistle to the Ephesians, are due to his contact with Roman life—to the rude experiences at Philippi, at Jerusalem, at Cæsarea, and during the first imprisonment at Rome. But at Tarsus the Greek literature and society did, if not its best, yet certainly much for him. That gifted, that extraordinary race, which was to the ancient world even more than, until a late period, France has been to Europe—the type and the mistress of its outward civilization—that race must have been understood in that age by any man who had great duties in the future towards the world, towards humanity.

At this time in his life, too, St. Paul would probably have become familiar with that large section of the Jews of the Dispersion whose centre was Alexandria,—who in everything but religion were nearly Greeks,—whose religion was taking more and more of the Greek dress every day. The great Alexandrian version of the Old Testament—the Septuagint, as it is called from the history (true or false) of the translation—which the Apostle so often quotes, while yet he treats it so freely, would have already been familiar to him; and the philosophical writer, Philo Judæus, whose efforts to establish harmonious relations between the Old Testament revelation and the Platonic philosophy have had such large results for the highest good, and, it must be added, for considerable evil, upon the history of religious beliefs, would have been often in his hands, although as yet he little knew that such vast consequences were to result from the study.

This education was moulding and developing a character which (not to dwell here on its subordinate features) may be described by one single word—intensity. There was much besides. There was sensitiveness; there was impetuosity; there was courage; there was independence; but, in all that he did, Paul of Tarsus, before his conversion as well as after it, threw his whole energy, whether of thought or resolution, into his work; and, as might be expected in a character of this mould, objects of thought and aims of action took their place in his soul according to the real, and not according to any fictitious, order of precedence. The central objects of thought and faith, the ultimate and supreme aims of life, disengaged themselves from all that was merely accessory and subordinate, and were pursued with a concentration of purpose that carried all before it. We may be sure that this was the case, so far as was possible in such a subject-matter, when the young student was still grappling with the accumulated traditions of Rabbinism. We know that it was so when, in the ripeness of his early manhood, the young Rabbi returned to the chief scene of his education to take part in a struggle whose issue would form the turning point of his career.

How mysterious is the thought that there are now living, in places and with names unknown to us, some who will hereafter profoundly influence at least some of our lives. True this is of all human beings at some time in their existence. Of Paul of Tarsus it was true in a sense which, perhaps, has never been repeated. Did he ever, we ask naturally—did he ever during his student life come into contact with One who was to exert so great an influence on his future career? They must have been at the same festivals; they must often have gazed on the same buildings, on the same human faces. They may unknowingly have met. The opportunity of seeing the Prophet of Nazareth, as He was popularly called, must have often presented itself to the young Pharisee: yet there is no proof, no intimation, that they ever consciously met as man meets man on the surface of this planet. The knowledge of Christ "after the flesh" refers to no personal experience of St. Paul, but to a mistaken mood of feeling in his Corinthian readers. The question, "Have I not seen Jesus Christ our Lord?" refers to that sight which made St. Paul the peer of Peter and of John, but which occurred after the ascension.

His first known contact with Christianity, with Christ, was that of a determined foe. It was standing, as it were, on the frontier of two worlds,—the Jewish or Semitic, on the one side, and the Greek on the other—that Paul of Tarsus reappears at Jerusalem not long before the death of Stephen. He would probably—inevitably, we may almost say—have been among the opponents of St. Stephen in the Cilician synagogue. Notwithstanding his earnestness and his accomplishments, he was not able to resist the wisdom and the spirit with which Stephen spake. He was checked, probably for the first time in his life, by the sense of a stronger power than any he could wield. There was a something that could do more in and for the human soul than ever the learned dialectics of the loved Gamaliel. He must have witnessed the arrest before the Sanhedrim: he must have listened to—it is a respectable conjecture that he reported from memory—the great apology in which the martyr justifies the spiritual worship of the Church by a comprehensive review of the whole past of Jewish history. And for the rest we have his own bitter, self-accusing words in later times,—" When the blood of the martyr Stephen was shed, I also was standing by and consenting to his death, and kept the raiment of them that slew him." The fact was, that the death of Stephen was, in Paul's eyes, a logical consequence of his own Jewish creed, and he was not the man to shrink from it. He, too, as he witnessed the violence of the brutal mob, the upturned face of the martyr, which was an angel-gaze into the depths of heaven, and then stood by outside the eastern gate, at a spot certainly not far from the scene of the great agony, and heard the thuds of the falling stones which, one after another, were crushing out the life of the man who had beaten him in argument,—he must have had, we think, some human sympathy with the object of the Sanhedrim's vengeance. We know that there was an undercurrent of such sympathy, but it might have been silenced or crushed out for ever, as completely as was the passing remorse with which the eye of his murdered master is said for a moment to have filled even such a soul as Cromwell's when it followed him from the canvas of Vandyck. For the present, a tempest of logically directed passion swept over the mind of Paul, and silenced or buried everything else; and the death of St. Stephen was followed by a general and sharp persecution of the Christians. The Roman procurator was probably absent, if he was not glad of the opportunity of showing his profound contempt for the theological disputes of an eastern province. So the Sanhedrim and the people had their way.

The Sanhedrim was mainly composed at this time of Sadducees, a sect which, believing little about the next world, naturally made the most of this, and whose leading members, generally persons of considerable eminence as rulers, were among the foremost personages of the hierarchy. These men knew well how to encourage, for political and worldly ends, the passions whose motives they regarded with entire contempt; but, for the moment, the passions of the ignorant people and the policy of these highly-placed sceptics practically coincided. It is at least doubtful whether Paul was actually a member of the Sanhedrim. A single expression has, perhaps, been overstrained to support the opinion. But he was certainly acting under its sanction and authority. Although this dread tribunal had been deprived of its old power of life and death, it seems at this period to have exercised this power anarchically, and other martyrdoms followed that of St. Stephen.

Paul could have had little enough in common with the high priest under whose commission he was acting. For the moment, they were making common cause against what they agreed to consider the new superstition. In many a synagogue Christians were arrested, scourged, compelled publicly to curse the name of Jesus. Women especially, it is more than once noted, were the objects of the violence of the persecutor.

At length the work was done, it seemed, effectually. The little community was broken up and dispersed, and the Sanhedrim, which claimed to exercise jurisdiction over a large part of the Jews of the Dispersion, turned its eyes upon the Church which had grown up in the important city, Damascus. That had better be crushed out too; and if the work was to be done, who could do it better than the young Pharisee whose accomplishments were so notorious, whose unflinching devotion to the synagogue had been proved by his activity as a persecutor? Paul was appointed as a special commissioner to destroy the Church of Christ in Damascus. He left Jerusalem on this errand accordingly. It was while he was on this journey that the new influence which was to make him what he is to Christendom was brought to bear upon his life.

There are many men for whom the phenomena of the spiritual world simply do not exist. It is impossible, within the compass of a lecture like this, to make any attempt to demonstrate their reality. It is necessary here that I should content myself with observing that they can be shown to be just as real as the facts and laws of what we call "nature." In both spheres we are in the region of mystery. We know just as little of the nature of what we call "matter" as of the nature of what we call "spirit." We only touch what we call matter, from without: we know not what it is in itself. And if we cannot deny, with some philosophies, any reality to matter at all, we are at least philosophically safe in saying that spirit is at least as real, and that the world of spiritual experience is as true, objectively—that is, whether we recognise its existence or not—as is the world of matter. Grace, with its operations, is as much a substantial certainty as is the law of gravitation ; and the facts which burst on the consciousness of Paul during that eventful journey are philosophically just as much entitled to respectful consideration as the last eclipse which was observed and registered at Greenwich.

Paul had nearly completed his journey. Some six weary days, at the least, it was from Jerusalem to Damascus. He had traversed the burning flats and uplands of Gaulonitis and Iturea : he was now in the beautiful valley watered by the streams of the Abana and Pharpar, about a mile and a half, it seems probable, from Damascus itself. Behind him was the great dome of Mount Hermon, capped with snow —on his right the Hauran—on his left the spurs of Antilibanus—before him the city which contained his destined victims, its white buildings just rising above the trees and gardens which lined the road. It is one of the very choicest spots on the surface of our globe — that approach to Damascus through the villages—beautiful in itself—more beautiful from its sharp contrast to the arid desert which encircles it. It is, as has been said not too enthusiastically, a very wilderness of gardens in which flowers and fruit are intertwined in a careless profusion— in which the prune, the apricot, the olive, festooned by the vine, grow on this side and on that, with a rich luxuriance, while everywhere the channels that are distributed, for purposes of irrigation, over the plain, cool the air with the clear fresh streams that run down from the base of Antilibanus and maintain this wealth of vegetation under that burning sun. Its situation alone explains the fact that Damascus is the oldest of known cities, and that while Tyre, Babylon, Palmyra—each of these, ancient as they were, more modern than itself—have long since perished, and perished utterly, Damascus is still a place of beauty and even of importance.

It was at noon, when all is hushed in these southern climes, even to the very birds upon the trees, that the event occurred which turned the whole current of the life of Saul of Tarsus. Suddenly—we can only repeat the words,— suddenly there was a light from heaven, above the brightness of the sun, shining round about Paul and them that journeyed with him. The stupefied companions of the Pharisee fell to the ground. They only rose to hear that a voice was being uttered which they could not understand. The vision was not meant for them, and, although the narrative makes it certain that it was not merely a something internal to the soul or mind of St. Paul, but on the contrary a strictly independent, or, as we moderns should say, an "objective" phenomenon, it was not intended for them, and they saw and heard only enough to know that it was in progress. Paul heard what they did not hear; he saw what they did not see. He heard in the tones of that voice, in the words of that language, which had fallen on the ears of Peter and of John, "Saul, Saul, why persecutest thou me? It is hard for thee to kick against the goads." He had, it is plain, felt the pleading of St. Stephen before the Sanhedrim—the death of St. Stephen outside the city—the constant, energetic, though sternly repressed working of his own conscience reviewing these facts of his own career. They were a cause at times of real secret distress to him; and here there was an evidence from without, confirming what had been already whispered within. The religion which he had argued against, which he had fought against, which he had persecuted, might after all be—it was—true. It made people, in every way inferior to himself, somehow, yet unmistakably, immeasurably his moral superiors. That he had already felt; and now here was the countersign of the feeling written in the very clouds of heaven. He could do no more. He asked submissively what he was to do, and he was told to arise and go into the city, and there it would be told him what he was ordained to do. The burning light of the vision had blinded him, and he entered Damascus, not at the head of his cavalcade, bent on schemes of violence and persecution, but led by the hand, as if he were himself a prisoner, to the house of Judas. There for three days he fasted, prayed—passed seventy-two hours in darkness, in silence, alone, alone with God.

The shock of the occurrence itself passed: its meaning, its consequences, its ineffaceable consequences, remained—unfolded themselves before his mind's eye. The world was another world to him; life was for him another order of existence; for he had given his will, his inmost self, to the Being who spoke to him. The strength, the secret, of the change was this, that he henceforth belonged no more to himself. He had abandoned himself without reserve to what he recognised as a perfectly holy will. That was the central, the determining, fact of his new life; and in the train of that act of self-surrender, all else followed. The old was fading away; all was becoming new. He was restored to sight at the entrance of Ananias, a humble, unknown minister of Christ at Damascus. He was received into the Christian Church by the sacrament of baptism.

The conversion of St. Paul was the subject of one of the most celebrated pieces of apologetic literature which appeared in this country during the last century. The Lord Lyttelton of that day had felt the force of the deistic objections to Christianity which were so eagerly urged by a large and cultivated school of writers, and he would seem to have recovered his faith mainly by concentrating his attention upon the significance of St. Paul's conversion. We are certainly concerned less with the evidential force of this event than with its real character; but its real character does undoubtedly invest it with a high evidential value, for it cannot be explained by the temperament or character of the Apostle. He certainly was not a visionary—a person of weak intellect. His whole conduct, and the arguments which he employs, prove that he was by nature a critical dialectician, quick at detecting objections, not merely in the case of an opponent, but in his own, and inclined by mental temperament to see to the bottom of such objections before laying them aside. Had he been of the facile and impressible temper which is assumed by the older deists, and, in a slight reconstruction of their argument, by M. Renan, he might have been expected to give at least one further proof of it, in an opposite or reactionary direction, at one of the many opportunities which presented themselves in his later life. But there is nothing afterwards in the way of change. The converted Paul ceased once for all to be a Jew in his conduct, in his feelings, in his inclinations, in his prejudices. If his conversion was not what it is represented in the Scripture narrative as being, the natural explanation of it is at least as difficult as the supernatural. The mental conditions which will explain the vision in the heavens above the brightness of the sun, the precise conversation with the heavenly Being, the being led by the hand into Damascus, the blindness, the instruction, the recovering of the sight, the total change of thought, feeling, conviction, purpose, which followed, would amount to a psychological miracle at least as striking as that which really took place.

Nor can the conversion be explained by the supposition that the account was in any way forged. What motive had St. Paul for inventing it? Was it, as has been supposed, some private pique or annoyance with the Jews, that led him to change his religious profession, and to account for the change in this kind of way? But there is no trace of any feelings of this kind in his early life. It would have been a sin against natural feeling, since the Jewish people had singled Paul out for a place of special confidence and honour; and, as a matter of fact, when the Jews were persecuting him afterwards to death, he expressed, in more ways than one, his deep love for his countrymen. He deplores their blindness; he excuses their conduct as far as he can. Even if, in one place, he paints it in dark colours, he would gladly, he says in another, were it possible, be accursed in their place. Was it the spirit of a sensitive independence which will sometimes lead men to assert their own importance at the cost of their party or their principles? That, again, is inconsistent with his advocacy of the duty of subjection to existing authority, in terms and to a degree which has exposed him to fierce criticisms from the modern advocates of social and political change. Was it, then, a refined self-interest? Did the young Jew see in the rising sect a prospect of bettering himself? But Christianity was being persecuted—persecuted, as it seemed, to the very verge of extermination. It had been crushed out, by the established hierarchy, in Jerusalem itself. It was doomed to destruction, every intelligent Jew would have thought, as well by the might of the forces ranged against it as by its intrinsic absurdity. It had nothing to offer, whether in the way of social eminence or of literary attraction. It was as yet, in the main, the religion of the very poor, of the very illiterate. On the other hand, the young Pharisee had, if any man had, brilliant prospects before him if he remained loyal to the synagogue. The reputation of his great master, his own learning and acuteness, his great practical ability, would have commanded success. If his object was really a selfish one, no man ever really made a greater or more stupid mistake, to all appearance; for no Jew could have anticipated for a convert to Christianity, within a few years of the crucifixion, such a reputation as that which now surrounds the name of St. Paul.

On the other hand, there is no reason to suppose that the power which effected this immense change in the purpose and life of Saul of Tarsus operated irresistibly upon his intellect and his will. When he tells Agrippa, " I was not disobedient to the heavenly vision," he implies that he was perfectly free to disobey. There is no such thing as irresistible grace in the moral world. If there were, man, in receiving it, would exchange his freedom as a moral agent for the passive obedience of a vegetable to the law of its kind. Paul might have persuaded himself that the vision was an hallucination—that his own brain had formulated the words of Jesus—that the blindness was due to physical causes—that the scruples about the blood of Stephen and the martyrs were of the nature of a foolish superstition; and when the shock was over, he would have carried out the purpose which brought him to Damascus. He would have entered the synagogue to arrest a fresh batch of victims for the Sanhedrim in Jerusalem. If he did not do this, it was because he was looking out, so well as he could, for truth, and was disposed to make the most of it when it came. Many a man in his circumstances would, as he could, have acted otherwise. St. Paul could say, " By the grace of God I am what I am; and His grace which was showed to me was not in vain."

And in this case of St. Paul, the new influence which remoulded his life belonged to a sphere which is above nature; but a kindred influence, scarcely, if at all, less powerful in its results, may be dispensed by persons or by causes which are strictly within our range of observation. The character of a friend, a startling occurrence, a new book, may form the frontier line between a past and a future which has little in common with it. And susceptibility to such influences, let me remark, is by no means a sign of feminine weakness. On the contrary, the most masculine natures, if true—if true to the higher promptings of conscience and to the higher sides of existence—are peculiarly open to them ; and even when they fall short of involving anything like a translation from darkness unto light, and from the power of Satan unto God, they still form that decisive turn in the affairs of men which, taken at the time, leads on to excellence.

It was natural that, in the first fervour of conversion, St. Paul should wish to make others sharers in his illumination and his joy. He appeared without delay in the synagogues at Damascus. His appearance had been expected as that of the accomplished Pharisee who was commissioned by the high priest, Theophilus, to exterminate the Christian heresy in the ancient Syriac capital. He would bring the most recent and the ripest learning to Jerusalem to confute the nascent error: he would use force if force was necessary, with prudence, but with unflinching determination. What must have been the blank astonishment of his own co-religionists when he "straightway preached in the synagogues that Jesus was the Son of God"! What must have been their indignation when the first stupor of surprise had passed! And how great must have been—we know that it was great —the thankful wonder of the trembling Christians when their declared enemy thus publicly, and at the imminent peril of his life, owned himself a disciple and preacher of the faith which he had so recently persecuted to the death ! The higher interests of human life are liable indeed to surprises, but few surprises that have ever happened can have rivalled this.

It would seem that this first effort at missionary work was of brief duration. It was, in fact, an anachronism, dictated by profound spiritual impulse, at variance with the orderly development of St. Paul's life. After a great change of conviction, nature, as well as something higher than nature, tells us that a long period of retirement and silence is fitting, if not necessary. The three days in the house of Judas were not enough in which to sound the heights and depths of newly recognised truth, or the strength and weakness of the soul which was to own and to proclaim it. They were to be followed by three years— I must not enter on the chronological reasons for insisting upon the literal value of that expression—three years passed in the deserts of Arabia. It is, indeed, thought that this retirement was dictated by a wish to preach the gospel to the wandering Bedouin tribes, or to the settled Arabs at Petrea. And there is no doubt that "Arabia" among the ancients was a very wide and inclusive geographical term. It might have included Damascus itself; it might have even taken in regions far to the north, extending to the very borders of Cilicia. But these are less usual uses of the word; nor can it be supposed that emphasis would have been laid on this retirement if all that had been meant had been a journey of a few miles into the desert beyond the walls of Damascus. Something may be said for a retreat to Petra, the ancient capital of Edom, which had its own synagogue in Jerusalem; but the probabilities are that, under the profound and awful inspirations of the hour, Paul sought to tread in the very footsteps of Moses and Elijah at the base of Sinai. There is a reference to the dialect of the district in the Epistle to the Galatians, which makes this at least probable for other than spiritual reasons. The spiritual attractions of such a course must have been, to a man of his character and antecedents, not less than overwhelming. There, where the Jewish law had been given, he was led to ask what it really meant,—what were its sanctions, what its obligations, what the limit of its moral capacity, what the criterion of its weakness. There he must have felt the inspiration of a life like Elijah's, the great representative of a persecuted religious minority, the preacher of an unpopular truth against vulgar but intolerant error. Would not the still small voice which had been spoken to the prophet—rather, *did* it not—again and again speak to him? They were precious years, depend upon it, for a man whose later life was to be passed, wholly passed, in action.

The value of such retirement, if circumstances admit of it or suggest it, before entering on the decisive work of life, can hardly be exaggerated. Many a young man, whose education is complete, as the phrase goes, and who knows, or thinks that he knows, what to do for himself or for his fellow-creatures, is often painfully disappointed when his plans for immediate exertion suddenly break down, and he has to remain for awhile in comparative obscurity and inaction. It seems to him to be a loss of time, with little or nothing to redeem the disadvantage. He is wasting, he thinks, his best years in idleness. He may, of course, so act as to make that phrase justifiable. It need not be so. A prudent no less than a religious man will thankfully, if he can, avail himself of such an opportunity for consolidating his acquirements, for reviewing the bearing of his governing convictions, for estimating more accurately the rescurces at his disposal, for extending or contracting his plans—at least, for reconsidering them. A religious man will, above all, seize such an opportunity for testing and strengthening his motives, and for cultivating an increased intimacy with those means and sources of effective strength which he will need so much hereafter. St. Paul, we may be sure, used the opportunity. It is even possible that the argument of his epistles to the Romans and the Galatians, although provoked by later circumstances arising in the bosom of the Christian Church, was the fruit of his meditation in the silence of the desert. In any case, in those dreary wastes his spirit would have been far from the pre-occupations of sense; free to measure the import and exigency of his recent vision and change; free to review the past years which had been a gain to him, but which, henceforth, so far as their proper end was concerned, he counted loss; free to prepare for the life of work and of suffering whose dim outline may—nay, must—already have sketched itself before his eyes, in a strength which could alone sustain him.

We have to consider in another lecture what were some of its results to the Church and to humanity.

H. P. L.

XVIII. The Life of St. Paul.

2. THE MISSIONARY, ADMINISTRATOR, AND MARTYR

A LIFE like that of St. Paul yields sufficient material for at least ten lectures such as these, and I therefore make no pretension whatever to deal with its main features exhaustively in one. It suggests, too, as some at least of my hearers well know, questions of great extent and intricacy which have created little less than entire literatures in the course of their discussion, and upon some of which no very positive opinion can possibly be arrived at. If these questions are passed by, or only glanced at incidentally, or referred to as being settled in this way or in that, without giving further reasons, it cannot be helped. All that can be done within such limits as ours is to suggest a few salient points of the general subject—to furnish the outlines which may be filled up by further and private study, —above all, if it might be, to stimulate interest in a great character, in a great saint and doctor, who on so many grounds is so entitled to command it.

The life of man is made up of action and of endurance—of the efforts which man puts forth—of the pain, discomfort, inconvenience, which he undergoes. And human life is noble and fruitful in the ratio in which it is laid out in vigorous action consecrated by a noble aim, and in suffering deliberately submitted to, or embraced from a generous motive. Nor do lives passed in speculative thought or in religious contemplation lie outside this devotion. Such thought is, or ought to be, an energetic, although it be an undemonstrative, variety of action. The thinker who is not dreaming—the contemplative whose soul is really engaged upon the unseen realities which interest him—is hard at work with that organ which, beyond all others, is capable of immense exertion and of distressing fatigue. To pass life in an aimless indolence—to shrink from endurance as well as from exertion—to exist but, as it were, in a state of moral coma—this is really degrading. Life is always—it is only—ennobled by effort and by suffering; and it is necessary to admit this as an axiom, as a truth lying fairly beyond discussion, if we are to understand St. Paul at all.

St. Paul's life became what it was under the influence of one overpowering conviction. He was certain that he, through no merit of his own, was in possession of truth of which men were almost universally ignorant, and of which it was of the utmost practical importance for them to know. This certainly rested upon two or three converging lines of evidence—the report of his moral sense or conscience as to the Christian character in the earliest Christians, the evidence of his bodily as well as of his spiritual senses as to what passed on the road to Damascus, and, thirdly, the remarkable coincidence between the conclusion which was thus reached and the fair meaning of those sacred documents which he had from his earliest years regarded as of Divine authority. And this certainty came to him at that decisive moment of his life which we have partly discussed. But the particular conclusion, from the nature of the case, only gradually shaped itself. To use his own words, he was a debtor to the Greeks and to the barbarians,—that is to say, to the whole human race. He practically owed it a share in that truth which he had, he felt, no right to monopolize. How should he—how did he—discharge the obligation?

St. Paul's missionary life extended altogether over a period of nearly thirty years; for, in one sense, he was a missionary from the moment of his conversion. His early efforts in Damascus provoked the hostility of the Jews, and not long after his return from Arabia, he was obliged to escape for his life from an officer of King Aretas, who, in those unsettled times, was commanding in Damascus, and who apparently was acting under Jewish influences. He fled to Jerusalem. To visit Peter was, he says, a leading motive for his going there. The Christians in Jerusalem were naturally afraid of a person who had been so conspicuous as a persecutor, and their confidence was only won by the good offices of Barnabas, who assured them of the facts and reality of St. Paul's conversion, and of his work for the faith in Damascus. He lived for a fortnight on terms of intimacy with St. Peter, and with St. James, our Lord's first cousin, and the first Bishop of Jerusalem. Some part of this time he spent in arguments with the Hellenistic or the Alexandrian Jews, for which his education had peculiarly fitted him. He thus excited the greatest hostility, and was obliged to take flight by way of Cæsarea to his birthplace at Tarsus.

Of his life at Tarsus during the next four years we know nothing, except that it must have been by no means a period of inactivity. Making his home his head-quarters, he seems to have preached in the city and its neighbourhood, as well as on the Syriac coasts on the opposite side of the bay; and several of the dangers and trials to which he refers in his second letter to the Corinthians probably belonged to this period, especially his three shipwrecks, and his being publicly scourged by the Jewish and Roman authorities.

M

In the year 44, Barnabas, who was working at Antioch, came to Tarsus to secure the co-operation of St. Paul. The Church at Antioch had been founded eight years before by refugees from Jerusalem who were flying from the persecution which Paul himself had directed. It had contained from the first a number of Gentile converts, and it was to superintend this new state of things that Barnabas had been sent with apostolic authority from Jerusalem. Barnabas and Paul worked together for a year in teaching the heathen, and in organizing the Church, and at the end of this period they took a considerable sum of money to Jerusalem to meet the wants of the poor Christians in that city during the famine which occurred at the time of Herod Agrippa's death. They returned to Antioch with St. Mark, a nephew of Barnabas, and the Church of Antioch rapidly became—for the time at any rate—the most central spot in Christendom. The political and commercial importance of the city, as well as its position, made it the natural starting-point for a great scheme of Church extension, while the presence of a great many Gentile converts irresistibly suggested it. If the gospel had come to Antioch—had come to men of heathen birth in Antioch—could it mean to stop there? Was it not by its very terms a message of health and of deliverance to the whole human race? And was not Antioch, with its half Jewish, half Gentile Church, the natural scene for originating such an enterprise? So it was that the Church of Antioch was taught by the silent movement of the Holy Spirit within men's minds to make a great effort for the faith in the Gentile world, and to give her greatest teachers to the work. The decisive conviction came while the liturgy or holy communion (such is the apparent force of the original word) was being celebrated; and the two friends, with the nephew of Barnabas, set forth on their mission.

Up to this time St. Paul had worked as a subordinate, a kind of curate, to Barnabas. Like all really great men, he was profoundly indifferent to any mere questions of personal or professional precedence, provided the sacred principles themselves were safe, and the true work was being done. He left Antioch still the second to Barnabas; but after the conversion of Sergius Paulus, the Proconsul of Cyprus, the author of the Acts of the Apostles no longer writes

"Barnabas and Saul," but "Paul and Barnabas." Not only is the order of the names inverted, but the Jewish name, "Saul," is deliberately dropped, and the Roman name, "Paul" or "Paulus," which the Apostle had probably possessed from his birth, was exclusively adopted, with, no doubt, a view to conciliating Gentile prejudice. It is at this point that St. Paul's missionary life in its complete form begins.

Between his leaving Antioch in the year 48, and his arrest at Jerusalem in the summer of the year 58, he achieved what are popularly known as his three missionary journeys. These journeys do not bear traces of any fixed plan. What plan there was was disturbed, sometimes by circumstances; sometimes it was set aside by a higher guidance under which the Apostle acted. They rather remind us, if I may draw an illustration from a very different field of exertion, of those efforts which the discovery of the new world, and the hope of finding the imagined El-Dorado, provoked at the hands of English and Spanish adventurers alike in the days of Philip the Second and of Elizabeth. It was a spirit of enterprise, only in St. Paul's case it was consecrated by a purely unselfish and noble motive. An enterprise, as we all know, is necessarily governed by circumstances, and can never be mapped out very systema ically. St. Paul's journeys were, in their way, like the expeditions of Sir Walter Raleigh in his—the creations of a noble impulse which must be doing something—raids conducted on no very obvious plan upon the dark domains of heathendom. And yet, looking back upon these journeys, we may see that they do bear a certain relation to each other. The first was tentative. It was what military men would call the reconnaissance of the forces of the heathen enemy. It extended no farther than to the northern side of that line of mountains upon which the eyes of Paul had gazed in his earliest childish days. It began with a great success. It well nigh closed in the Apostle's martyrdom. In Cyprus, he converts the Roman proconsul; he punishes the magician, Elymas. Crossing to the mainland, he makes a great impression by a single sermon at Antioch in Pisidia, which provokes an outbreak of Jewish hostility. At Iconium, the scenes of Antioch are repeated. At Lystra and Derbe, he is among uncivilized Pagans, who are reaby to pay him divine honours in one mood, and to stone him to death in another. Jewish hostility was at the bottom of the incident at Lystra, and the Apostle turned homeward by the way he came, making as sure of his work as he could by leaving presbyters in every town he visited, and at last embarking at Attalia direct for the Syrian Antioch. This was in 49; and the next year, 50, was marked by his visit to the apostolic council at Jerusalem. In 51, he set out on what is called his second missionary circuit. He would not take St. Barnabas's nephew, who had shown a want of apostolic resolution, and this leads to a separation between Barnabas and himself. Silas, or Silvanus, took the vacant place.

This second journey is, on the whole, the most important. It is quite certainly the richest in incident, and the boldest in its range. Again the missionaries start from Antioch. They pass through Syria, Cilicia, and Lycaonia; they revisit the old scenes of Derbe and Lystra, where Timothy is taken into the Apostle's company. And then the Galatian mission followed, of which we know little from the Acts, but much from the letter to the Galatian Churches. St. Paul was detained in the district by some bodily ailment, whether it was weakness of the eyes, or, as is on the whole more likely, epilepsy; but this did not prevent his working on as an evangelist; and he probably founded at least three Churches in the three chief towns of this, the central district of Asia Minor, amid an amount of exuberant enthusiasm characteristic of people of Celtic origin, and soon to be followed by a serious reaction. He then intended to work along the western coast of Asia Minor, or subsequently along the north-eastern coast of Bithynia. He was in both cases prevented by Divine intimations, and finally was directed by a vision to cross from Troas into Macedonia. This decisive moment marked the entrance of the gospel into Europe. Accompanied by St. Luke, who joined him at Troas, he crossed, touching at Samothrace, to Neapolis. And then there follows a series of incidents to which the greatest prominence is assigned in the narrative of the Acts, and with which we are all more or less familiar. The Roman colony, to all intents and purposes a western town, Philippi, is the scene of the conversion of Lydia, of the exorcism of the slave girl, of the scourging and imprisonment of the apostles, of the conversion of the jailer. At the purely Greek city of Thessalonica the successful preaching on three sabbaths is followed by an attack on the house of the Christian, Jason, by his arrest, by the Apostle's escape by night. At Berea, where the resident Jews are capable, we are told, of a more generous bearing, and where there are many converts, yet the Apostle has to be privately removed in order to secure his safety. At Athens he is face to face with the great traditions of the past of Greece—with the scorn, and yet with the curiosity, of modern Epicureans and Stoics, with an anxious idolatry that would leave no possible object of superstition unvenerated. And Corinth—Corinth, famous even in Pagan days for its gross impurity connected with its popular worship of Aphrodite—is his residence for a year and a half. It witnesses the conversion of Crispus, the ruler of the synagogue, the formal secession of the Church from the synagogue to the house of Justus, the failure of the Jewish appeal to Gallio; and then there follows, in the spring of 54, the Apostle's return, by way of Cenchrea and Ephesus, to Jerusalem, for the feast of Pentecost.

St. Paul's third journey is clearly intended to supplement and to confirm the work of the second. He had not yet visited Ephesus, the capital of Asia Minor, and one of the great centres of the ancient world. Ephesus, to which a famous temple and commercial interests drew together men of many races and of many tongues, had a natural charm for the heart of an apostle. He spent three years in Ephesus, so great was his sense of its importance to the future of the faith. The progress of his work here was marked by his secession, as at Corinth, from the synagogue to the lecture-room of Tyrannus; then by his triumph over the professors of magic; lastly, by the great riot organized by the discontented silversmiths who made shrines for the temple of Artemis or Diana. And the other noteworthy point of this circuit is his visit to Corinth, which, as we know, from his two epistles to that Church—one of them written from Ephesus, and the other while he was travelling through Macedonia—urgently required his presence. On his way he went so far west as to pass the frontiers of Illyricum. He remained in Corinth three months, wrote the epistles to the Romans and the Galatians, and, in the spring of 58, returned by way of Philippi and Miletus, at Miletus taking leave of the presbyters of Ephesus, and, with presentiments of coming trouble strongly upon him, reached Jerusalem.

The remaining ten years of his life, from 58 to 68, were still, although in a less active sense, missionary years. He still works on, but he works in chains. He is less in synagogues; he is more in law-courts, in guard-houses, in dungeons. His arrest at Jerusalem, in the summer of 58, was followed by his long imprisonment at Cæsarea. He was only sent to Rome, by Festus, in the late autumn of the year 60. He reached it in the spring of 61. But he misses no opportunity of doing what there can be done. Speaking before Felix or before Agrippa, he turns a legal argument into a religious apology. When he is on board the vessel which is carrying him to Rome, when he is shipwrecked at Malta, when he is chained to a soldier in the Via Lata, near the prætorian camp, he is still a missionary. His two years of imprisonment at Rome are devoted to work— first, work among his own countrymen, and then work among the Gentiles; and on his acquittal, he seems to have spent four years first in Macedonia and Asia Minor, and then, probably, a year or a year and a half in Spain. Then again he is in the East, at Ephesus and Nicopolis. Even in his second imprisonment, when his work was all but done, he could influence such persons as Linus, who was to be Bishop of Rome, or Pudens, the son of a senator, or Claudia, a British princess.

But, speaking broadly, the last ten years of his life were spent more in administering and governing the Church than in enlarging her frontiers. Before, however, we pass to this side of his work, it is natural to ask the question, What were the qualities which made St. Paul the first of missionaries?

And in answering this question, I do not forget his apostolic prerogatives. He could work miracles, he could command a degree of inspiration which might well seem to place him outside and above the category of all ordinary Christian missionaries. And yet his success, we may be bold to say, was largely due to qualities which any who tread in his steps, at however great a distance, may certainly share. There are, among others, these points to be remarked in him. He never for one moment forgets that he is uttering a Divine message,—that he is preaching a creed, and not commenting on a philosophy. His creed was, indeed, as he told the Corinthians, the truest and the best philosophy; but then it came, as he believed, out of no human brain, but from the mind and heart of God. Accordingly he proclaims it simply, unhesitatingly, uncompromisingly, as a man would do who had no doubt about its inherent power—about its ultimate success. St. Paul, in fact, was what would be called in the present day a dogmatist. Dogmatism is very unbecoming in those who can appeal only to human authority for what they say, and who ought to know that, this authority being human, they may very possibly be mistaken. But a man who believes himself to be charged with a message from God to his fellow-man must be clear, positive, straightforward, in his assertions. A dogmatic address is simply due to the character of what such a man professes to have to say. Men who object to dogmatism in Christian teachers, on account of the claim which it implies, would smile at the claim to bring a message from heaven in the mouth of a declaimer against Christian dogma. If St. Paul had preached Christianity as if he were half ashamed of its mysteries—as if he were thoroughly afraid of offending Jewish or heathen opinion—he might, no doubt, have got through life much more easily, but he would not have made half a dozen sincere converts, or have roused the jealousies of a single synagogue.

And St. Paul is disinterested. He sought not what his converts could give him: he sought themselves. And disinterestedness, in whatever cause it may be enlisted, is always power. The Corinthian and the Galatian Christians knew perfectly well that their great teacher had nothing on earth to get by them; they knew in their better moments that he had given them all that was worth having in life and in death.

But then, side by side with this sincere and unaffected accent of certainty, and this lofty independence of motive, St. Paul is capable of the greatest possible consideration for the difficulties and prejudices of those whom he is anxious to win. Strong men, like strong systems, can afford to be generous, while the uncertain and the timid are almost necessarily suspicious and unsympathetic. Their own hold of truth, they instinctively feel, is so precarious that they cannot venture to take liberties. They will be suspected themselves of vacillation or disloyalty if they appear to enter into the difficulties of others. St. Paul knew that no weight of human authority, and no ingenuity or strength of human argument, could touch a truth which he had received, as he believed, neither of man nor by man, but from God and His Divine Son. But for this very reason, he could become "all things to all men," that he might by all means win some; and to the Jews even he became as a Jew that he might save the Jews. Nothing in his whole life appears to me to illustrate this quality of the tenderness of strength in St. Paul, and which he pre-eminently possessed, more strikingly than his circumcision of Timothy. He did this, you remember, in his second missionary journey, when he was carrying with him and distributing to his Gentile converts that decree of the council of Jerusalem which was the guarantee of their freedom, and which proclaimed that they need not observe the Mosaic law. Timothy's father was a Greek; his mother was a Jewess; and St. Paul felt that to be accompanied by one who was half a Jew, and who professed the Jewish faith, and yet was uncircumcised, would be a cause of great and unnecessary offence in every synagogue he entered. He therefore, even under those circumstances, circumcised Timothy. "How inconsistent!" men might exclaim. "How illogical! How wanting in adherence to principle!" The real question always is, when principle is and when it is not at stake. Paul could resist the pressure of opinion at Jerusalem when the circumcision of Titus was said to be religiously necessary. He could withstand St. Peter himself to the face when deference to a narrow Jewish prejudice was compromising the faith. A man of real principle is not afraid that his generosity will be mistaken, or that, if it is mistaken for the moment, it will in the end be misunderstood.

And once more. St. Paul is always eager to recognise the truth, the measure of truth, which is already admitted by those whom he wishes to convince or to convert. When he makes war upon the strongholds of religious error, he is never an indiscriminate destroyer. Truth, the truth which is mingled with it, being, as it is, the strength of all error, the Apostle recognises such truth as truth; he makes the most of it; he shows how, if rightly understood, it leads on to the full, uncorrupted, unmutilated truth which he is himself recommending. And thus his method generally was, on reaching a town, to begin his work at the synagogue, because, you observe, the synagogue furnished him with the premises of his argument, and with people who already believed what ought to lead them to agreement with himself. He had rights in the synagogue, too—rights which were not yet formally cancelled—and he made the most of them. In the synagogue he and his hearers were united at least in this,—in a common reverence for the Old Testament Scriptures. Read his sermon in the synagogue at Antioch in Pisidia as a sample of his method. During the whole of the earlier part of that sermon, every Jew present must have followed him entirely. He solemnly acknowledges the God of his people Israel; he traces God's hand in Israel's history down to the days of David —the great days upon which every Jew looked back with enthusiastic interest. Then he enlarges upon David, a name so dear to the sympathies of his audience; and then at last he names, as David's promised Son, Jesus. He justifies this by referring to the ministry of the Baptist, and to the facts of our Saviour's life. The rulers who crucified Jesus, he says, did not really know the Jewish prophets, or they would have acted otherwise. The resurrection of Jesus, he says, was the fulfilment of God's promises to the fathers of Israel: it was the God of Israel, then, who proclaimed true righteousness and forgiveness of sins through Jesus. And the sermon closes with a warning against unbelief, which is carefully conveyed in the familiar language of Jewish prophets. The effect of such a sermon as this was to say, "You Jews suppose Christianity to be a something altogether hostile to the old faith of Israel. On the contrary, if you will examine the matter, you will see that Christianity is its necessary, its legitimate, development—that it completes that unveiling of the Divine mind which the Jewish law only began." Or take the most modern of St. Paul's sermons, as it has been called—that which he pronounced on the steps of the

Areopagus at Athens. Here of course he does not quote Jewish scriptures, of which his hearers would know simply nothing. He had observed, he says, that the Athenians were a particularly religious people, and that, in order to be quite safe with heaven, they had even erected an altar to some unknown God. Well, then, he says, he is able to tell them something about that God. They too had heard of one Being who was the source and sustainer of universal life; they too had been taught to look at human history as an education, as a discipline, for some higher truth which they had not yet mastered. So far they would have gone with the preacher. And now he passes the frontier of their sympathies. That all men of all nations were of one blood, or that there was One who stood in a universal relation to all, who would judge all, who had died and who had risen from death to attest this as his mission,—this, no doubt, was beyond them, and yet how skilfully, how tenderly, is this further step introduced. How carefully does the Apostle feel his way from what was admitted to what was unknown; and it was, we may be sure, but a sample of his usual method.

Yes, beyond all controversy, Paul the apostle is the first of Christian missionaries. All the great labourers for the extension of Christ's kingdom in later ages—Boniface and Augustine, Patrick and Columba, Xavier and Martyn—all have breathed his enthusiasms; all in their degree have lived his life; all have accepted his methods; all have trodden his steps. Peter, indeed, was first at work. Peter, in his own single person, was the rock on whose personal exertions the Church was to be built. Peter laid its foundations; and, as we gather from somewhat dim traditions, the other apostles of Christ had each his appropriate field of work; and they can have been no common efforts by which the earliest Syriac Churches were founded on the Upper Euphrates, on or beyond the frontiers of the empire. But, as compared with St. Paul's more abundant labours, everything else in the apostolic age pales and fades away. He it is who is the typical missionary—the man who still, almost before our very eyes, with truth upon his lips, with a burning love of his God and of his fellow-men in his heart, goes forth to win a reluctant world to obedience to a mysterious and exacting creed which, yet, alone could bring it the great, the surpassing gifts of peace and righteousness. And his example is as energetic as ever. Depend upon it, he has not yet done the work he has to do before the end.

St. Paul was not only a missionary who laboured for the extension of Christianity : he was a great ruler and administrator of the Christian Church. He had to tend, support, guide, govern, the Churches which sprang into being as he passed along his way. "The care of all the Churches, that which cometh upon me daily," he represents as the climax of his trials. As an apostle, he had a responsibility towards the whole Church. There was no restriction of such responsibility to particular cities or districts, such as was afterwards, for example, the case with bishops at the close of the apostolical age. Certainly there was a general arrangement between himself and the three apostles who were called pillars of the Church, that they should work among the Jews and he among the heathen nations ; but his own activity at his visits to Jerusalem, and the later labours of St. Peter and St. John in heathen lands, show that this was not understood to interfere with the inherent rights of each member of the apostolic college.

As a great ruler in the Church, St. Paul had to pronounce decisions on very various questions affecting Christian duty ; and as he deals with them, we must be struck with the strength and tenderness of that sympathy which was his characteristic gift. The Church of Corinth was divided into parties, one of which made free and unauthorized use of his own name. He remonstrates tenderly but firmly. The Corinthian women were agitated by a discussion as to what sort of head-dress they should wear at public worship. He goes into this seemingly trivial question with the greatest patience. He decides, for very weighty reasons, that their heads are to be properly covered. A Christian is guilty of an odious incest : St. Paul cuts him off from the communion of the Church. The man repents : St. Paul orders his restoration to Church communion. Might people, it was asked, eat meat which had been offered for the purpose of sacrifice in the heathen temples ? It entirely depends, St. Paul says, upon whether offence is thereby given to weak uninstructed Christians or not. Is it well for Christians to marry again, or not to marry at all ? St.

Paul enters into these questions with the utmost minuteness. Two Philippian ladies, Euodias and Syntyche, have a private quarrel while St. Paul is in his prison at Rome. He hears of it: he sends them a special message, desiring them to make it up. Onesimus, a converted slave, wishes to return to his master, Philemon, whom he had injured and then deserted: St. Paul gives him a letter of recommendation full of the most delicate consideration for Philemon's own feelings and position, as well as for those of his own recent convert. The holy communion was profaned at Corinth through the proceedings at a lovefeast which preceded it. St. Paul uses language of stern severity, and then adjourns the discussion of details until his arrival. The last chapter of the Epistle to the Romans has been described as a mere list of names. Its value, its interest, are of the very highest order. It shows how true, how discriminating, was the Apostle's care even of the individual members of the several flocks that were under his jurisdiction.

And besides these questions of conduct, St. Paul had a great deal of what would be called purely ecclesiastical business on his hands. In the epistles to Timothy and to Titus, we see him organizing the Christian clergy, making rules for their lives, making provision for their sustenance, insisting that their wives are to be persons of ascertained Christian character. He gives Timothy full instructions for instituting an order of widows devoted to charitable work. Indeed, nothing was nearer his heart than making Christian faith useful and fruitful for the purpose of relieving human want and human suffering. If the body was one, he argued, then its members had duties towards each other. One of the persistent efforts of his life, again and again referred to, was to raise money among the wealthier Christians of Gentile or Hellenistic origin in order to support the poverty-stricken populations in and about Jerusalem.

But the duties of the Apostle towards the faith and knowledge of the infant Church were even more exacting than his duties towards its organization and conduct. Everywhere there were sides of truth to be elucidated or insisted upon; there were misapprehensions to be removed; there were errors to be rebuked. Each Church, it might almost be said, had its peculiar misapprehension of the Apostle's teaching. At Thessalonica, what St. Paul had said about Christ's second coming was exaggerated into a reason for neglecting ordinary duties. In the Galatian Churches some clever preachers were persuading the majority that it was necessary to observe the Jewish festivals and fasts, to be circumcised, to be, in fact, good Jews, as well as, or before, being good Christians. At Corinth, the cardinal doctrine of the resurrection was denied because of the difficulty of giving an adequate physical explanation of it. At Colosse, a strange mixture of Jewish cabalistic rules and of Greek modes of thinking had produced a philosophy which, while retaining Christian phraseology, dethroned Christ in the Christian heart. At Ephesus, at any rate in the later apostolic age, there must have been some of those attempts to make capital out of Christianity, with a view to framing theories about the universe or about human life, which, under the name of gnosticism, abounded so largely in the following century, and the remains of which are quite plainly discoverable in the first. At Alexandria, if, as is probable, the Epistle to the Hebrews was addressed at St. Paul's instance or dictation to the Christians living in that city, there was a disposition to fall back altogether to Judaism.

It is in St. Paul's epistles that we see him at work in this vast field of labour, and, if those epistles had not a far higher claim on our attention, their purely literary interest would be simply exhaustless. They are probably only a portion of the letters which he actually wrote—preserved because instinctively received by the apostolical Church into the sacred canon, while the others perished. They were written amid the distractions of a life of ceaseless effort and of ceaseless struggle. It was in the midst of the mission at Corinth, in 52 and 53, when Jewish passion and heathen impurity were giving him so much to think about, that he wrote the two letters to the Thessalonians. It was at the close of his three years' sojourn in Ephesus—so rich in its results, so serious in the proof it had given of the vehemence of popular passions—that he wrote his first letter to the Corinthians. It was while travelling—we know how difficult it is to write letters when we are on our travels,—it was while travelling through Macedonia that he wrote the second letter to Corinth. At Corinth, in the midst of absorbing preoccupations, he found time to write the great Epistle to the Romans—itself a theological treatise—and the brief vivid remonstrance to the Galatians. A prisoner at Rome, he seizes the opportunity of writing not merely the circular epistle which was addressed to the Church of Ephesus, and some other Churches, but also those to the Colossians and Philemon, and, later, the tenderest of all the epistles—that to the Philippians. He was again engaged in missions when he wrote to Titus and to Timothy. When he wrote to Timothy for the last time he was in prison, in full view of the inevitable end.

While the division of our Bibles into chapters and verses has great practical recommendations, it has also some serious drawbacks, and they are nowhere more obvious than in reading the epistles of St. Paul. Unlike St. John's, St. Paul's style does not always readily lend itself to this minute subdivision. And each one of his epistles is, as a rule, like its several paragraphs, an organically connected whole. In order to enjoy, if not to understand him, it is well occasionally, after reminding ourselves of the circumstances under which an epistle was written, to read it right through at a single sitting. In this way the force and relative subordination of the arguments, the drift of the incidental observations, the varied plan of exhortation, of remonstrance, of irony, of affectionateness, becomes in turn obvious. We are no longer dealing with disconnected fragments, but with a complete composition which, in its completeness, speaks for itself.

Amid all the distractions of our own day it is almost consolatory to reflect that the apostolic Church itself was disturbed by serious controversies—controversies which ran up into offensive personalities, which were at times, as at Corinth and in Galatia, conducted with the greatest bitterness. The great controversy in which St. Paul was engaged within the Church turned upon the question whether the Jewish observances, and circumcision in particular, were necessary for Christians. A large party of Christians whose centre was Jerusalem, who were probably influenced by the current opinions in the school of Shammai, and who made free use of the names of the apostles Peter, James, and

John, maintained that these observances were necessary. To these men St. Paul's work appeared to be radically revolutionary ; and, as in Galatia, where they could, they went over the ground which St. Paul had evangelized. They insisted that, if the Gentile converts would be really good Christians, they too must be circumcised. St. Paul maintained that, while, if a man happened to be circumcised, it did him no sort of harm, to insist upon circumcision as necessary for a Christian was to deny fundamental truth, for there were two points of the gravest importance which really were involved in this apparent trifle. First, was the work of Christ as the restorer of man to a state of righteousness before God complete in itself ; or was it merely a supplement to the Jewish creed ? Was the system of the Jewish law, after all, able to make men righteous ; and, if it was, where was the need of the work of Christ ? If this was the case, moreover, was it even conceivable that Christ was greater than Moses and the prophets—greater in His essential nature ? The Judaizing theory that the law in its entirety was still obligatory meant, at bottom, that Christ's work was not nearly complete, and so that His person was really only human. And a second question was, Was Christianity meant to be the religion of mankind, or only of a small subdivision of the Jewish world ? Was it—to use later language—to be merely national or to be catholic ? If Christianity was serious in claiming to be the true, the absolute religion, it could not but also claim to be universal. The two claims, men instinctively felt, went together. In resisting circumcision, then, St. Paul was contending not merely for the Divine dignity of his Master, but for the world-embracing character of the new kingdom in which there was to be neither Jew nor Gentile, barbarian nor Scythian, bond nor free, but all were to be one. St. Paul has, indeed, been said by a distinguished writer against Christianity, to have been its real author, and to have changed it from a beautiful moral sentiment into a dogmatic creed—to have invested the person of its Founder with a rank which He never would have claimed— to have given the new religion a world-wide extension which was not contemplated by the Prophet of Nazareth. It is instructive to compare this, which is, substantially, Toland's idea of St. Paul's work, with that which, proceeding from a writer of the same school, represents it as practically a failure, the Judaizing tendency having, it is contended, successfully asserted itself, even in the second century, in the ordinances of the Christian Church, and in the prevalent conception of the Christian life. The two ideas might well be left to neutralize each other.

St. Paul only taught in other terms what his Master had taught—in different terms, certainly, and with application to new circumstances. Our Lord had said that in the coming time the Father would be worshipped neither on the Samaritan mountain nor in Jerusalem. He had ruled that a man is not defiled by what he eats. He had called Himself Master of the sabbath—an unpardonable assumption in Jewish eyes. He had made claims upon the love, upon the trust, upon the obedience, upon the reverence of men, which could only be justified if He was what St. Paul taught. He had told His followers to preach and to baptize, not among the Jews only, but among all the nations. St. Paul insisted on these features of our Lord's teaching at a critical point in the history of the apostolic Church. That was all. Nor was his work in vain. The greatest minds in Christendom are his distinct creations. It is from Paul that Augustine learns the doctrines of grace of which he was so great a master. It is from Paul that Chrysostom imbibes his vivid sense of the range and applicability of Christian morals. It is at the feet of St. Paul, not less than at those of St. John, that Athanasius discovers what was really meant by the incarnation of the Son of God. He was caricatured by Marcion; he has been abundantly misrepresented by modern antinomian systems of divinity. These teachers pass and are forgotten: St. Paul remains. If, as at the first, there are in his writings not a few things hard to be understood, which they that are unlearned and unstable wrest to their destruction, this does not obscure the glory of the apostle of the nations, or render him responsible for inferences from, or for paraphrases of, his words, which he would have been the first to disallow.

In all ages truth has demanded sacrifices, and no man ever lived who understood this better than Paul of Tarsus —the power, the fruitfulness, of sacrifice as a means of advancing the cause of truth and goodness. He must have seen from the first, as martyrdom lay in the nature of things, a sufficient presentiment of the end. In the course of discharging his duties he was again and again close to death. He gives the Corinthians a list of the dangers which even before the year 57 he had to encounter. He explains to the Philippians while he is in prison for the first time, in Rome, that he already looks upon death as gain. It would seem that he must have been arrested at Nicopolis, late in the autumn of 67, and sent, probably by the local duumvirs, to Rome for trial as soon as it was safe to cross the Adriatic, for since St. Paul's release in the year 63, events had occurred which made a Christian's position much more insecure. After the great fire in Rome in the year 64, the Emperor Nero endeavoured to divert the popular indignation of which he was the object, by turning it from himself upon the Christians. The pagan historian, Tacitus, has described the atrocities of this first persecution of the Church,—how some Christians were crucified, how some were dressed in the skins of wild beasts and hunted to death with dogs, how some were clothed in dresses of inflammable material, and set on fire at night in order to illuminate the imperial gardens. This was three years before St. Paul's last arrest. St. Paul was well out of the way when it happened, but the name of so noted a leader of the Christians would now have been known to the Roman police, and they would have been on the look out for him. Probably he reached Rome by way of Brindisi early in 68, and his case would have come on for early trial before the city prefect, to whom the emperor at that time delegated cases of this kind. He would have been tried in one of the great basilicas or law-courts which abutted on the forum. The tragic interest of the Second Epistle to Timothy consists in its belonging to these, the closing months—we may almost say the closing days—of the life of the great apostle. It was written when his case had been brought into court for the first time—when he had been acquitted of the first charge against him; that is, probably, his being concerned in the burning of Rome. He says that on that occasion no man stood by him, whether as patron or as advocate. He had had to plead his cause all alone. And yet he was not alone: he was more than ever conscious of the strengthening presence of our Lord. But for this, the isolation of those last weeks would have been quite unbearable. Demas had forsaken him for worldly motives. Crescens, for some unnamed reason, had gone off into Galatia. Even Titus—we cannot suppose it was through cowardice—Titus had left for Dalmatia. Only Luke remained. He longed to see Timothy once more before he died, but he knew that the end was near, and it is impossible to say whether his wish was granted. The second charge against him—probably that of introducing a religion unrecognised by the State—would no doubt have gone against him. But then he could die as a Roman citizen. There is no serious critical reason for rejecting the ordinary account of his martyrdom. He was beheaded with a sword outside that gate of Rome which looks towards the port at the mouth of the Tiber, and which is now called in his honour the Gate of St. Paul.

A splendid church, first erected by the Emperor Constantine, and lately rebuilt since the great fire of 1824, marks the neighbourhood, at any rate, of the spot on which Paul of Tarsus passed to receive, as he believed with all his heart, "a crown of righteousness." But his enduring monument at this moment, and to the end of time, will be his great, his unrivalled place as a writer in the sacred canon, and the gratitude of millions of hearts to whom he is the incessant minister of the truth whereby the two deepest longings of the human soul may be permanently satisfied—the longing to be inwardly righteous, and the longing for an inward peace.

H. P. L.

XIX. The Results of Justification. ROM. v. 1–12.

IN these stirring verses the apostle Paul has made this much plain—that God's way of justifying sinful men by the gospel, by their "standing in Christ," affords the most ample grounds of hope for the perfect and complete salvation of every believer. The developments of that hope he does not tell us; into the holy life he does not yet enter.

The difficulties of a believer—his hopes, his fears, his motives are postponed for the present; but taking his stand upon the bare fact of the atonement, St. Paul states the obvious result, that he who believes in it must expect the fullest possible deliverance, and to be admitted into the very glory of God.

To be acquitted of guilt is the beginning. But this blessing does not come alone—it brings along with it this, that it opens a door by which each reconciled sinner may look for further blessedness. Hope, therefore, is the keyword of the section, and the other ideas are merged into this sentence.

First, our hope reposes on this new relation of ours towards God, when we are at peace with Him. Second, our hope is not impaired, but confirmed. Third, our hope is warranted by the proof we already possess of the love of God to us. A few words on each of these points.

First of all, being justified by faith we have peace with God through Jesus Christ, by whom also we have access by faith into this grace wherein we stand and rejoice in hope of the glory of God. There is room now in the hearts of believers to hope that God will bless us with His blessedness since we are at peace with Him. This peace with God, or peace in respect of God, is neither our friendly feeling towards God through Christ, nor that deep serene peace of the Spirit which is Christ's bequest. It is true, no doubt, that our conscious reconciliation with God ought to bring us into a holy calm; but, still, the hope of what God is going to do for us cannot spring out of any experience of our own. It must spring out of what God *has* done. It is the friendly relationship which God has established *Himself.* We must go back behind our own experience. It is the change of an armed attitude towards us; the change is that which we owe to the atoning work of Christ. Before God in Christ had reconciled us to Himself we are described by Paul as *hated.* God hates not us, whom He has made, but sin, which He has not made. Sin compelled God to an attitude of painful antagonism. This is not hate. It may exist with the most tender affection. David refused to receive Absalom, but loved him. In our sin God cannot speak to us words of friendship.

This may have been a greater trial to Him than it was

to us. Who can doubt it? Men chose evil rather than good with their evil deeds lying unatoned upon their consciences. While we were on our part disliking God and resenting His claims—this was the previous condition of things, the natural (or rather unnatural) condition produced by sin—notice what a revolution Christ's death wrought. It restored a right relation between us and God, and the obstacles which had separated us from God were taken away. We have had access, as Paul phrases it, into the favour of God. The offended One is offended no longer. The mighty One, whom—against His will—our sin had arrayed against us, is glad to become our friend.

The blessed Mediator has done this, and we who were banished have been received into the place of favour.

So that now we may even hope to behold the glory of God. Greater than the change from midnight to noonday, more blessed than any other change, is this sudden change in the experience of the soul that is brought nigh to a reconciled God. For the threatenings of a broken law, love; for condemnation, there is complacency; for a frown, there is a smile; for the unanswered question, "How can a man draw nigh to God?" there is now a near hope of glory.

Standing thus within sight of the Divine, standing thus near and in favour with our Father, what is there for the believer to fear, what is there that he may not hope?

Second. This glorious likeness to the Divine splendour is still future. The present is a life of trouble for the Christian believer; in Paul's day especially was the life of the Christian a life of sorrow. But these present troubles do not weaken the believer's hope; on the contrary, in the long run they confirm and increase our hope. How so? Why, these our troubles bravely and meekly borne for God's sake, work in us a steadfast endurance holding on to the end; and the Christian who is thus enabled to bear his trials is a consecrated believer. Not a shallow hope that God is his friend, but a *knowledge* of it, for the friendship has been put to the test; and having stood that test, and having come out of it with a complete confidence and knowing himself to be in friendship with God, he stands stronger and confirmed in his hope, and knows that the end of it is blessedness and glory some day.

And in this way must not his hope wax more intelligent? He had hoped that one day he should see God; but now tribulation worketh patience, and patience experience, and experience hope, and he learns that this works out a far more exceeding weight of glory. Not like fanatics, who love martyrdom for its own sake. Worldly troubles the Christians of Paul's day had cheerfully met. The hope to be one day glorified with God is a theme of triumph with them, triumphing over all worldly sorrow. So the believer learns to transfer his exultant hope from earth to heaven, and—strangest of all strange paradoxes— he glories in tribulation.

So this triumphant hope of the Christian in what God is going to do for him, finds a foundation in what God has already done.

This is the argument upon which the section beginning with the fifth verse is built. The love of God for us has been already shed abroad in our hearts. This love of God for us, which the Spirit pours into the heart of a believer, is that unparalleled love which was shown by God for us when we were sinful men. And this is specially dwelt on by the Apostle. If when we were still strangers to God, He reconciled us by the death of His Son, much more can we believe He will love us and bestow upon us favours now we are reconciled to Him. It is a much greater effort of generosity to reconcile an enemy than to save a friend. It is barely possible for any man to give up his life for a righteous man, although it might possibly be done; but the altogether incredible feature in the sacrifice of Christ lies here, that we were actually at enmity with God. His great love was the love that loved us when we were in sin. This made us need His love, helpless and without strength to help ourselves. When He saw us outcast, perishing, then He had compassion upon us, at the right moment, at the predicted moment of our moral need and helplessness. At this time, when we were utterly unable to help ourselves, the Son of God died for men.

That test of love was supreme; it was put to the hardest conceivable test. It did not fail in that great thing, how can it fail in this less thing? What we hope now from God is less than what we have already received from God. God's attitude towards us has changed **for the better.**

Instead of having to show kindness to men in sins, He has to show it to justified men. We have become His friends, reconciled to His favour by the blood of His Son. Suppose He was called upon to do as much for us as He did when Jesus died, would not the love that went cheerfully to death for the enemy go much more cheerfully for the friend?

In the next place, there is no such grievous thing for Him to do now. To bring us back to the glory of God, to live up to His Heaven, is to be the work of the Saviour. Not now in pain and toil and anguish must the blessed Redeemer throw His love away. All that which had to be done in weakness upon earth, in the suppression of sin, has been done by His love; and what remains is easier work, for He is now the uplifted Christ, radiant in bliss, with matchless forces at His command. Surely He will not withdraw His hand from the easy completion of what He once in blood and tears began—reconciliation by His death!

So stands the fact. As He saved us in our sins, much more will He save us now.

Let me add a few remarks for practical purposes. Only let us comprehend the meaning of the death of Christ, and everything will put on a different aspect. So with Paul. The human race had been sunk in hopeless gloom. There was war between heaven and earth. The fact of sin and broken law severed man from his Maker. Death stalked through the homes of men.

And now what a change! God Himself is changed because He is now our friend. This life's gloom is all changed. The troubles of life are still upon us, but they do not mean what they did before. They were taken to be the spiteful efforts of a power that grudged happiness to men; but now we are God's friends, and the afflictions that come thick upon us are experiments upon our confidence, raising us to a more complete trust, and vindicating our trust in Him whom though He slay us we will yet trust.

And, last of all, the future is changed. The leaden pall which overhung our moral existence is changed. We are now upon a rock, with God upon our side, and no longer threatening us as an adversary. We have now boundless anticipations. Who can say what is too much to hope for by the man for whom God died? The body is vile, and creation still groans in sympathy with groaning humanity, and of all men the Christian seems in this life the most miserable. But if God be for us, who can be against us? And if God spared not His own Son, what is there that He will grudge to give us?

We shall have His risen life, which is eternal life, which shall quicken the body; and the majesty of the firstborn, the very glory of God, shall open out for us a heaven, for already we rejoice in the hope of it.

Brethren, does not such a change, wrought by the single fact of Christ's death for us—a change more infinite, more striking than the change that occurs when day dawns, and all things live again—does it not justify the triumph displayed in the verses I have read? "We boast," that is the meaning of it, "we boast in tribulation," says the Apostle. It shows his joy, not so much for himself as for the love that redeemed us. Is it not a wonderful thing for a man to be proud of God? This is what Christ's death enables us to do. Such a display of Divine love, sweeping us into its mighty bosom, puts into the mouth of the reconciled enemy a marvellous song of praise.

It is much to know, and some have got no further, that we are saved. It is more to rejoice in Him who saved us. It is much to know and realize the heavenly logic, that if when we were enemies, as we were once, we were saved, much more shall we be saved now we are reconciled; and not only so, but we also boast in Him through whom we have received such reconciliation. Amen.

XX. Joy and Tribulation. ROM. v. 2, 3. *"We rejoice in hope of the glory of God, and not only so, but we glory in tribulations also.*

"WE rejoice in hope of the glory." We rejoice — we glory—these two expressions in the original are the same word, and our version misleads us, not only by covering over and hiding the repetition of the idea, but by confusing the glorying in tribulations with the altogether different idea of the previous verse, the glory of God. So that it is a great deal better to retain, as I think the Revised Version does, the idea of rejoicing in both cases.

"We rejoice in hope of the glory of God." Anybody can rejoice in hope. "And not only so, but we rejoice in tribulations." That is a very different business; a much harder and more difficult thing to keep the light burning in the midst of the storm, than when it is sheltered and enclosed within the lantern. The notion of rejoicing does not go the whole length of the Apostle's idea; the word that occurs in both clauses may literally be rendered, "We boast ourselves." It is the same word that is employed over and over again in the New Testament, and in the Old too, about boasting one's self in God, and a number of other and similar expressions.

Well now, that is the first thing I want you to think of. There is such a thing, and it is a good thing, as Christian boasting—knocking out of the word all notions of exaggerated talk and all ideas of self-glorying, and retaining the idea of a triumphant confidence that finds utterance in the words of bold cheer and hope. A boasting which is not vain boasting, a boasting which is not about myself, a boasting which does indeed consider that I have great needs, but considers much rather the greatness of the things than the smallness of me, poor creature, that have got them.

And the thing that I want to impress upon you, dear brethren, is this—that the type of Christianity which is not triumphant is imperfect. The type of Christianity which is always downhearted and abject, with its face to the earth or its eyes turned in upon its own unworthiness, is only one half the true thing; and that we should not only be able to sit with our enemies in the gate, so to speak, but that we should, in our inmost consciousness, have a confident, rejoicing, triumphant grasp of the great things that God has freely done for us and given to us.

Take away the vain glory, the self conceit, the self-inflated regard, and keep the notion of a large confidence, with its head up and its mouth wide open to speak great things, not about itself, but about God that loves it, and the gifts that He has given.

"In God will I boast all the day long." Well now, the

next thing, look at the double object, strangely compact, of light and dark, woven together into one paradoxical unity. Look at the double object on which this triumphant boasting and confidence that has got a tongue in its head, is built, and rests, " in hope of the glory of God." That is one side of it, all flashing with brightness; "and not only so, but we boast ourselves in tribulations also." That is the other side of it, all dark and stormy; and the two things may equally lead on to the one thing, a tongue charged with gladness and the music of praise and the triumph of trust. "We glory," "we rejoice," "we boast ourselves in hope of the glory of God."

What is the glory of God? The whole sun of the absolute and the perfect splendour of this Divine nature manifesting itself, the rushing out of the light from the great Fountain and central Sun of light. Wonderful that you and I should be able to cherish a hope of that, which plays upon us as the sunlight may upon some opaque surface—it falls upon us as the sunlight may upon some reflecting mirror, but it falls upon us, too, as upon the flowers that open their petals to its light and drink in its beams, and then give back the light in flashing reds, in rich purples, in pure seraphic whites.

So the light and the glory of God comes down on us; ay! but more than that, it comes into us, it fills us and saturates us, and when transfused and changed into its own perfect beauty for the glory of God in us, so far as man can apprehend, it is communicated to him in Jesus Christ, not only that he may know it, but that he may be it. As the Master said, "The glory which Thou hast given Me I have given them." Everything therefore of Divine which there is in the perfect character and manhood of Jesus Christ our Lord, is there that it may be here, and here not merely as knowledge, but as life that changes us into itself; and, as the old mystics used to say : " If thou becomest this thou knowest it." If thou hast glory thou comprehendest the glory, the ultimate end, of course far away ahead, in which this glory becomes an object of our hope as the complete assimilation of even our poor manhood into the likeness of Jesus Christ our Lord, who is for us the likeness of our Father God. That is far-off hope; but look at the context, hearken what, if I may use a pedantic word, what the genesis of this hope is: "Being justified by faith, we have peace with God through our Lord Jesus Christ, by whom also we have access by faith into this grace wherein we stand." That is to say, the shining apex, the summit of the pyramid, like the gilt ball on the top of some campanile, which catches the rays of sunshine, is "the hope of the glory of God"—travelling down and down and down; and the foundation of the structure is, "being justified by faith," and the first storey of it is, "we have peace with God through our Lord Jesus Christ," and the next is, "by whom also we have access into this grace wherein we stand." And then again up at the top: "And rejoice in hope of the glory of God." This is to say, my conscious confidence that I shall one day be changed into the same image from glory to glory, as by the law of the Spirit, lies in this, that away down there, in the depths and root of my being, among the filth and dirt that is there, there has been laid the first course and beginning of this great spiritual building—that I have been cleansed and forgiven and have access to God, and have His favour in my heart, and so have a place where I can stand. As the Apostle says with such emphasis; and because of all these things, imperfect and initial and rudimentary as they obviously are, in our life's experience here, we may so dwell in them that it will all run out into this—unless God is going to make a fool of us and to stultify Himself—the glory of God living in my heart and changing it into all brightness.

Well! that is one side; what is the other. "And not only so," says he, but in this song of boasting of ours there is a minor as well as a major key. Somehow or other they harmonize, and are beautiful and melodious together. We rejoice, or we boast ourselves, not only in that far-off hope yonder, but in this present sea of troubles and afflictions and temptations that beset us. Why is it that the Apostle thinks that a man may reasonably rejoice and lift up his head even in the midst of sorrows and trouble? The words that follow my text are quite as significant and important for the purpose as the words that precede them.

"And not only so, but we glory in tribulations also, knowing that tribulation worketh patience, and patience experience, and experience hope." We get back to the old thing again; we found that there was this line of cause and effects: "Justified by faith, peace with God, access into the grace," and that—that ran out into hope.

There is one line, and there is another converging line: "tribulation, patience, experience," and that runs out into hope too. You may get to the Cape of Good Hope whether you sail round the world eastward or westward. You can come to the same thing, the bright hope of God's glory, whether you start with the blessed thought of forgiveness through Jesus Christ and of that which He brings to us, or whether you start with the black thoughts of sorrow and tribulation, and will follow them out. The one and the other alike tend to this. You cannot get a rainbow without both sunshine and cloud, and so hope's rainbow is painted on the cloud without which it would not be half bright, and it is painted by the sunshine, without which it could not be at all.

So, "we rejoice in hope of the glory of God," "and not only so," but in it "we boast ourselves in tribulations also," knowing their meaning and their nature. That is to say, the thing that makes a man master of his sorrows is, that taught by God, he should see the meaning of the sorrow, and understand whither the drift of the tempest is carrying him and all that are exercised thereby. We shall not be afraid if we are caught up in the hideous whirlwind, for we know where the storm is sweeping us too; and it is sweeping us yonder home, where the wind dies down, and He says, "Peace! peace! be still; and there is a great calm."

So then, dear brethren, big troubles and little ones, pinpoints and lance-thrusts, the sorrows out of which our heart's blood seems to pour and the little annoyances that only bring out drops of bad temper; they all have one mission, and that mission is that the sorrow may work not merely patience and passive endurance, but may work brave patience and an endurance which acts as well as suffers, and that brave patience may prove to us the power of the gospel, and so the proof, the experience, may lead on to hope.

And the last thing I have to say is, that as far as the form of these words in the original is concerned, they may both of them be either, as our Bible takes them, statements of a fact, or they may be exhortations to a duty. And I think, if I remember rightly, the Revised Version has adopted the latter alternative in both cases. I am not prepared to say without sacrifice of context, or no. "*Let us* rejoice in hope of the glory of God. And not only so, but *let us* also rejoice in our tribulations.

And all I want to say about that is just this one thing; you can cultivate this habit of triumphant confident boasting in hope of the glory of God, and in the sorrows that to other people dash and darken the hope; you can cultivate it, and if you are Christian men and women it is your duty to cultivate it. It is not a thing that comes and goes independent of a man's own moral nature and own relations. A good many people seem to think that there is no kind of account to be given of their ups and downs, or of their religious experiences. There is always an account to be given, not necessarily inculpating them, but always to be given by some better explanation than that of God arbitrarily withholding His hand and hiding His face. And there is one simple explanation to be given very often of the "downs" of our religious experience. You cannot expect that you will have "boasting in hope of the glory of God" if that great blessed prospect that closes our horizon is never looked at by you; if your hearts are never turned to it, if your desires are never drawn out to it, if your eyes are constantly fixed on the material things, cares, duties of business—joys, sorrows, botherations of this present, that you have neither heart nor eye to look up and to look forward.

Ah, dear brethren! there are a great many things in which our Christianity now-a-days is very deficient. I am not very sure that there is one in which it is more deficient than in the few faint, heartless, scarcely believing hurried glances which you and I cast onwards to that great hope that ought to burn like a rising sun at the end of the avenue and vista of every life. If you never think of it how can you boast of it? Cultivate as a duty this attitude and temper of joyful, triumphant, and if need be, eloquent confidence; for when the heart is full the mouth will not be closed. And cultivate it by these three things. Think about the hope. Remember its foundation and make that firmer. Peace with God and access to Him. And try to read the meaning—the sweet, wise, wholesome meaning of sorrow and joy—that life in its darkness and life in its brightness may equally reveal to us the great beyond, in which is light, and no darkness at all.

XXI. St. Paul's Messages to Individuals. ROM. xvi. 12. *"Salute Tryphena and Tryphosa, who labour in the Lord. Salute the beloved Persis, which laboured much in the Lord."*

I HAVE chosen this text, because I am not going to speak of St. Paul's letters to individuals, but of St. Paul's messages to individuals. Among the myriad of sermons which have been preached in the Christian Church during nineteen centuries, I should doubt whether any sermon has ever been preached on this text before. Now, I certainly disapprove of all fantastic or sensational texts, but you will, I think, soon see, that without any attempt to strain this text, or to deal with it unfairly, and quite apart from that rhythmic beauty which is often found in lists of names, it may become suggestive of deep and sacred truths. I should, indeed, deem it dishonest to represent it as being anything more than it is. It is but one of a number of messages to unknown private persons, mostly old women and slaves. If a modern clergyman were writing to the parishioners of a former parish, what would be more natural than that at the end of the letter he should add by name friendly greetings and affectionate remembrances to any poor pensioners or aged widows whom he had known. Felix Neff, the Apostle of the High Alps, as he was called, two days before his death, being scarcely able to see, addressed at different intervals in large irregular characters which filled a page, words of loving adieu to many of the poor persons whom he knew. Now, St. Paul was not dying when he wrote this letter, but it is exactly this, neither more nor less, which he does in this chapter and others at the close of his epistles. No less than twenty-six men and women, for the most part absolutely unknown to us, have greetings sent to them. For instance, immediately after the verse I have read to you we have, " Salute Tryphena and Tryphosa, who labour in the Lord. Salute the beloved Persis, who laboured much in the Lord. Salute Rufus, chosen in the Lord, and his mother and mine. Salute Asyncritus, Phlegon, Hermes, Patrobas, Hermas, and the brethren which are with them"—and so on. These chapters, full of strange and obscure names, are read in churches twice in the year in the course of our Sunday lessons. Now why are they read? Is it mere hypocrisy? Is it the mere survival of an old custom? Doubtless, when they were first read aloud to the little Churches to which the letters were originally addressed, then they would have been listened to with the deepest interest. The slave, or the poor woman, or the converted Gentile, who heard his or her name mentioned in St. Paul's letter would say, " How kind, how good it was of Paulus to remember me. What a help it is to me to know that the dear and holy apostle with all the care of all the Churches upon him, and living as he does in the midst of plots and perils, yet thinks of such an one as I am, and prays for me. If I be dear to him, must not I also be dear to his Lord and to mine?" But what do we mean by reading these salutations to the always obscure and now totally forgotten dead? Why should it be to us a part of our worship to hear read to us such words as "Salute Tryphena and Tryphosa, and Urbane, and Amplias, and Stachys, and Mary," and a number of other persons of whom not so much as one single word or one single syllable is known or recorded.

Well, brethren, I will try to show you—only asking you to dismiss altogether from your minds the foolish and superstitious notion that in the names themselves there is anything whatever more sacred than in your name, or mine, or any one else's, or that there is greater enchantment in these greetings than there would be in any other greetings in any other serious letter. To speak in unmistakable language, there is no more in these names of Amplias, and Stachys, and Tryphena and Tryphosa, than in the names of Brown, or Jones, or Smith. They are no more names to conjure with than those. Eighteen hundred years ago they were just the names of poor, ordinary, every-day persons in Rome or Ephesus—slaves, on whom the nobles or the careless women who lived at ease in those cities would have looked down with scorn as they passed by them in their glittering chariots, and would have treated them as though they were the merest dust beneath their feet; and yet, I would try to show you that very genuine lessons may be learned from these lists of names, though those lessons do not lie so much in the names themselves as in the whole surroundings and circumstances in the midst of which the greetings were written.

First of all, do not these numerous greetings prove to us very simply and decisively the overflowing affectionateness of the heart of St. Paul? May we not learn from them the lessons of kindliness, of family affection and Christian life? Is it not a lesson which we ought and need to learn? Does not this practical indication of the Apostle's abounding love to his converts give fresh force and beauty to such pathetic exhortations, never, alas! needless among Christians, as "Be kindly affectioned one to another with brotherly love; in honour preferring one another," or "See that ye love one another with a pure heart fervently." Christians needed each other's help in those days. They were as lambs among wolves; they were as torches blown by the wind and buffeted by the storm, but still steadfastly upheld amid the darkness of a perverse and crooked generation. Their common and their mutual love was to each and all of them their help and consolation amid the fury and hatred of the world. "Little children, love one another," said St. John, when he was too aged to preach any other sermon as he was carried in the litter from church to church through the streets of Ephesus. And what a grand and beautiful sermon those four words were if only we could learn their meaning. "See how these Christians love one another," said the envious heathen then. Alas! they would not say so now, and they would have little cause to say so now.

But this list of names may at least serve to remind us of the beauty of that lost ideal as it shone forth in the purple dawn of Christian enthusiasm, in the early glow of Christian love. They loved one another, and their great apostle loved them all. He had "the heart at leisure to itself:" with him to be out of sight was not to be out of mind; he had that intense sympathy in the strength of which, as has been truly said, he had a thousand friends and loved each one of them as he loved his own soul. He seemed to live a thousand lives in them and die a thousand deaths when he must quit them. May not, then, this mere list of names serve to remind us of the duty of a wider sympathy, a more kindly unselfishness, a more tender regard for all men, and especially of them that are of the "household of faith"?

Then I would ask you to observe another point about it: Many of these greetings are to women. The world has never, I believe, recognised the vast debt which Christianity has owed to the work of women. Even in this day, though women do more than men in the great works of quiet, unobtrusive charity; though, in the tending of the sick, and the visiting of the poor, and the teaching of the young, and the consolation of the sorrowful, women are incomparably more thorough, more patient, more tender, more skilful, and more self-denying than the vast majority of men; yet even in this day Christian women might well complain that they and their needs and their sympathies are far less cared for in our public exhortations than those of men. Well, it was not altogether so with St. Paul. In this chapter alone seven women—Phebe, Priscilla, Tryphena, Tryphosa, Persis, Julia, the sister of Nereus, the mother of Rufus, whom St. Paul, in tender gratitude for her kindness, calls also his own mother—are all recognised with words of gentleness and praise. Even in this day, I imagine, the minds of holy and noble women may well be pained by the sort of mock deference and mock homage with which they are often treated, by the banter and badinage, and by hypocritical compliment and foolish humorousness, and the general terms of exaggerated meekness with which many speeches are publicly addressed to them. There is not the faintest trace of this in St. Paul. For foolish and unworthy women, for women weak and base he had words of deserved scorn. The very loftiness of his ideal for true Christian women made that ideal, when meanly dwarfed and miserably debased, an object of mere indignant contemplation to him. In days when women lived for the most part (as they did in ancient days and ancient cities) in unavoidable ignorance, and enforced seclusion, and were shamefully regarded, as they are now by all who are base, as the mere chattels and servants of man's caprice and wickedness, St.

Paul's illuminated soul had recognised the sacred and beautiful type of Christian womanhood—of woman the friend, the helpmeet of man, of sisterhood, of wifehood, and of motherhood—everywhere two aids in council, two beside the heart, two beside in the liberal offices of life, two in the tangled business of the world, two-celled heart beating with one full stroke of life. He realized in prescient vision the mothers and the holy virgins of the many Christian centuries; he saw in the poor Phebe and the poor Persis, the precursors of St. Perpetua and St. Felicitas, of St. Barbara and St. Agnes, of St. Celestia and St. Theresa, of St. Dorothy and St. Catherine of Syria, of Elizabeth Fry and Florence Nightingale, of Sarah Martin and Mary Stanley, and all the holy women who adorned themselves, not with braided hair, or gold and costly array, but in modest apparel and shame-facedness, and becoming propriety, and, above all, as became women who profess godliness with good works.

And many, again, whom St. Paul here salutes were slaves and men of poor and mean condition. What lesson have we here, again, in this mere list of names! It is the nature of the world to fawn, to flatter upon the great, to speak smooth words of their sins. They are ashamed to know the poor, ashamed to be friendly with the poor—almost regard it as a condescension to own with them a common brotherhood. This was not the preaching of St. Paul; to him man, simply as man, was as great as he is in God's sight, and could not be greater; to him in the essence of things a slave was as great as a Cæsar, because every whit as much for slave as for Cæsar Christ had died: Nay, a despised slave might be much more to Him, and much greater, than a deified Cæsar. For man in himself, however great he think himself, is less than nothing. Man is great in God only, if he is great at all. A Nero sat among his lictors, clothed in imperial purple; the kings of the Orient laid their diadems before his worthless feet; riches of the world were at his disposal; there was life and death in his mere nod. The slave was the almost nameless creature who starved and herded with his fellows, who might be branded if he spoke a hasty word, and flung to feed the lampreys in the fish-ponds if he broke a crystal vase. But all that was nothing to St. Paul. A few short days, and both would die, and then one second and the angels alter that, one second and Nero might be wailing in abject shame in the outer darkness, while the poor slave may be acclaimed of angels, and tread—

"The heavenly Jerusalem's rejoicing streets."

But notice, again, St. Paul's greetings were not mere indiscriminate eulogy. Being addressed to Christians in days when Christianity, remember, was an indictable offence, in days when to be a Christian was to be persecuted as a Christian, he was writing presumably to good and holy men; yet even between good and holy men there is a difference, and St. Paul uses only the language of deserved and appropriate praise. Phebe is "a servant of the Church." Priscilla and Aquila—the wife put first, as nearly always, because she happened to be the more able and active of the two—have hazarded their lives for St. Paul; Epenetus is "well-beloved"; Mary has laboured much among you; Andronicus and Junia are fellow captives with St. Paul; Urbane is a helper in Christ; Tryphena and Tryphosa "labour in the Lord"; "the beloved Persis," "labour．．．in the Lord," and so on. One little fact shows how ．．．of insight these descriptive touches were. "Luke, the beloved physician, and Demas greet you;" that is in the Epistle to the Colossians. Luke is "the beloved physician"; but why is no word of praise said of Demas? Look on five years later—from the first imprisonment of St. Paul at Rome to the second, which was so much more shameful and severe—and you will there read, "Demas hath forsaken me, having loved this present world." Had the prescient eye of St. Paul seen already the latent possibility of that dishonourable defection? It may be so; at any rate, five years earlier he does not praise Demas, and he does praise Luke, who continued faithful to the last. And this being so, seeing that even apart from Demases, there were these differences between Christians, even then, may we not, every one of us, take courage in the thought that as God bestows on us different gifts, so He also expects from us different forms of service. All branches cannot bear the same fruit; all members have not the same office; all Christians cannot do the same work. We must, each of us, do what we can, and if only our work be faithful in our own best way, and up to our little best in that way, let us hope that God will accept it with all its imperfections—with all its miserable imperfections—even as we hope that He will accept us in the Beloved. Mary has her work and Phebe hers, Urbane has his work and Apelles his, and some of us, perhaps, think, with a sigh, that we do little or no work, either for God or for man. Well, if we are but trying to do what little we can, let us be content. We may then be like Asyncritus, Phlegon, Hermes, Patrobas, Hermas, of whom nothing is said. We may be content, if we can do no more, to be of the common herd, of the vulgar crowd, of the nameless multitude of Christianity; content to be of the faithful, if only we be faithful, but not famous:—

> "Content to go to the crowd untold,
> Of men by the cause they served unknown:
> Who lie in the myriad graves of old,
> Never a story, and never a stone."

Better to be called, were it but at the eleventh hour, than not at all. Better to be of the forgotten throng, the mere ciphers of Christianity, than to be of the world's guilty conquerors or guilty kings.

So far, then, my friends, we have seen in these names, first, Paul's affectionateness and the duty of Christian love; then Paul's regard for Christian women, and the glory of Christian womanhood; then Paul's honour for slaves, and the dignity of man simply as man in the sight of God; then Paul's discriminating eulogies, and his loving acceptance of all his friends, and so in that the loving acceptance by our common Master of our differing gifts.

Once more, and lastly, think of this. The mere casual mention of these names by St. Paul has given them a sort of earthly immortality, has enshrined their names till the end of time in the sacred Book of all the world. The poet Horace might have sung of them; he does actually mention one or two of the same names in his days in his gay lyrics; the philosopher Seneca might have mentioned them among his brilliant aphorisms; the historian Tacitus might have introduced them amid his sombre and intense records; yet, in that case they would still have been incomparably less eternised here on earth than when St. Paul mentioned them, and casually, with loving messages of Corinth and Tertius, wrote down their grotesque designations on the fugitive papyrus.

F. W. F.

XXII. "A Cheerful Giver." 2 COR. ix. 7–15. "*Every man according as he purposeth in his heart, so let him give; not grudgingly, or of necessity: for God loveth a cheerful giver.*" (Also remainder of chapter to the end).

IF you will glance with me over this whole context, you will see that it is really a little treatise which contains almost the whole matter, the whole theory and philosophy, of the Christian administration of material wealth. Here is, first of all, set forth very distinctly in the words which I have read, the great rule of Christian liberality. Then there follows, in the subsequent verses, the great law of recompense. "God is able to make all grace abound toward you, that ye, always having all sufficiency in all things, may abound to every good work." "He that ministereth bread to the sower, both minister bread for your food, and multiply your seed sown, and increase the fruits of your righteousness."

Then the subsequent verses tell us of the great blessed tie which knits giver and recipient. "Who long after you, and by their prayer for you, do give thanksgiving unto God, for the exceeding grace which is in you."

Then there is, with a beautiful sudden abrupt turn, a setting forth, in one sentence, of the great motive which underlies it all. "Thanks be unto God for His unspeakable gift."

Now, let me deal with these points briefly, as is necessary, from the comprehensiveness and largeness of the figure.

First, look how the Apostle puts forth here the great rule about the Christian administration of material wealth. "*Every man* according as he purposeth in his heart, so let him give." There is, first of all, universality. You take up a newspaper and read down the half dozen subscription lists that may be there. Do they give to the Lord? Out of half a million, three or four hundred men are all the collectors for everything. "Wheresoever the carcase is, there the eagles will gather." It is the same people who do it all.

And so it is in a congregation. Like bits of coloured glass in a kaleidoscope, shape them into one form—that is the subscription list for this thing. Shape the identical pieces, no more pieces, put the same pieces into another shape—that is the subscription list for something else. And then other people go and say: "We give very largely;" or, "we don't do as we ought to do." *We!* It is by no means a universally diffused thing in this, or in any congregation.

Now the next thing that I want to say is this: Notice the absolute freedom of the gift, as well as the deliberation, "according as he purposeth in his heart." First of all, what we call now-a-days a voluntary principle; no compulsion of any sort whatever, whether legal or otherwise.

That is a very unworthy kind of thing to bring into a Christian Church. Like a force-pump, working up reluctantly a few drops of muddy water. The other thing like the tapping of an artesian well, where the pure, unstinted supply comes upward to the surface by its own inward energy, so to speak. "Let every man, according as he purposeth in his heart." It is not the right to do as you like, or to refuse if you like; but it is the right fully to choose to do what you ought, and that "ought" I think you know. Well then, not only uncompelled must be the gift, but after deliberation, and intelligently. I believe that there are very few things that Christian people do that are done on the average with so little bringing of an intelligent Christian conscientious consideration to bear on the subject, as this question, how they are to administer the money that God has given them, to His glory.

Impulse! A hasty hap-hazard plunge of the hand into the pocket, and bringing out the first coin that comes; sometimes, habit, a certain form of Protestant indulgence; a guinea to all the subscription lists that come to hand. Habit, hap-hazard, a hundred other motives, instead of a quiet deliberate consideration in the light of the principles that are not very recondite, and which we profess to believe—What is my duty in given circumstances, and in the present case; and that rule of Christian liberality should be a deliberate and intelligent act of shaping our gifts, in accordance with the whole tendency of the gospel, which does not pretend to destroy human impulse, but does aspire to regulate it, and bring everything under the principles that belong to the gospel of Jesus Christ. Then, if one requirement is that Christian men shall give thoughtfully, intelligently, after due deliberation, what a lot of low theories there are by which, I am sorry to say, a great many good people try to get money out of folk, and which theories stand self-condemned by this text. If the only legitimate way of giving is to do it intelligently, without coercion, for the love of God, I am afraid that a great deal of what is called "moving appeal"—which has for its object the collecting box—must be an abomination in His sight.

We can lift the whole thing up to a far higher region than we usually move in with regard to this matter; and not look down upon Christian money-giving as if it were a very subordinate thing, but one in which spiritual consequences of all sorts are mixed up. And then the last point here about this rule of Christian liberality is, it must be free, deliberate, intelligent and cheerful. Not grudgingly, as if we were drawing a tooth, coming out with a twinge; not grudgingly, as if the question were, "How little can I get off with?" One hears perpetually, "Oh! there is no end to these collections; it's always, give! give! give!"

Always! Suppose a man's lungs were to say: "Oh! there is no end to this expiring of air that I have to do. It is perpetual breathing out, and out, and out." Well, are not you perpetually breathing in, and in, and in? Is it your air that you breathe in? How have you come to have it? We have nothing that we have not received freely. Therefore give freely as you receive freely. Suppose God were to say about you and me: "There is no end to this give! give! give! to these mortals." What would become of us?

Don't! don't forget, dear brethren, don't forget that if your demand is unceasing the supply is unceasing too. "Not grudgingly, or of necessity." Some of you, when you are waited upon, say, "Well, I suppose I must give you something! My reputation, my position, a matter of the A B C order, I am on your list, and I cannot well pass it by. I suppose I must give you something. Let me see! How much shall it be?"

Ah! "For the Lord loveth a cheerful giver." How much of conscious sense of the Divine favour a man loses when his liberality is without a heart and without a head! If you give, and your mind does not follow you,—if you give, and your heart does not follow your gift,—you will get no good out of it; but if it is accompanied with both, you will have a sense of the Divine love and favour resting upon you, because your giving is from the heart, and that giving is intelligent and cheerful. All pure Christian deeds have a pure joy bound up with them, and this amongst the rest, when it is done from a right motive and done in the right fashion. We are filled by a conscious glow and blessed warmth coming from a sense of Divine sympathy. We Protestants are too much afraid of what is distinctly a New Testament doctrine, that when men do right for the sake of God and the love of Christ, they feel the blessedness of the love of God resting upon them in a peculiar fashion. There is a recompense for our works, and a reward given to goodness which is based upon Christ and giving, as well as a hundred other forms of Christian love, if done on the right lines from the right motive, with the right accompaniment, which does bring down upon a man's head the cheerful sunshine of the Divine love.

So then, says the universal rule, it is free, deliberate, ungrudging giving, with the head and with the heart, that God wants. And then follows the long paragraph about which I can only speak superficially, setting forth the great law of recompense, the recompense for this gift. "God is able to make all grace abound toward you." Well, I think the word "grace" must be widened out to its widest significance, so as to mean not only spiritual gifts, but all the gifts of God which come from His love and power. "He is able to make all grace abound toward you," to give you all that and a great deal more. To give you all graces of an outward kind as well as all the far higher graces of an inward kind; to give them all in order that—that is beautiful—God is able to make all grace abound toward you that ye may abound in every good work. So you are not to think of money-giving, or other forms of Christian liberality, as a good investment. If a man says, on the strength of a promise like this, "It will pay," he will get no blessing, because the purpose of the recompense of the gift is that I may have more to dispense and bestow. God gives to us that we may abound to every good work. And then the Apostle quotes one of the old Psalms which seems to contain the same principle, and then clinches the whole metaphor: "He that ministereth seed to the sower minister bread for your food, and multiply your seed sown, and increase the fruits of your righteousness." The farmer goes to his field, sows his corn, and all the harvest that comes from it he divides into two portions; part of it for seed, and part of it for bread. He eats the bread and it perishes with the eating, there is an end of it; drops out of the wealth of the world, it is no more good to anybody; that which he had for his own enjoyment dies and passes; but the portion of his crop that he took for seed, he sows it and it springs and lives. And so goes the perpetual series of circulation, of sowing and reaping. That which he cast abroad is eternal, whilst that which he used for himself is transitory and has disappeared. And, says Paul, that is the law with regard to all outward things, and all inward things too, that God gives to a man. Now it is true in a very modified way about even outward things. A man does not give money because he is liberal, but because he has certain other qualities. I do not suppose that anybody ever ruined themselves by Christian beneficence. I believe, and I hope you believe, in a Providence. You Scotch people that may be here this morning will remember poor Burns' words about a little gift that was bestowed on the little nibbling creature in the field:—

> "We'll get a blessing wi' the lave
> An' never miss't."

And that is true! Nobody ever made himself poorer by giving to his brethren and to God. "He that is able to make all grace abound toward you" will supply the seed that is to be sown. Then, far beyond that, notice the great principle that is here in that metaphor of the twofold distinction of the crop, and the twofold results that come of the two things; notice the great thought there of the transitoriness of everything that a man bestows on himself, and the eternity that is bestowed upon what a man gives away, for God's glory, unto others.

> "What I gave I have.
> What I spent I lost."

So runs the quaint old inscription. The bread that we eat may nourish us for the moment, but, as I said, it drops out of the wealth of the world. The seed-corn springs next year, and from it comes corn in another year. That which a man does for God, and gives to Him, is invested with a kind of quasi-eternity, and lives on and on and on in ever-widening circles, like the ripples upon a pond; each branch becomes a stem or a root, like the Indian banyan-tree. So that of all my poor possessions, only those are reserved which have been laid up His altar, and given up to Him. Dear brethren, there higher recompense than material, and a loftier region than the outward, in which this low motive of payment for services and payment for results of service is absolutely set aside. Every emotion of sympathy and tenderness is strengthened by being indulged. That is to say, if action follows it. If you sit crying over a novel, you get up a bit more sentimental than when you sat down. But if you cry over a story of real distress, then,—instead of the hardheartedness which follows mere sentimentalism,—then you set to work to remove it, and try to brush away some of the filth and the snow from your own door at any rate.

Well, then, an emotion is strengthened by being indulged and carried to its legitimate action. Yielding to the impulse, the intelligent impulse, of sympathy and liberality, makes you a better man and a nobler one, a man ready for Jesus Christ. For Christian men and women to hear of necessities, and to be appealed to to help them, and to refuse to do so on any other ground than conscientiousness, makes them more of a niggard and a hunks; makes them less Christlike, turns out of them something of the Divine image, and takes away the spirit and the generosity of nature.

So then, there is in you going on a process of making you brighter or darker, deepening or shallowing (if I may coin a word). One of the means by which, under God and through faith in Him, we get emancipation by degrees from the chains of sense and the material, is by listening to the claims of God in His gospel, and of men in their misery.

And so, in the deepest and most wonderful way, that old text of Scripture comes out: "There is that scattereth and increaseth, and there is that withholdeth more than is meet, and it tendeth to poverty."

I do believe that the crying sin of the Christian Church is covetousness. We cannot deal with it, we do not deal with it, in our Church censures, because it is one of the intangible things that it is impossible to define; but sure am I that there are hundreds of thousands of Christian men and women who are shutting up their souls against the influx of Divine light and love and joy, and are hardening their characters day by day, by a niggardly and illiberal and grudging administration of the material wealth that God has put into their hands.

Dear brother, if you think that I am preaching too much about salvation by works, remember your Master's words: "Make for yourselves friends out of the mammon of unrighteousness, that when ye fail they may receive you into everlasting habitations." And now there is another point that I must touch very superficially, and that is the great blessed bond of union that knits together the giver and the receiver. "The administration of the service not only supplies the wants of the saints, but is abundant also by many thanksgivings unto God." I cannot profess to interpret the whole of these words, but just draw out of them the general thought. This thing that Paul is talking about in our text was an entirely novel thing in the history of the world; there had never been anything like it before, it was a gathering together of money among the Gentile countries for the poor Jewish Christians. The strangest thing of the sort that had ever happened, an entirely new phenomenon! These Jewish Christians had looked with very great suspicion upon an extension of the gospel to the Gentiles, they had never had a very warm side to the Gentile Churches, nor to Paul, who had been their leader. And so says Paul, Now, look here; here is a world all tumbling to pieces, great clefts and rifts between nations, race animosities, religious animosities, parting them wider and wider; and here is a bridge for you.

Those Christians—Jewish Christians—up there in Jerusalem, they don't think much about you, or at least they did not; but when they get this sign of your brotherly sympathy, "the experiment of this ministration," all their doubts about you will disappear, and "they will glorify God for your professed subjection to the gospel." It will convince them if anything will, and then you will be knit together in bonds of love and sympathy. He follows the gift in imagination. It is not so much money here, but it is the melting away of the frost of suspicion there. It is the pledge of love in the stranger's heart to the giver; and a mysterious silken thread of union going across the gulf of national separations. And it is not only a sublimating thing, a thankfulness and confidence and a sense of brotherhood and friendship, but it is put upon the altar and goes up at last in prayer and thanksgiving to God, turned into the curling wreath of the incense of prayer. That is the end of the money, says Paul; and so, dear brethren, it may be only a five-pound note at this end, but at the far end yonder there are hearts that turn to unknown benefactors, with a sense of sympathy and prayer that goes wreathing up to God in the incense of a sweet smell, an odour acceptable in His sight.

Is there anything that binds yon Indian Empire to England's crown like the possession of a common faith? Is there anything that knits our rulers to those heathen races, to whom we are debtors by injuries inflicted and by sovereignty assumed? Is there anything that knits our rulers to them so closely, and puts them on so blessed and permanent a basis, as the help of the Christian Church in this field of missions? I do not dwell upon the matter, only I say, follow your gift to its legitimate issue and see what it comes to, and look how strangers are knit together. There may be prayers for you and me going up to God from far off hearts that may never see us.

And the last word, the swift, abrupt introduction, of which we cannot find any explanation of any sort, is to me very beautiful,—the great motive on which all rests. "Thanks be unto God for His great unspeakable gift," unspeakable in the greatness of the life from which it came, unspeakable in the depth of the sacrifice which it embodies, unspeakable in the glory to which it tends

And, says Paul, there is the root of all Christian life; and the only true noble idea of it is, that it shall be a yielding up of the nature unto Him that has loved us, and a giving back of ourselves to that dear Lord who has done so much for us. So we have the root of all Christian obedience, and the deepest designation of the Christian life. "Thanks be unto God for His unspeakable gift." What heroism that brings into our hearts. How it changes the aspect of duty, "grudgingly, of necessity, feeling that is a burden." Is that possible? If you and I are living in the light of the Cross, and are taking our burdens there to Him, it is not possible. There are professing Christian people, true Christian people perhaps, but very imperfect ones, who seem to think that what Solomon calls, the horse-leeches' two daughters, always crying, "Give! give!" is a type of the Christian Church. Men may give to the pulpit's appeal indeed, but I do not think you can keep up that feeling long, if you just get away from man's pleas, and quietly think about the unspeakable gift, and who gave it you, and what it is, and how it comes to be a recompense.

And so, for your own sakes, that you may be happier Christians, that you may have a deeper and a firmer hold of the exceeding mercy of our Lord Jesus, I beseech you take this whole matter for your edification, and in the light of Christ's cross ask yourselves, "How much owest thou to my Lord?" That grace is the motive, and the pattern: I will not offer burnt-offering, nor that which costeth me nothing. "Freely ye have received, freely give." Christ gave Himself for you, do you give yourselves to Him.

XXIII. St. Paul's Prayer and the Answer.

2 COR. xii. 8, 9. *"For this thing I besought the Lord thrice, that it might depart from me. And He said unto me, My grace is sufficient for thee: for My strength is made perfect in weakness."*

ST. PAUL stands out before us in his own letters with a distinctness and a vividness such as belong to no other person in history. We shall touch on a remarkable circumstance in this extraordinary life—that which occasioned the prayer, and the answer to the prayer, which form the two parts of the text. He tells the Corinthians that about fourteen years before the date of this letter, he was, first, the recipient of a mysterious and miraculous revelation, and that then, as though to correct a possible self-conceit springing out of it, the subject of a very painful experience in the form of what he first describes as "a thorn in the flesh," and afterwards "as a messenger or angel of Satan to buffet him."

I. *The Thorn in the Flesh.*—Much has been written in earlier and later days of the Church as to the probable nature of this affliction. Some have thought of a very terrible temptation to sinful desires, others of human antagonists to his ministering, while the earliest, and also the latest, idea of it has been that it was an aggravated kind of bodily disease, at once sudden in its access, periodical in its return, and humiliating in its character. The most vivid description of it, though even there quite in enigma, is given in the Epistle to the Galatians, where he mentions that his first preaching among them was occasioned by a compulsory detention owing to an attack of sickness; and speaks of it as a great proof of their devotion that they were not repelled from him by the peculiar symptoms of his malady, but received him, notwithstanding all, as an angel of God, or even as Christ Himself.

It has been conjectured by some that the awful circumstances of his conversion may have left their trace behind them in this mysterious manner. But the expressions here used, "a man in Christ," "caught up to the third heaven," seem rather to point to a later experience, when he was already a Christian, and when, instead of being arrested by a voice from heaven, he was himself transported "in vision" into heaven, whether during that sojourn in Arabia of which he speaks in the same Epistle to the Galatians as having intervened between his conversion and his first subsequent visit to Jerusalem, or at some other point in that later ministry which we know from the history in the Acts to have been often comforted by direct communications, at times of emergency, with his risen and glorified Lord, it is impossible to say.

"For this thing," he says, "I besought the Lord thrice, that it might depart from me." Two brief remarks occur to us on this verse; first, St. Paul's example certainly authorises prayer to our Lord Jesus Christ. It is quite evident that He is the Lord spoken of. The words "My strength" in the answer are explained afterwards by himself to mean "the power of Christ." Our Lord Himself, therefore, is the Divine Person spoken to and speaking.

Again, St. Paul's example sanctions prayer on account of external or material subjects. The "thorn in the flesh" was a bodily malady. However connected with spiritual matters in cause or consequence, it was as much corporeal in itself as any fever or any disease to which flesh and blood is liable.

"For this thing I besought the Lord thrice." On three separate occasions, he seems to say, of the recurrence of the attack. At intervals, sometimes at long intervals, the same violent, painful, humiliating interruption occurred to his labour and ministry. Three occasions of its breaking in upon his work for God and man seem to have stood out with special prominence in his recollection. Once he besought the Lord, and no answer came. Twice he besought the Lord, and still the Hearer of prayer answered him not a word.

St. Paul, therefore, had experience of that Divine silence which the Psalmist so touchingly prayed against, and which is the trial of trials to Christians now.

St. Paul was one with us in these troubles. He knew what it was to have no conscious answer, and he knew what it was to find the evil prayed against still unremoved. And there was a special trial of faith in this silence in the case of St. Paul. To his own view, and in the sight of others, his malady, whatever it was, formed a direct hindrance and obstacle to his ministry. He never knew but he might be suddenly arrested by it on a missionary journey; or that he might not be made by it an object of dislike and contempt to those whom he was devoting himself to save. It must often have seemed to him as though the gospel itself was a great loser and a great sufferer with him. Once or twice he had made supplication, and no answer came. For the third time he found himself laid low by what he could not but speak of as an evil angel. To St. Paul there was an evident agency and presence of the devil following up the work of the Divine Sower by a spurious and noxious sowing of his own. The same apostle who felt the hand of God over him, guiding and controlling and strengthening every word and work of his ministry, was yet conscious of an opposing influence counteracting and obstructing, so that he could say with perfect reality, and with all fulness of meaning, to a Church which might have profited by seeing him, "Wherefore we would have come unto you, even I, Paul, once and again, but Satan hindered us." The "messenger of Satan" prevented, or else followed everywhere the messenger of Christ; and to pray for relief from his adverse working, was to pray to the holy and merciful Saviour, "Thy kingdom come."

II. *The Answer.*—For the third time he prayed thus in reference to his own haunting and thwarting foe. This time an answer came. But what answer? No granting of the petition; no mitigation of the pain, the shame, or the hindrance; only this—yet let us think twice before we say "only"—"and He said unto me" (St. Paul wrote, "He hath said," to express, I suppose, the decisiveness, the finality, and also the satisfactoriness of the reply), "He hath said unto me," and I accept, and live by it as my sufficient strength and stay, "My grace is sufficient for thee; My power is made perfect in weakness." The malady shall not be removed. Its humbling influence is still needed even for the blessed and holy man who might have seemed to require no such discipline. Still must he toil and travel, and have no home, and no resting-place, not knowing from day to day when he may be stopped and prostrated by the stroke of sudden palsy or epilepsy. This he must accept as the appointed cross to be borne upon him to his martyrdom. Sufficient for him is the grace, that is, the favour, of Christ. It is enough for him to know that Christ loves him; enough for him to know this, too, that human weakness, and not human strength, is the very element and atmosphere in which the power of Christ has free course and is glorified. There are many places in St. Paul's writings which illustrate this Divine rule and maxim. "But we have," he says in an earlier part of this epistle, "But we have this treasure," the treasure of the Divine light, "in earthenware vessels," like those pitchers of Gideon's three hundred which concealed the lamps until the moment of the attack. "We have the Divine light in earthenware vessels, that the excellency of the power may be of God, and not of us." And again, "we which live are alway delivered unto death;" we are always being handed over to a condition, as it were, of dying or dead men "for Jesus' sake, that the life also of Jesus "—that is, the living life now in heaven—"may be manifested in our mortal flesh," supported and enabled in its weakness by a strength evidently not its own.

Brethren, we are here in the very heart of the Christian mystery, as it works in the life's life of the man. Behold, first, in this example, the meaning and use and compass of prayer. St. Paul was a sufferer as well as a toiler. All those journeyings by land and sea, all those perils in city and wilderness, all those watchings and fastings, all that weariness and painfulness of which he tells in the chapter before this, must have left their mark upon him. That anxiety of all the Churches, that quick and sensitive sympathy with the weak and the tempted, that perpetual intercession, which was his life, for friends and converts, for Churches and countries, must have told upon his constitution, and made him what he calls himself to Philemon, "Paul the aged," long before he reached—probably he never did reach—the traditional limit of the threescore years and ten. He leads us to suppose that he was a man of humble and unattractive appearance at the best, and that he was liable to seizures of illness which made him even repulsive to those who looked on him.

III. *The Relief of Prayer.*—But we need not enumerate over again all the personal trials which would have deeply depressed, or very probably sadly soured, the spirit of most men. Whatever they were, he had one resource and one refuge: "For this thing I besought the Lord." Evidently it was as easy to him and as natural to carry anything which troubled him to Jesus Christ, as it would be to one of us to speak of any subject of personal interest to the trusted companion of the life that is seen. The communication between him and heaven was always open; and the word intercourse, and even the word conversation would not be too strong, and would not be too familiar to express what prayer was to him, either in the variety of its topics or in the directness of its access, for question and answer. We may remember, too, that with St. Paul this kind of communion with an invisible Lord was comparatively a new thing. Before a certain year, month, and day he knew nothing of it. He would have declared it an impossibility, he would have scouted it as an impiety. If at a later point of time it was so easy and so natural to him, as we have said, to carry everything to Jesus Christ as a man to his friend, we can by that infer that he had good reason for the change, and we can also encourage ourselves to believe such a change, if it be yet necessary, quite possible for any one of us.

I do not make any practical distinction, nor do I urge any one to make any, between prayer offered in so many words to Jesus Christ Himself and prayer offered to God the Father through Him. St. Paul evidently used both methods, keeping the unity of the Godhead unbroken, and above all things careful never to suppose any motion of the Divine will which is not equally the volition of the Son and of the Father. There are, even among true Christians, those to whom it comes most sweetly and naturally on any particular occasion to address themselves to the Divine Saviour, in whom God is; and those to whom it is easier and simpler to address themselves through the Saviour to God Himself, who so loved us that He gave His Son, and who in Him is evermore well pleased. But whichever be the form of prayer, the thing itself must be the life. Whatever it be that troubles, that alarms, that perplexes, that tempts—for this thing we must beseech the Lord. There is no distinction in this aspect between the bodily subject and the spiritual. The unfavourable season which diminishes the personal income or threatens the national prosperity, is as suitable a subject of prayer as the conscious lack of the fertilising grace which alone can give increase to the spiritual sowing. The pestilence walking in darkness, and the destruction wasting at noonday; the blow of distress or bereavement threatening home or kindred; the sight of a country sick with crime and woe; the dread of national dishonour or national decay; all are as fit topics for beseeching the Lord once, twice, and thrice, as the innermost secret of sin or backsliding, which is causing the heart to cower and tremble, lest, after all that has been done, and all that has been suffered, itself should be a castaway. Only we must remember, St. Paul certainly did not forget, that for all earthly or outward blessings asked at the throne of grace there should be a double "if," a tenfold "peradventure" in prescribing the form in which the Prayer Hearer should make answer. It may please Him to keep silence; it may please Him to refuse; it may please Him to continue the discipline of severity till patience has had a more perfect work. And the prayer of faith will count this no reproof of the praying, but only so many solicitations, so many indications of a possible performance, of which "My grace is sufficient for thee" may be the key-note or the under-song.

We will only add that there is one great advantage in prayer for temporal blessing or bodily relief, that it has a direct tendency to make praying real, and so to react for good upon our more spiritual petitions. It is no reproach to any of us to say (it must be so while we are in flesh and blood) that the thing seen must always be more substantial to us than the thing or the person that is not seen; and that consequently, if we can, so to say, carry the one into the presence of the other, it must help us in realizing that other by the mere meeting and contact of the two. That petition, for example, which stands last but one in the Litany: "That it may please Thee to give and to preserve to our use the kindly fruits of the earth," if it at all seems to intrude itself among prayers of a higher and deeper import, does yet throw an emphasis of reality upon these last, and serves in many minds rather to emphasize than to disparage the one immediately following: "That it may please Thee to give us true repentance, to forgive us all our sins, negligences, and ignorances, and to endue us with the grace of Thy Holy Spirit to amend our lives according to Thy Holy Word."

IV. *Reconciliation of the Outward and the Inward.*—Observe, secondly, and finally, in the example before us, the reconciliation of the two lives, the circumstantial and the spiritual. "He hath said to me," and I accept the saying, "My strength is made perfect in weakness." It is natural to us to suppose that although of course the Divine is stronger than the human at its best, yet the human heart at its best, must be stronger than the human heart at its worst, and therefore must help rather than hinder the operation upon it of the Divine. To take the instance before us, who would not say that if St. Paul had been naturally a more impressive or a more attractive person than he appears to have been; if St. Paul, to say the least, had not suffered under the humiliating and disqualifying malady, whatever it was, which made it a matter of wonder and thankfulness if any new people amongst whom he came did not despise and reject him, it would certainly have been better for the success of his gospel, for the acceptance of Christianity in the world? In the same way we all think it a great gain, so far as it goes, if a preacher of the Word, or a Bishop of the Church, has great gifts of eloquence, or admirable powers of persuasion—we all say, "What an influence is here on the side of good, what a power must this man be meant to exercise over his generation!"

Brethren, we will not fall into the snare of paradox, or speak of the curse of natural powers, as some people have dared to speak of the curse of health or prosperity. Still, I think there is something to be said for the gain to the cause of Christ on the whole, from St. Paul's personal insignificance, or from the humble station and want of human learning of the original apostles. Surely there is great force in what St. Paul says about the argument for Christ's resurrection life drawn from the sight of his own frail and suffering mortality. Surely the mere fact that the gospel made its way to its present position in the world, not by the help of swords or sceptres, of oratory or intellect, but in spite of all these, starting from a remote district or an insignificant dependency, and using as its instruments men of obscure station and humble gifts, does redound, now that the thing is done, to the testimony of its truth and to the divinity of its origin. Surely the principle itself is one which commends itself. True strength is always perfected in weakness. If we tried to illustrate, we should but weaken; otherwise we might ask what more powerful instrument of conviction was ever devised than the transparent simplicity of a little child, drawing after it by the cords of love some hard or dissolute father to a life of temperance or to a life of grace? Again and again has the saying been almost literally verified: "Out of the mouth of babes and sucklings hast Thou ordained strength, that Thou mightest still the enemy and the avenger."

And when any great work of Christ is wrought on a larger scale—not inside the walls of a house, but in the chief place of concourse—who are the men that touch consciences, and stir hearts, and reform lives? Are they, generally speaking, the picked men of the Church, the learned and eloquent, who "sit in Moses's seat," and do a decorous and useful work in formed and gathered congregations? Or are they rather the humbler, and less gifted by nature, who simply possess the earnestness of conviction, the tenderness of love, and the fire of grace, just looking up to Christ for strength in weakness, and taught by the Holy Ghost, in the same hour, what they ought to speak? Thus Christ specially attests Himself from generation to generation. It is not that He sets on one side His own gifts (for are they not all His?) of speech and thought, of toil and learning, of influence and eloquence, it is only that He suffers not "the wise man to glory in his wisdom, or the mighty man to glory in his strength." From "wise and prudent," as such, He hides His secrets that He may reveal Himself to babes. As babes so come to Him, ye wise and prudent, and then to you He will reveal Himself. In weakness His strength is perfected. Come to Him as weak and you shall be strong.

Yes, He is no respecter of persons the one way or the other; and, therefore, He casts not away the rich and the great, the wise and the mighty. Only for their own sakes, that they may not deceive themselves, that they may taste the sweetness, and "drink of the rivers of His pleasure;" therefore will He humble first those whom He is to exalt in due time, that they may learn the blessedness of being little, and lay low at His feet the powers and talents by which He has made them to differ.

"My grace is sufficient for thee," for it is more to have the love of Jesus Christ than to be rid of any cares or any sorrows. "My strength is made perfect in weakness." Then teach me, Lord, the mystery of that blessed contradiction, "When I am weak, then am I strong."

C. J. V.

XXIV. Spiritual Blessings in Christ. Eph. i. 3.

"Blessed be the God and Father of our Lord Jesus Christ, who hath blessed us with all spiritual blessings in heavenly places in Christ."

Such is the cheerful and joyful tone in which St. Paul begins this letter to the Christians of Ephesus; and yet at the time of his writing it he was a prisoner in bonds at Rome, and did not know whether he should be acquitted and set free, or condemned and put to death. But still you perceive that he is very cheerful, even triumphant, and begins this epistle, not with complaining about his trials, but with blessing God for His goodness to him. And from the fine spirit of manliness which we perceive in the Apostle as he writes thus to the Ephesians, let us learn something—let us learn to think less of our troubles and more of our mercies. "Blessed be the God and Father of our Lord Jesus Christ, who hath blessed us with all spiritual blessings in heavenly places in Christ." Blessing God for His having so greatly blessed us, that is the theme that is set before us in this passage, "Blessed be the God and Father of our Lord Jesus Christ, who hath blessed us with all spiritual blessings."

God blesses us in very many ways. He blesses us with the mercies and bounties of His daily providence, and for these we may be very sure that St. Paul would not have us be ungrateful. Of these he would not have us be unmindful; but still, according to him, the spiritual blessings which God bestows are so far superior to all temporal mercies, that the temporal mercies are almost lost sight of, eclipsed by the far superior splendour of the spiritual blessings that are given to us in heavenly places in Christ.

"Spiritual blessings in heavenly places." Now you will observe that this word "places" is printed in italics. It has no existence in the original, and, as the margin suggests, we may read either "heavenly places" or "heavenly things," and "heavenly things" seems to be, upon the whole, the better rendering here. And the word "heavenly" probably has reference more to character than to locality. He hath blessed us with all spiritual blessings in heavenly things, that is to say, spiritual heavenly blessings, as contrasted with the earthly and temporal blessings. He hath blessed us with all these spiritual heavenly blessings, with *all* of them. Now, friends, there are some earthly temporal blessings with which God does not bless—with which He has not blessed you, with which He has not blessed me. Do not let us grumble, or be unthankful at all; but I suppose that every man feels that there is something in his temporal lot that gives him dissatisfaction. He knows that God has some good gift in this world that He has not yet bestowed upon him. He would like a little more bodily health and strength; he would like a little more money—everybody would, or nearly everybody I have ever met with, when he is honest; and this and that we should like to have, this and that that we do not possess, and more of this and that that we do possess. But no; God will not give us *all* the temporal and earthly blessings, and undoubtedly for very good reasons, for He knows, and every man of common-sense also knows, that it would be the easiest thing in the world to spoil him utterly by giving him a very large amount of this world's good. And so God deals out these temporal blessings rather sparingly, giving every one of us far more than we deserve; but He has to dole them out in scant measure, because He knows very well what utter moral and spiritual ruin would be the result in most cases of an over-exuberant manifestation of His temporal kindness towards us. So He does not bless us with all temporal blessings; but when it comes to the spiritual blessings there is no need of His dealing scantily and carefully here—no need of His withholding any one of them; and He does not withhold any one of them, for He has blest us with *all* the spiritual blessings. There is not one of these that can do us any harm; there is not one of these but must do us good. And so God gives them all, and with a right-royally liberal hand.

But He blesses us with these blessings *in Christ*. They are all in Christ for us. God gives us these blessings through Christ. Christ is God's great depository of all spiritual blessings. Christ is God's almoner. Christ bears God's purse, and whatever spiritual blessing you or I desire, and go to God for, whether it be pardon, or peace, or holiness, or strength, or what not—if we go to God for this spiritual blessing He refers us to Christ. "This is My beloved Son, **hear ye Him."** And God gives us nothing directly in the shape of spiritual blessings, for He has blest us with these things in Christ, and it is only in Christ and through Christ that we ever can obtain any of them.

He *hath* blessed us with these spiritual blessings in Christ. 'Well," some one will say, "God has through Christ blest us with a number of spiritual blessings, but surely there are some that we have not yet received. There are some that we are looking forward to. Indeed, we need spiritual blessings —great spiritual blessings—every day of our lives, and how can it be said that God has already thus blest us? We are looking forward to the great supreme and crowning blessing of all—eternal life and happiness in God's presence—and that has not yet been bestowed upon us, and yet we read that 'God hath blessed us with all spiritual blessings in Christ.'" Well, these blessings have not yet come to hand, but God has given them to us, and placed them in Christ's hand to be by Him dispensed according to our need, and according to our capacity of receiving and enjoying them. There are many spiritual blessings which we are not yet fit to have. We should not understand them; we should not appreciate them. A little boy who is the heir to a very large estate, of course does not actually come into possession of that estate while he is a child; he could not at all appreciate it. And there are spiritual blessings which the most experienced Christians are no more fit to receive now, in this world, than a child of five or six is fit to receive the title-deeds of his estate. And so these blessings have all been given, *all been given*, and Christ holds them in His hand for us; and according to our need and according to our developing capacity for appreciating and using well the blessings, they are bestowed upon us. And, undoubtedly, it will be the joy and rejoicing of our Lord's heart, for ever and ever, to be bringing out of that treasury one spiritual blessing after another; to all eternity doing this, and so discovering and ever making new discoveries in the greatness of God's love. "Blessed be the God and Father of our Lord Jesus Christ, who hath blessed us with all spiritual blessings in heavenly places in Christ."

The rest of the chapter is filled up with descriptions of some of these spiritual blessings, to a few of which let us advert.

And, in the first instance, we read of election as one of

these spiritual blessings. "According as God hath chosen us in Him before the foundation of the world, that we should be holy and without blame before Him." There I stop, leaving out the last two words, "in love," for a reason to be assigned presently.

"According as He hath chosen us." And whom hath He chosen? Well, the first verse will tell us as much about election as I, for my part, very much care to know. "Paul, an apostle of Jesus Christ, by the will of God, to the saints which are at Ephesus, and to the faithful in Christ Jesus." These are they whom God hath chosen—Paul himself, the saints that are at Ephesus, and the faithful in Christ Jesus. That is to say, all holy and believing persons have been chosen of God, and instead of troubling ourselves by curious speculations upon this subject, I think it is enough for us to know that wherever there is a saint—a holy person, one that is faithful in Christ Jesus—you have one of those whom God hath chosen. "According as He hath chosen us in Him." For, as our Lord says, "All that the Father giveth to Me shall come to Me, and him that cometh unto Me I will in no wise cast out." "Chosen in Him" and "before the foundation of the world;" because from the beginning or ever the earth was, the idea of Christ and His people—the Saviour and the saved, the Vine and the branches, the Shepherd and the flock, the Bridegroom and the bride—that idea has ever been before God. "According as He hath chosen us in Him before the foundation of the world."

But chosen us to what intent and purpose? "That we should be holy and without blame before Him." God has chosen us not only that we may be saved from eternal destruction, not only that we may be happy for ever in heaven, but He has chosen us for this special purpose—"that we should be holy and without blame before Him." Now, it is one thing to be holy and without blame before the world; it is one thing to be holy and without blame before the Church; it is one thing to be holy and without blame in one's own esteem. It is quite another thing to be holy and without blame before Him "to whom all hearts are open, and all desires known, and from whom no secrets are hid." A man may be holy and without blame in the estimation of himself, and in the estimation of his neighbours, and be but a very "so-so" character after all. But to be holy and ness. A man may do a thing voluntarily, and yet not do it "with a will," as we understand the expression. What God does He does with a will; and He does it "according to the *pleasure* of His will," and He does it "according to the *good* pleasure of His will." Look at all these terms, and how they heap up. "Having in love adopted us according to His will,—according to the pleasure of His will,—according to the good pleasure of His will." And if there be all this love about our adoption, well then, what may we not expect from God as His adopted children? We surely may look forward to being dealt with with the greatest possible lovingkindness; and when we study the Scriptures, and read, in so far as we can read, the future of God's people, we shall find that there is not so much difference between the adopted sons and the well-beloved Son. Just as, were you or I to adopt a little child, the right thing would be to make the adopted child feel so perfectly at home that it would hardly know that it was only an adopted son. Thus God does; for, although, of course, the adopted sons can never be worshipped as the well-beloved One, yet they sit upon His throne, and they are served by the angels that serve Christ; and thus does God manifest His love to the adopted ones, even as to the only-begotten one Himself.

And all this is "to the praise of the glory of His grace, wherein He hath made us accepted in the Beloved." Here is another spiritual blessing—acceptance in the Beloved; but it is all "to the praise of the glory of His grace"— the glory of God's free favour, for it is of grace from first to last; and I have sometimes thought that one obstacle to people's accepting the gospel is that it is all of grace. Mind you, I would not, on any account, withdraw this idea of grace, though people through its withdrawment should universally accept the gospel; but I say that if the gospel were not all of grace, it would, perhaps, commend itself to some minds that cannot receive it now. If the terms ran thus, "Now, you do your best, and God will do the rest," there are many people that would say, "Yes, that looks fair; that is about the right thing." But when God says, "No, I give you all these blessings in a spirit of free grace"— well, you know, that does not look like business. We are not accustomed to do that sort of thing ourselves. If we give anything, we expect something in return, and so, measuring God's corn by our poor little bushel, we find it hard to believe in this principle of salvation entirely by grace. But by grace it is from first to last ; and according to the riches of His grace, and to the praise of His grace, He hath made us accepted in the Beloved.

"Accepted." This word is hardly good enough to do all the duty that the Apostle requires it to do. "Accepted" is a cold word. There may be very little heart in it. There may be anything but willingness and joyfulness. For example, you accept an apology; but, perhaps, you do not do it in a very good spirit. You accept an invitation, but only when you have in vain tried to find a decent excuse for declining it. You accept a composition of half-a-crown in the pound, but you grumble at it, and think it ought to be at least five times as much. And so this word "accepted" does not say much, and I think that we might substitute for it that God hath "made us welcome" in the Beloved. God's "come" is always "welcome," and it is not a bare acceptance that God gives us. It is a right joyful acceptance, like that which was given to the prodigal on his return.

But we are made "accepted *in the Beloved*," for all these blessings are given to us in Christ—chosen in Christ, adopted in Christ, and now accepted in Christ the Beloved. And I do not think that of all the fine and glorious names that are given to Christ in Scripture, there is one better than this, or more truly descriptive of Him—"the Beloved;" the beloved of God, the beloved of all angels, the beloved of all saints. You may say that He was despised and rejected of men; and of men, to a large extent, He may be despised and rejected still. Nevertheless, can you mention the human being that ever was the object of a thousandth part of the love that has been felt and is felt for Jesus Christ? For whom has so much service been done? For whom has so much suffering been undergone? For whom have so many lives been laid down, as for Jesus Christ? And when we think of all the love wherewith He has been loved, of all the love that loves Him now, and of all the love wherewith to all eternity He will be loved, I think you will see that this name "the Beloved," is just exactly the name for our Lord Jesus Christ. And God makes us accepted in Him. No acceptance out of Him; no coming to the Father but by Him; no entrance into heaven save by Him. And if there were, if there were another way of going to God—if I could go and by my own merits gain some sort of acceptance with the Father, I tell you candidly that I would rather not, for this is a far more excellent way than even if I could, upon my own merits, go to God. It is a fine, a glorious way of being introduced to God to be introduced by the beloved Son—to be introduced as the friends, as the brethren, yea, as the bride of Jesus Christ; and were there other ways of acceptance, our good sense and good feeling, I am sure, would dictate that it were better, better far, to be "accepted in the Beloved."

And Paul goes on to speak of yet another spiritual blessing—"In whom we have redemption through His blood." We have redemption in Him—all in Him, you see. The first words indicating that God gives us these spiritual blessings *in Christ* are repeated all through; and now we have redemption in Christ, and through His blood. This redemption means an act of purchase; and when Paul says that we have redemption in Christ through His blood, He means that Christ hath bought us with His blood. Bought us, then, from whom and from what?

Well, now, I have heard it often said that Christ has redeemed us from Satan. I do not believe that. He *saves* us from Satan, but He does not redeem us from Satan; for to redeem is not only to deliver but to purchase, and we never were the devil's that we should be purchased from him. He may have stolen us: it is very likely. We may have sold ourselves to him: that is more likely. But we never were his lawful possession—never; and Christ would no more buy us from the devil, than a shepherd with power to rescue a stolen sheep would buy it from the thief. No; but what He has redeemed us from is, as the apostle Paul tells us plainly, the curse of the law, being made a curse for us. That is the redemption—from the curse of the law which condemned us as sinners to eternal destruction.

From that curse Christ has redeemed us, and redeemed us with His blood, "not with corruptible things such as silver and gold." If we had been redeemed with corruptible things such as silver and gold, I, for my part, could not put very much trust in the redemption; but if we be redeemed with the blood of Christ—that is to say, if Christ thought that it was well and worth while that He should lay down His life to make us His own—then I know that I am His own for ever more. What men give little for, they may lightly part with; but what men have purchased at a very great price, they will on no account lose, if they can possibly preserve it. And so, since Christ has redeemed us with His blood—not by means of two or three years of virtuous living and wise teaching, but with His blood—I know that He will hold fast that which has cost Him so much, and I am very sure that He will not disown me because of imperfections and failings. It is not because I love Him, but because He loves me, that He will keep me; and I feel persuaded that He will keep all whom He hath thus purchased. Like the Apostle, I am "persuaded that He will keep that which we have committed unto Him against that day." It is redemption through His blood. Much as this doctrine is derided at the present time, the fact that He bought us at such a price as His own precious life makes our redemption and eternal life so absolutely secure.

And once more. The Apostle speaks of this further blessing—"the forgiveness of sins, according to the riches of His grace."

"Forgiveness of sins." Now, brethren, between redemption and forgiveness there is a differnece. They are nearly akin, but they are not exactly the same. You can imagine a case of redemption in which there should not be forgiveness. For example, if some friend of mine got into trouble and required that some one should go bail for him, or pay some debt for him, and so deliver him from the consequences of the imprudence that he had committed—well, I might go and stand bail, or I might go and pay the debt. That would be redeeming him; but I might not forgive him. I might be very angry with him; I might rebuke him; I might day after day and year after year make the very fact of my having redeemed him a ground of reproaching him. That is very easily understood. But here, in this case, there is not only the redemption, but there is the forgiveness; and Christ has not redeemed us from the curse of the law that He might afterwards reproach us for our sins. There comes, with the redemption, the forgiveness. There comes, with the act of love that saved us from the curse of the law, the act of oblivion in which all sin is forgiven and forgotten.

And this is "according to the riches of His grace;" and if forgiveness be according to this measure, then I should think that every one has a right to feel encouraged, to feel sure that there is forgiveness for him, forgiveness according to the riches of His grace. Mark you, not according to our merit, or according to our penitence, or according to our tears; but according to God's grace and the *riches* of His grace. Now, all forgiveness is, of course, according to the measure of grace that the forgiver is ready to exercise. If I forgive I forgive according to the grace or kindliness that is in my heart. Some people can forgive much and some can forgive little; but when the forgiveness is according to God's grace—when it is according to such a magnificent standard as this—well, then, while I should be sorry to encourage any man in sin, I feel emboldened to say to any man and to every man, "My friend, you cannot sin beyond the riches of God's forgiving grace."

And now, looking over this text once more, here we have spiritual blessings—being chosen in Christ, being adopted in Christ, being accepted in Christ, being redeemed in Christ, being forgiven in Christ. Let us, then, brethren, join with all our hearts, and bless "the God and Father of our Lord Jesus Christ, who hath blessed us with all spiritual blessings in heavenly places in Christ."

H. S. B.

XXV. Sainthood. Ephes. i. 1; v. 3. "*Paul, an apostle of Jesus Christ by the will of God, to the saints which are at Ephesus.*" "*As becometh saints.*"

Most of the words in the New Testament which are familiarly used amongst us, are obviously undergoing a constant process of deterioration; they are becoming lowered in their meaning; they are indeed the expression of the Divine thought; they have come down from God out of heaven, but in their contact with the minds of men they have contracted something of earthliness, and have lost something of their first ethereal purity. Now, apparently at least, the word which occurs in the verses that I have read to you; the word "saint"—apparently, I say, this word "saint" forms an exception to this general rule; for now-a-days Christians of all communions appear to use the word saint in a somewhat higher, and more transcendant sense than that which we find in the New Testament. And, I say this, because that vile form of slang has now, I suppose, passed away for ever; all slang being in its nature temporary, and representing some form of transitory vulgarity; that form of slang, I say, I suppose has passed away for ever, which used to lead men of the world to shoot out the lip, and shake their heads, and say about men who lived on higher principles than other men, "I never like your saints; I think that after all they are no better than other men are." Christians of the Roman Catholic communion, as we all know, appear to restrict the word "saint" very much to those who, after due examination of their virtues and their supposed miracles, have received a sort of patent of spiritual nobility; and who are for the future technically called saints; those who may be addressed in the language of the great old Roman Catholic poet,

> "Thou daughter of the skies
> Made in the last promotion of the blessed."

And whom do we, my brethren, ordinarily and certainly so far, not wrongly, entitle saints? When we penetrate through the mists of the past, and look at the company who surrounded our blessed Lord and Master; when we go into some cathedral and gaze through the glorious gloom at the painted figures upon the pane; when we see this form or that form with its appropriate emblem, we say, "that is the figure of St. Paul," or "that is the figure of St. John." When we take down some of those books which Christendom will never let die; when we read the effusions of St. Augustine, first we are charmed and elevated for a while with its subtle mysticism; we forget for the moment that the word saint, applied to the ancient, simply means an orthodox writer. And thus it comes to pass that while it cannot be said that we use the word erroneously, yet we do as a matter of fact restrict it to those who possess, or who are supposed to possess, very exceptional holiness indeed. We restrict it to those whose faces haunt our imaginations with that deep look of yearning in their spiritual eyes; those whom we seem to see almost in our dreams, with the cross upon their shoulder, and the glory upon their brow, winding on through the cloud in a dark path to the very throne of God; that is to say, in our imagination; and in our account, those only are saints who live and move and have their being in no ordinary sphere; these elect of the elect, whose souls are like stars and dwell apart; who, in the language of a living writer have been well called, "The very aristocracy of the kingdom of God;" in short, in the language of St. Paul, to the members of a Church like the Ephesian Church, "saints" or "called to be saints"; we habitually apply the term to those only, who in a special and signal way above all the rest of the sons of men, have walked "as becometh saints."

Now it may be instructive, in the first place, to turn for a short time and consider the use of the word "saint," as we find it in the New Testament.

In the first place then, as a matter of historical fact, the word saint is transferred from the Church of the Elder dispensation, to the Church of the New dispensation; the chosen people, so emphatically a holy nation—a nation whose ideal was that it was a saintly nation amongst the people. The Israelites are repeatedly called, and especially in the book of the Prophet Daniel, "the saints of the most High God"; and together with the privileges of the Elder dispensation, the Christian Church inherits its titles also. So as St. Peter wrote, "Ye are a chosen generation, a royal priesthood, an holy (or saintly) nation, a peculiar people"; and we find the use of this word emphatically recognised in the book of the Acts of the Apostles; thus to take one instance out of several, in the ninth chapter of the Acts of the Apostles and the thirteenth verse, when the Lord appears to Ananias, Ananias answers, "Lord, I have heard by many of this man, how much evil he hath done to Thy *saints* at Jerusalem." The meaning of the term "saint" there cannot be that Saul picked out those who were pre-eminently holy among the members of the Church and persecuted them; it means the whole body of professed believers; those who called themselves by the name of

Jesus, or were separated from the world; and towards the close of the ninth chapter and thirty-second verse, and again at the forty-first verse, we find precisely the same use of the word "saint." "Peter passed through all quarters, and came down to the *saints* which dwelt at Lydda;" and at the raising of Tabitha "when he had called the *saints* and widows, he presented her alive." Now this comes out still more clearly, when we look at the use of the word no longer historically, but as may be properly said, doctrinally. Of the epistles of St. Paul, six at least are addressed to entire Churches of saints, or called to be saints; and yet when we unfold these epistles and trace their argument we find warnings so solemn, and reproofs so stern and piercing, addressed to the members of those Churches, that we can hardly wonder that one is reported to have said, " That the epistle to the Corinthians seemed to him, in spite of its beginning, to be an epistle which was addressed to sinners, and not to saints;" but the two short passages which I have read as the text will I think, if put together, show us very clearly that the word "saint" cannot possibly be intended to signify one who is exceptionally holy.

There are some communions among our separated Protestant brothers, who have institutions that are called "Believers' prayer meetings." I can well suppose that that must be an institution which to some minds would possess peculiar attractions. It is so very pleasant by a short title of the kind to imply all that you are, or think that you are, and to imply also that which you think other people not to be. It sometimes appears to one who is obliged to take somewhat of an external look at matters, that the Anglican and insular rigidity which we used to hear so much used as a reproach to the Church of England, is fast passing away; and that in exchange for it, English Churchmen are giving way to boundless experimentalism, to a sort of plagiarism of every communion under heaven. I venture sincerely to hope, that there will be no plagiarism in this institution of believers' meetings; for I am convinced that the table of the Lord is the only true and scriptural believers' prayer meeting. But suppose that such a meeting were held, consisting of this or any other congregation that you like to suppose, and suppose that at this meeting —meant and adapted for advanced believers—the clergyman, or leader of the meeting, were to take down his New Testament and to open it at that part of the Epistle to the Ephesians which was read as the Epistle for last Sunday, the very part of the Epistle at which John Newton found his congregation began to ebb away, and almost leave him alone,—suppose, I say, that the convener of such a believers' prayer meeting were to look around upon those whom he saw assembled before him, and gazing sternly in their faces were to read out such words as these, " Putting away lying; be ye angry and sin not; let no corrupt communication proceed out of your mouth; let no filthiness nor foolish talking, nor jesting which are not convenient be heard amongst you;" and I am convinced that emotions that are not ordinarily considered saintly would arise in the hearts of those assembled before the speaker. They would say, perhaps not altogether without reason, that he was guilty of cruel irony, of a most bitter piece of unfair sarcasm; that he had assembled them as being pre-eminently saints, and had treated them as though they were pre-eminently sinners. But if the word "saint" in the Epistle to the Ephesians was intended by the Apostle to mean advanced believers, those who are pre-eminently of saintly character, it appears to me that this is very much the course that St. Paul would have pursued in writing as he did in the fourth and fifth chapters. We, therefore, on the whole conclude that the term "saint" means professing disciples of Jesus Christ, those who have been separated out of the world, or baptized into His name; and it would appear that we are very much in the habit of confining to those who are exceptionally holy, that term which St. Paul addresses to all the members of the Churches to whom he writes. Nor, brethren, can we possibly, do what we will, restore the word exactly to its original use; and possibly in some respects it may be well that we cannot do so; but let us endeavour to derive profit from it by looking fixedly at its original meaning. The main idea of the word here translated "saint," and very often translated "holy" in other places, is beyond all doubt the idea of separation and yet of dedication, the idea of consecration, of separation, of dedication of those who are baptized into the body of Christ.

My brethren, there are many controversies raging around

the baptismal font; those who ought to be brethren "fall out by the way"; but as far as our own Church is concerned, I suppose all Christians of our communion are agreed in this point, that at least baptism does mean dedication to Christ. Now consider for a few moments what this dedication involves. We have an obvious and an instructive analogy in the Jewish temple. That temple as we know was a holy temple. Why was this honour put upon it? It was a material fabric; it was a fabric made like other buildings, of stone and wood, and adorned with precious stones; it was made of material things, and when its work was done it was destined like other buildings to pass away, like an exaltation from the earth. But then it was a building that had been set apart from the world to God; it was dedicated to Him; and because it *was* dedicated to Him it was meet for the wondrous ritual which it enshrined. But, my brethren, if this temple, if this material fabric, was thus capable of dedication to God, how much more is the human spirit, made in the image of God, and redeemed with the precious blood of Jesus Christ, the shrine it may be of heroism and sanctity. The Apostle says, "Know ye not that ye are the temple of God, and that the Spirit of God dwelleth in you. If any man defile the temple of God, him shall God destroy; for the temple of God is holy, which temple ye are." And when did that dedication of body, soul and spirit, to our God take place? The words sound in our ears, "know ye not therefore it is the first principle of the spiritual life; know ye not that so many of us as were baptized unto Jesus Christ, were baptized into His death." Here then, observe, is the first and chief element in the idea of the word "saint"—it is separation, it is dedication to God; and observe that the irregularities even of the Corinthian Christians did not obliterate this title, and did not do away with this saintship; the title still remained, if it were only to condemn them. All were saints, that is, all were dedicated to God, but some defiled the temple of God while others walked as became saints.

But this is not all. There is another word, a rare word in the New Testament, that is also translated "holy." The word to which I refer occurs in the compound word, hierarchy, and means nothing less but that the person or thing is consecrated to God without reference to character or moral qualification. It mainly means, when applied to a person, that he ministers in sacred things. He may be an unholy priest, but as a priest of God that name is given to him still. But in the word which occurs in the text and elsewhere, and which is rendered "saint," there is something more than that; the thought lies near to that which is separated by God from the world, and is also separated itself by an inner consecration to Him. The word "saint" does not assert what we call saintliness as a fact about all to whom it applies; but it does imply that it is a duty.

Now brethren, I cannot help thinking that this view of the matter is a very instructive one; and for this reason it seems to take the idea of saintship down from the clouds, it seems to take it out of the region of sentiment, and even of that which is heroical and transcendental, and it brings it very near to each one of us. In the first place, is it not well fitted to correct that despondency about the Christian life and the Christian character, which is so apt to rise amongst us? When we, the ministers of Christ, speak to you, and tell you that you are in a certain sense saints, that you at all events are called to be saints, that is, called to be separated from the world, called to be pure, called to be gentle, called to be holy, called to be self-denying, one knows very well from one's own heart what the answer of many is. "It cannot be; I cannot do these things; I have learned my catechism; I know that as a matter of theological fact it is true that in a certain sense I am dedicated and set apart to God; but I cannot be pure, the chains of habit are coiled round and round me, that harlot face of sin which looks so fair in the lamp-light of passion, but so wan and haggard when God's daylight streams in upon the soul, lures me again and again to my destruction; I cannot be heavenly-minded, the pursuit of business, the babble of society around me, thoughts about investment and percentage which I cannot help, and must be, these things have deafened me to all the songs of heaven, and I can hear them no longer." No, brethren, that which we are called upon to be we may be, not by ourselves, but by the power of the Holy Spirit of God. All may have that;

there is within each one of us a fountain of life deep as eternity, and inexhaustible as God. If there is not inner help of the Holy Spirit, what is the meaning of our dedication?

I remember to have heard from one who was a spectator at the time, of his having once seen a little child playing upon a headland over the sea, who took a telescope from the hand of one near him, and handed it to a blind old sailor, who was sitting on the cliff, and the child asked the blind man to sweep the far horizon and tell him with the glass what ships were there. The old man, however, could only turn bitterly towards the child, with those sightless eyes of his; and it seems to me that you might as well give a telescope to a sightless man, as to give the Bible to a man whom you do not suppose to possess the guidance of the Spirit. You are not called because you are holy; you are to be holy because you have been called; and whenever God calls men to a duty or a privilege, depend upon it He gives them the necessary grace.

But again, this view of saintship seems to me to correct many of the false standards of saintship. Some of us may have, perhaps, read in the old Church history the story of a hermit who had passed many years in fasting and prayer to God, night and day, and who had at last, as no doubt frequently happened in such cases, become puffed up with spiritual pride; and the man, we are told, in his pride prayed to God, that if there were a saintlier soul than his, or one man who took a more lofty view of the Christian life, that God would reveal it to him by His Holy Spirit; and the legend goes on to tell how the mist fell from his eyes, and he saw in a vision, a dark lane in a great city near; and there in a squalid and fetid chamber was a shoemaker bending over his last, by the wretched light of a lantern; and the angel told him that "there was one who was far holier than he was." Brethren, not apostles, missionaries and martyrs only, are, and may be, saints of God; nor again, not such as we read of in modern religious biographies only. With all the gratitude which Christians give to modern lives of modern saints, there are some dangers connected with reading their biographies; for is it not the case that many of them are the objects of a morbid analysis and had better never have been printed? At the best it does but show, spiritually, in the same way as some transparent glass enables one to count the fibrous threads which are at the root of the hyacinth, without showing the real life which is unfolding into beauty, colour, and form. Sometimes passages in the life of good people strike profane persons outside as if they were occasionally written by those who had their eyes alternately turning towards heaven, and turning round to see who was listening behind the half opened door. A letter appeared lately in one of our great public organs in reference to the death of one whose name can never be mentioned without emotion by any English Churchman—Bishop Patteson—and in that letter the writer said, "Such was the man, and no doubt there are many, who but for his death might have passed away without his worth being known. There are many great and good men, it may be quite as good and great as he, who pass away unnoticed by the world; but that is the very reason why we should be ready to recognise and honour him, who himself looked for no recognition and no honour; but, as by a terrible flash of lightning, was suddenly revealed to us by his death. It is well we should know what stuff there is in the men we meet in common life, doing work and carrying in their breasts those lion hearts which neither treachery nor death can force one inch from the path of duty." Such truly was the man who is described in these eloquent words; and it came naturally to him when the opportunity was presented to be a martyr for the sake of Jesus Christ. When in that great cloud of witnesses with which we are encompassed, ready as it seems to reveal itself and break out into life, the voices come again and again: Who are those, who are clothed in white robes, and from whence come they? The servant in the house of whom we think but little, doing his duty; the governess, submitting to the vulgarity of the rich for the sake of duty; the pure-hearted boy taken at school or college from us, who leaves no trace on the world behind; the old man bearing cruel pain so bravely and so gently that those around can scarcely help bursting into passionate tears. Ah! brethren, amongst us in our everyday life there is many a life which, although we know but little about it, is a long lane with no refreshment, where is felt somewhat of the Saviour's agony and sorrow; where the thorn pierces into the brow and the nail pierces into the heart :—

> "When earth last saw them they were bleeding
> Thorn-crowned and sore perplexed,
> They shall be changed and beautiful exceeding
> When we shall see them next."

It has been sometimes speculated that there must be grief to the blessed beings when they miss many in that great throng. Yes, but if we miss some, shall we not also see many; and those whom it may surprise us to see there! When Christ shall come to be glorified in his saints and admired by all that believe, many a hasty judgment shall be reversed; "the last shall be first, and the first shall be last; for many are called, but few chosen."

And now, brethren, in conclusion, in speaking of the saints of God, I desire not to forget: "Other foundation can no man lay than that is laid, which is Jesus Christ;" all holiness comes from Him, and Him only. The oft-repeated motto of the Elder dispensation was, when God said to His people: "Be ye holy, for I am holy;" that is, become ye holy, for I am intrinsically and essentially holy.

My brethren, in the great philosopher of old we read of a high and spiritual love, but the love of which Plato speaks is the love which looks to an idea; the love which makes the Christian holy is the love which looks out from himself, and which clings to the person of Jesus Christ. The object of the philosopher is a misty and an abstract one; but the object with us is real and true. Have we not often in our own experience seen the distinction between loyalty to an idea, and the loyalty which can fasten around a person? Loyalty to an idea is a great thing; but there is something far grander and deeper to such beings as we are, in the enthusiasm of love, which falls in passionate tears, and gives strength to the idea also. No mere idea can grasp the soul of man like that deep and perfect holiness in Jesus Christ our Lord. Christ, conceived of the Holy Ghost and born of a virgin mother, who suffered and died for us, unwarped by our selfishness and untarnished by our impurity and sinfulness, is the Saint of saints, the Holy of holies; we have an unction from the Holy One, and a chrism from Christ, in virtue of which we may be holy as He is holy; and, though ever so faintly and feebly, may realize the grand idea contained in our text; and as by our baptism "we are called to be saints, so let us walk as becometh saints."

W. A.

XXVI. The Apostle's Alternative. PHIL. i. 21–26. "*For to me to live is Christ, and to die is gain. But if I live in the flesh, this is the fruit of my labour: yet what I shall choose I wot not. For I am in a strait betwixt two, having a desire to depart, and to be with Christ; which is far better. Nevertheless to abide in the flesh is more needful for you. And having this confidence, I know that I shall abide and continue with you all for your furtherance and joy of faith; that your rejoicing may be more abundant in Jesus Christ for me by my coming to you again.*"

THESE are words which one may well shrink from taking as a text of a sermon. Their simplicity requires but little exposition, and their greatness and elevation dwarf all that come after them, which must necessarily sound, if I might say so, like some poor, thin, reedy pipe trying to imitate the open diapason of an organ. Then, when we remember the hundreds and thousands of souls that have rested upon them and felt their grief and great darkness lightened, and that have gone to the sleep of death with the music of them sounding in their ears like a mother's most gentle lullaby, one may well shrink from preaching about them. My object is a very much humbler one than to try to exhaust their meaning in a sermon. I only want to follow as well as I can the course of thought, and to set before you the devious windings of the Apostle's mind in these words, and the conclusions into which he settles down. If I might take such an illustration, I would say that the language of my text is like a great river, which, flowing through some country, bends first to the one side and then to the other, and then comes back again into its straight course.

There is a triple movement of thought and feeling in

these words. First, there is the strong absorbing devotion which a man has to Christ. For him it transfigures life and adorns death; the one is simple consecration to his Master, the other is simple advancement and progress. So simple, so continuous, so uniform do life and death and the problem of the choice between them come to be to a good man when he is only thinking about himself. "To me to live is Christ, and to die is gain." Then comes in the bend of the stream; a rock on the margin sends the waters away in another direction. He begins to think about other people. "No man liveth to himself." There are his brethren, and there is his work to be considered; so he is confronted with considerations that complicate the problem, make it by no means so easy and simple as it looked at first sight, and he comes to a stand; he is drawn this way and that way, there is attraction in life, there is attraction in death, and he hesitates between them. Then comes in the third feeling, and he settles down into rest, not because the two attractions are equal, and so he remains poised in the middle between them, but because he takes hold upon something deeper, and he apprehends it gladly to be his present duty to stop and work. He puts it in a wonderfully beautiful form. He says, "If I may not depart and be with Christ, I shall stop and be with you, which is, in some sort, a being with Christ too; if my joy will be less, my brother's joy will be more. If I cannot get the gain of death, I shall, at any rate, get the fruit of work; and so I do not merely hesitate—I acquiesce." Now, I will venture to try and work out for a few moments this very meagre and bald outline of the general system of thought, with its wimples and windings, which we find in these verses.

I begin with that first attitude and movement of the Apostle's mind, and I venture to throw it into these words. Here we get the grand, noble simplicity and unity or continuity of life and death to a devout man thinking about himself. "To *me*," he says—and the position of the word in the sentence shows the emphasis which is to be put upon it—"to me, not merely in my judgment, but in my case, so far as I personally and by myself am concerned —to me the whole mystery and perplexity comes down into two clauses, with four words in each—to live is Christ;

to die is gain." The outward life is what he is talking about, obviously from the antithesis; and in the latter clause, what he says is not (as our Bible makes him say, or suggests that he means), that the act of dying is gain, but (as the form of the words in the Greek seems to show) that to be dead is gain. Like everybody else, he shrank from the act. No man ever said that the act and article of dissolution was anything but a pain and a horror and a terror; it was not that that he said was an advance, but it was the thing beyond. To die—that is loss; but to be dead—that is gain. Let me then for a moment dwell upon these two considerations.

Look at the noble (shall I call it?) theory of life, the grand simplicity and breadth that there is in these words. I said that the Apostle's meaning in this clause is the external life of service, so that it is not exactly the same idea as that which comes in one of his other epistles, the Epistle to the Galatians, where he says, "The life which I now live in the flesh I live by the faith of the Son of God, who loved me, and gave Himself for me." But we must take the idea that underlies that passage also into consideration. In all senses in which you can use the words, Christ is this man's life, the secret of its origin, its source and basis. He lives in Christ, by direct and, as I believe, supernatural communication of a real life to him through faith in His name. It is a continuous miracle that is being wrought, if you will rightly understand the meaning of the word "miracle," in the experience of all souls that are born again. In the deepest, profoundest sense, which some of you do not approve, and put away, and say it is mystical—in that deepest and profoundest sense, "to me to live is Christ." My brother, the deepest truths of spiritual experience are all mystical. There is a genuine mystic as well as a spurious mysticism, and the confusion between the two has been the ruination of much of Church life. "To me to live is Christ." Rooted in Him, deriving my being from Him, drawing all its energies from Him, my true life flows into me from the Lord, the basis and the source. I live in Him, I live by Him, and then and therefore, and in the proportion in which that is true, I live for Him; the outward life becomes the manifestation and expression of its inward union, and He who is the source and basis becomes also the goal and the aim; and He who is the source and basis on one side, goal and aim on the other; from whom it rises, towards whom it sets, like some great stream, if such a thing were possible in hydraulics, that flowed back to the source from which it originated,—He who is thus source and aim, Alpha and Omega, beginning and end, starting point and goal, is also law and pattern. "To me to live is Christ." The complications of ethics become simple, the hard abstractions of morality become vital and glowing with tenderest power, when through them there shines not some ideal countenance of an imaginative beauty, but the living face of the living Lord, and the marble statue becomes instinct with life, and reaches a hand down from its pedestal to help us poor strugglers here to become like Himself. *De Imitatione Christi*, the title of the old book, *The Imitation of Christ*, is the sum and substance of our practical duty. "To me to live is Christ"—source, origin, end, aim, law, pattern, power, reward. In every aspect a Christian's life is genuine and real only as it is derived from, devoted to, shaped after, energized by, and passed in communion with the Lord Jesus. Life from Christ, life for Christ, life with Christ, life like Christ. "To me to live is Christ."

My brother, one word before I go further. Contrast the blessed simplicity, the freedom, the power that there is in such a life as that, with the misery that comes into all lives that have a lower aim and a less profound source. To take only one illustration, for time will not allow me to dwell upon other points. Instead of having your days frittered away by the pursuit of a succession of trivial objects, which in comparison all objects are that terminate below the stars, is it not something to have one great purpose, one great aim, one great business running clean through them, which knits them into a unity, and makes them all concordant to one great end? My life, if I be in Christ, may become a chain of golden deeds; my life, if I be out of Christ, is almost sure to become but a heap of unconnected links. Or if I may turn to another illustration, the one is like the timid navigators of old that crept from headland to headland, and never lost sight of a low-lying shore, nor saw the wonders of the deep, and the majesty of mid-ocean, nor ever touched the happy shores which they reach who steer by the stars, or rather who carry a compass in their barks that always points to the unseen pole. "To me to live is Christ." A blessed unity, simplicity, continuity, and homogeneousness, being without limitation, without narrowing, without cutting off of anything that is broad and grand, is thereby breathed through the whole of a man. Now turn to the other side a moment. The Apostle goes on to say that wheresoever life is thus simple, and of a piece, death will be simply gain. That carries two ideas distinctly in it—continuity and increase. The direction is the same. Shall I say— will it be too vulgar an illustration ?—that he passes the points, and gets on to the other line without a jostle or a shock? He never knows that he is gone from the one to the other; he keeps on doing the same thing, only in a better way. There is no bridge, there is not even a momentary interruption of the continuity ; there is scarcely a modification, except merely superficial. All that was the true man in himself and in his occupation lasts, and is intensified. The life is simply lifted out of the common atmosphere, and plunged as it were into an oxygen jar, and it blazes out the more brightly for the change. Death is gain. Dear friends, let us put this very simple, plain question to ourselves: "Can I say the first of these two things?" In the exact measure in which you can say it, you can say the other—in the exact measure, and no more. And oh, what a difference between the man to whom death is the breaking short of most of his habitudes and the abandonment of all his treasures, and the man to whom it is simply the superlative degree of all that in its positive condition made life sweet and blessed! Shall I say that before some of us there rise the high, cold, great snow mountains, on the summits of which nothing can live, and when we come to the base of them, we look up and feel the trackless, impassable wastes, and know not what lies beyond; and for others of us, this man and those that hold with him, there has been a tunnel cut through the Alps, and it goes straight on, and comes out, keeping on in the same direction, beneath a bluer sky, and with a brighter land, with sunnier plains and a happier life spread before us in the warm south? "For me to live is Christ."

Now let me say a word as to the second bend or reach, as I called it, of this river, the hesitation that arises in his mind from the contemplation of life as a field for work. The broken language of the original (which is only partially represented in our version, and which makes the exact translation of a portion of my text somewhat questionable) seems to express the broken water in the river, as it takes the turn—the hesitation and confusion of the Apostle's mind. It would appear as if this was substantially what he meant to say, "If living in the flesh is the medium or condition, or necessary preliminary to my getting fruit from my work, then I cannot acknowledge even to myself which of the two I would rather choose. I am in a strait betwixt two." The word suggests the idea of a man hedged up between two walls, and not knowing how to turn. "I am in a strait betwixt two, having," more than a desire, one amongst many, a vagrant passing thought, "having *my* desire, the faculty, the mind, having my longing turned towards departing and being with Christ, which is far better. Nevertheless, to abide in the flesh is more needful to you." So then we get two counter-attractions —the attraction of death, the attraction of life. Notice how he talks about the former, "I desire to depart." The word seems to mean literally to loose by lifting; and it carries in it, according to one interpretation, the metaphor of weighing an anchor, and according to another the metaphor of lifting the pegs of a tent or other nomad dwelling, also conveying the idea, which our Bible gives, though it is not an exact translation, of migration. Ah! that is beautiful. It is only another day's journey, and I have had a great many like it, though this time it is across the Jordan, and I have not passed that way heretofore; and then tomorrow in the morning, no more packing up and hurrying away somewhere else, but I shall be at home, and lay aside the luggage and the pilgrim's staff. I want to depart.

And then notice one thing that fills his thoughts and his horizon—to be with Christ. I am not going to talk about how these words seem to bear the fair inference that has often been drawn from them of the immediate, conscious passing into the presence of our Lord, and therefore into restful felicity, of those that depart in His faith and fear. That seems a perfectly fair inference, but I have nothing to do with it at present. I want rather to fix upon the practical side of this thought. Dear brethren, our imaginations work best with little material, and for the clearness and operative power of the great hope of immortality, I believe that it is of prime importance that it should not be over-burdened with a multitude of petty, and, if I may so say, accidental, certainly non-essential details. The simplicity of the one thought is far mightier. The veil is the picture, according to the old story. "To depart"—no physical theory of another life, no curious prying into what lies beyond—"to be with Christ."

> "I shall clasp thee again, O soul of my soul,
> And with God be the rest."

That is the attraction. He draws us, and we run after Him. You remember the beautiful old Rabbinical lines about the death of Moses, that it came because God "kissed him with the kisses of His mouth," and drew the soul from him in the sweetness of the contact; and so death, who has made his darkness beautiful, draws us in proportion as we feel that he is heaven and heaven is he.

Then notice how this attraction of death, so true, so wholesome and healthy, is differenced by a whole universe from other reasons that men have had. This is no morbid sentimental religion; this is no such man as people tell us now-a-days Evangelical Christianity produces, who is smitten with a diseased desire for another world, and so wants to scramble through this one; this is no man that is sick, and morbid, and sorrowful, weary of work and tired of life. He is not saying like Job, "I loathe it; I would not live alway:" he is saying, "Thy face, that is my life; and the nearer I get to it, the fuller it shall be."

Then think of that reason for living that masters and overbears such a reason for wanting to die. "Nevertheless, to abide in the flesh is more needful for you;" that is to say, "There is work to be done, and so I feel that life tugs at me." He is not saying, "Oh, I dare not go away into that great unknown." I do not wonder at a man that can only say, "There may be an immortality, but it does not rise beyond a faint presumption; it can never reach to a certainty:" I do not wonder at a man whose creed is that clinging to life: but this man saw yonder a great light, and he turned away from it, and said, "No; there is work for me here." I do not wonder at men—and I am afraid I am speaking to some of them—who, with a fear which is partly physical and partly arises from their consciences, saying to themselves, "I shrink from it." I do not want to frighten you, dear brethren; but let me remind you of one word, "After death, the judgment." This man believed that, and you believe it, and you shrink away from it. But it was not that that turned him. I remember when I used to live in the South of England, there was a story that went about—I do not know whether it was true or not, but it will do for an illustration—about some man that was thrown over the face of the Isle of Wight chalk cliffs. They found him in the morning lying down there among the white boulders and black seaweed, and below the finger-nails there was powdered chalk that he had scraped in his desperate clutch as he fell, to save himself. My friends, there are some of you that grasp at life like that, and for something of the same reason, because you are afraid of the smash when you get down to the bottom. I preach to you a great message, a message that takes away all that fear, and I ask you, do you know anything about the attraction of death because it is getting close to the Lord, and do you know anything about the counter-attraction of life because it is stopping to do His work?

And that brings me to the last word I have to say. Notice the beautiful, calm solution of the question—not in an equipoise of hesitation, something pulling two different ways, and so the rest of equal forces acting—notice the calm solution, the peaceful acquiescence, "I know I shall abide and continue with you all." Then the innate delicacy of the man comes out in the way in which he phrases his perception of the necessity there is for his stopping. He sinks self, and represents himself as sharing his brethren's gladness. "Having this confidence, I know that I shall abide and continue with you all for your furtherance and joy of faith." Well, I have only two things to say about that. One is this: The true attitude is neither desire, nor shrinking, nor hesitation, but a calm taking what God wills about the matter. As Richard Baxter says in that simple, quaint old hymn of his—

> "Lord, it belongs not to my care,
>   Whether I die or live;
> To love and serve Thee is my share,
>   And this Thy grace must give."

Ah, yes, friends, that is the thing. He is not much of a workman that is always listening—if you will allow me take a Lancashire illustration—for the six o'clock bell to rung in the mill turret; and although it seems very devout sometimes, it is not much better for a man to be always casting his eye away from his work to the future. Stick to your tasks,

> "Nor seek to leave thy tending of the vines
>   For all the heat of the day, till it declines,
> And God's mild curfew thee from work assoil."

Then you may be quite sure that, when the long day's work is done, and we have gone home and obtained our wages, He will come forth, and gird Himself, and will serve.

Now, dear brethren, if you forget everything else that I have been saying, I ask you to carry away with you my one last word. Here are two theories of life for you. They are mutually exclusive; taken together, they cover the whole ground; that is to say, if you do not have this one, you must have that one. Here is one of them: "To me to live is Christ, and to die is gain." Here is the other: "To me to live is self, and to die is loss and despair." *Which?* Which?

A. M.

XXVII. **Silvanus.** 1 Pet. v. 12. *"By Silvanus, a faithful brother unto you, as I suppose, I have written briefly, exhorting, and testifying that this is the true grace of God wherein ye stand."*

These words are of more importance and interest than may strike one at first sight. They are, as I shall show you in a moment or two, an endorsement by the Apostle Peter—who was the great apostle of the Jews and of the circumcision—of the teaching of Paul, the great apostle of the Gentiles. And from that point of view they show us —what I daresay none of us seriously doubt, but what is doubted by a great many people now-a-days, and what has been thought to have been a wonderful discovery of recent criticism—they show us the folly of the hypothesis, that there was a gulf of antagonism between Peter and Paul, one the representative of Jewish Christianity and the other the representative of the Christianity of the Gentiles —a gulf of separation within the Church itself. I am not going to dwell upon that at any length, but I want to draw out one or two of the points of biographical and other interest which these words represent, in order to bring out one or two lessons that lie in them.

And now, the first thing I want to notice is, Who is this good brother Silvanus that Peter praises so warmly?

The "as I suppose," looks as if he was not altogether sure of him; but the original word in the Greek has none of that uncertainty which the English word "suppose" has about it.

And here he says he is sending this letter "by Silvanus, a faithful brother," to them, who had some special connection with these Churches whom Peter is addressing.

Which were the Churches? They were mainly the Churches in Asia Minor, the Churches scattered all about that great peninsula.

Who founded these Churches? Paul, as you read in the Acts of the Apostles; and Paul's friend, Peter, had never even seen them, he did not know anything about them. Peter had always been true to the division of labour laid down at the beginning between himself and Paul; Paul saying in effect, "Now you go to them of the circumcision, and I will go among the Gentiles; this is your walk, that shall be mine." And so in true bonds of brotherly affection, like two wise men, they split the field between them and divided the labour. And so it happened that Peter had had nothing to do with these Gentiles, and yet here he sends them this letter.

And who was this Silvanus? Well, this name hides a well-known person; one form of whose name is Silvanus, as we see here, and in one or two other places, and the other form of the name is the familiar Silas. And now you get on the track.

Who was Silas? He was a good brother whom the Church had sent from Jerusalem on Paul's first missionary journey, when the Jews heard of the success of Paul and Barnabas, and began to be afraid that this new gospel was going to be rather too liberal a thing. Some of them fancied it to be highly dangerous to get the Gentile nations into the Church without first making Jews of them and having them circumcised. We get a brief account, a kind of shorthand report, as it were, in the Acts of the Apostles, and the upshot is this : They called together the elders and the disciples, and put the collective wisdom and the united strength of the whole Church into the nature of a generous letter, and selected Judas "surnamed Barsabas, and Silas," and said to them, "Now, you go and visit the Gentiles, and take this letter with you."

So they went to Paul and Barnabas at Antioch, and delivered the epistle. Well, when Silas got to Antioch, he caught the fever of, and was infected by, the enterprise that Paul and Barnabas were working ; and being a good earnest man he determined to throw in his lot with these brethren, who had been a little suspected by Peter and his friends. He joined these, and said to Peter and the others in effect, "You may go to them of the circumcision ; I am going further afield." And so we read that on that all-important missionary journey of the apostles, Paul took Silas instead of Barnabas, and the two went out together. As we read in the story of the persecution at Philippi, it was Paul and Silas that were flung into prison there. And these two worked that missionary tour together during at any rate its first half, and then towards the middle of it we lose sight of Silas, and hear no more about him for many years, until here he crops up again ; no more by the side of Paul you see, but by the side of the other apostle, Peter, the representative of the other great activity in the Christian Church. He has gone over from the one work to the other ; and having stood like a good, true, faithful man beside Paul as long as he wanted him, he has transferred his sympathies and energies to the other man, Peter, and so Peter sends him with this letter.

And now there are one or two things I want to say, and the first is this. How these strange, fragmentary little bits of a kind of grudging notices of good men that we get in the New Testament, that did the work—how they fit in with the whole character of the Book. If the meaning of the

Bible had been simply to tell the story of the rise and
progress of Christianity, you would have had the history
of all these people, when and where they began and why
they left off working, and all about them, just as you get
in a biographical dictionary. But that is not the principle
on which the Bible goes at all. A man crops up for a
moment, and then goes down again, and we hear no more
about him ; there is not the least care about any man's
history ; sometimes you get only a word about him, sometimes whole pages. As long as God's breath is breathed
through him, he is vocal, and you can hear the music ; and
when God's breath is gone, he is like a dead pipe in an
organ—you hear nothing of him, he disappears. There is
only one in the whole Bible that runs through it, and that
is God ; because the Bible is intended to describe the acts
of God and not of man. And so it picks up a man and
lets him drop again, and oblivion swallows them up, except
in so far as the grace of God speaks through them.

And so of Silvanus, we see him working away in that
missionary tour, and then comes a great gap ; and then,
for an instant, one beam falls upon him in the darkness,
where he stands by the side of the Apostle Peter, and
then we lose sight of him altogether, because that no man
" should glory in me " ; and that we should learn that the
meaning of Scripture is to teach us the mighty acts of the
Lord, and there is only one Man whose biography is a
gospel, and that is Jesus Christ, God manifest in the flesh.

And then there is another thing that I need just drop in
passing, and that is how these glimpses that we get of
good, earnest, hard-working Christian people that appear
for a moment and then are lost sight of, and all their work
swallowed up in oblivion—how that should reconcile us
to the conditions under which you and I have to do our
little bit of work for God. Never mind whether anybody ever hears about it or not, what does that matter ?
Never mind whether they see it or not, that is of no
moment. Silvanus did his work, and there was none to
approve, and very few to blame. There is no happiness
in any man merely having people talking about him and
what he does. Never mind whether God sets us upon a
pinnacle, so that people can see what we are doing, or
whether we are in some little hole or corner where nobody

knows anything about us—work away and never mind. If you were to drain the sea, you would get all the things visible that are lying at the bottom of it; and the sea of oblivion will be drained some day, and all the works will come up again, and "I will never forget any of their works," He says. And so Silvanus, and you and I, need not mind. He approves of them, and if they are written in the Book of Life, it matters nothing whether they are written anywhere else or not.

"By Silvanus I have written briefly." Why in the world does he say that he has written briefly? It is not such a short letter. There are five good chapters of it. It is long as compared with letters in these days, or as letters in any days. What made him say that? Well, I will tell you what I think made him say it. I think it is obvious throughout the whole of this Epistle, that he must have had Paul's letters before him; and it seems to me that he is thinking about the same thing that he speaks about in his second letter. "Our beloved brother Paul, also, in all his epistles, has said so-and-so;" and he says to himself and to them, "You have been no doubt taught by Silvanus, and by the Epistles of Paul." My little letter is very insignificant, compared with such a colossal monument of Christian energy and certainty as the Epistle to the Romans. My letter is a very small affair, beside that great building of those Epistles to the Corinthians. My brother Paul can argue, I cannot. I write as God has given me; I write briefly; and my work is not to argue, not to demonstrate, not to plunge into the depths of theological subtleties, as he has done for the enlightenment of the Church in all ages. My work is to exhort and to testify. I can, at any rate, do that. I can appear as a witness to what I have found. And what I tell you is this, "That this grace that he brought to you long ago, that this grace in which you stand, is the true grace of God. It is for my brother Paul to argue, it is for me to exhort and to testify."

Well, I think I could show you, if I had time, that all through this letter there are references to Paul's letters, and once or twice there are distinct verbal quotations; and it seems to me that the explanation—and a beautiful explanation it is—is this: let us try to recognise the kind of service for which God has fitted us, and let us try to recognise the kind of service for which He he has fitted our Christian brethren that are most unlike ourselves. And let us not fancy that every man's coat must be cut according to our cloth, and every man's service must be the kind of service that we do. There is room in the canon of Scripture, amongst the possessors of authoritative inspiration, for the more mystical John, for the more argumentative Paul, for the more practical James, for the exhorting and testifying Peter. All these various rays blend together to make the one perfect light; and as he himself says in another part of this letter: "As every man hath received, even so minister the same as good stewards of the manifold grace," the manifold grace, " of God."

And now the last thing. Look at the substance of this point that he makes. "This is the true grace of God wherein ye stand." Let us take a verse or two from the Epistle to the Romans, to which I said there was a constant reference in this letter. Peter says: "I testify that this is the true grace of God wherein ye stand." Paul says in Romans v.: "By whom also we have access by faith into this grace wherein we stand." That is uncommonly like a verbal quotation, is it not? It looks to me as if Paul's very words were being repeated by his brother here; and as if he was in effect saying: "I, the apostle of the circumcision, whom ye people down in Asia Minor have known a great deal less about than you have known of my brother Paul that is imprisoned in Rome now, and who cannot speak to you himself; I, the apostle of the circumcision, who have had nothing to do with founding your Churches, I tell you that what my brother said to you is the true grace of God, and that grace in which you stand is the very word of the living God that abideth for ever. And there is my witness, and I send it to you in his own words to make it a little more emphatic, and by his own chosen companion, that you may know there is not a shadow of a difference between me and him; but that we are one in heart and one in work, serving one Master and preaching one gospel."

And now the lessons out of that. Well, the great one, the only one worth while dwelling upon even for a moment, is this: That we shall never understand the great and blessed revelation of God in Jesus Christ, in this New Testament of ours, unless we recognise the two facts; the diversity and the unity; unless we see, as I have said, Peter, Paul, James and John, each man apprehending according to the grace given unto him. The central mystery of it all, of all of them preaching in their various ways, according to their different idiosyncracies, inspired and illuminated by God's invisible Spirit, all preaching the one truth, which, blessed be God, has a thousand sides, and in which every man sees that which he needs most. The diversity between these men has been most absurdly and wickedly exaggerated. There is no diversity about this, that Jesus Christ is the Lamb of God that taketh away the sins of the world. There is no diversity about this, that all men have sinned and come short of the glory of God. There is no diversity about this, that the Spirit of the living God dwelling in men will purify and strengthen them and fit them for heaven. There is no diversity about this, that one means of salvation is provided for them in that crucified Saviour. Paul, Peter, John, James, all of them believe that, and they all of them preach it. And whatsoever be the difference, it is one Lord, one Cross, one faith, one God and Father of all.

There are differences of administrations but it is one Lord, and there are diversities of ends but it is one Spirit. And no man can rightly understand that majestic harmony of witnessing who has not an ear equal to catching the diverse notes of sounding concord, for there is no harmony without diversity, and the true unity is the unity of the stars that differ from stars in glory, but are all irradiated from the one central sun round which they move, and to which they bow in obedience.

And the last thing that I leave with you is this. Dismissing altogether those thoughts that have occupied us for the last few minutes, remember this one last point—the substance of the witness which all do bear in their varying manners, is this; that there is one thing and one thing only on which, as on a rock, our poor feet can stand—that only by resting on the grace of God, and the love of God in Jesus Christ our Lord, and the communication of spiritual strength and gifts from that love, are we able to resist the enemies that come against us, the storms that beat, the winds that blow, the evils that threaten, the temptations that seize; and in Christ alone is the grace by which our feeble feet shall be made to stand, to withstand in the evil day, and having done all to stand.

Dear brethren, He sets our feet upon a Rock, and establishes our goings, and unless we stand fast in the Lord, dearly beloved, our feet shall slide in due time.

XXVIII. Christian Meekness. TITUS iii. 1-4. "*Put them in mind to be subject to principalities and powers, to obey magistrates, to be ready to every good work, to speak evil of no man, to be no brawlers, but gentle, showing all meekness unto all men. For we ourselves also were sometimes foolish, disobedient, deceived, serving divers lusts and pleasures, living in malice and envy, hateful, and hating one another. But after that the kindness and love of God our Saviour toward man appeared.*"

THE instructions given by St. Paul in the second chapter of this letter had reference to domestic or household life. Those to which he now proceeds in this third chapter relate to the public and social demeanour of the Christians in Crete. They fall under two classes; for a Christian's duty to society includes a right attitude to the State or civil authorities on the one hand, and on the other, a proper behaviour in his private intercourse with his neighbours. On both points Paul has something to say appropriate to believers; and, therefore, our subject falls under two heads: first, how the Christians were to act towards the State; second, how they could act in intercourse with ordinary heathen society. If we would do justice to the first group of apostolic counsels, we must remind ourselves of the political circumstances with which his agent Titus had to deal. Throughout the ancient world, authority, both domestic and civil, assumed a more severe complexion than it does with us, and pressed with a weight which we should deem excessive upon the subject classes. It was so with the model kingdom of a family. Roman, as well as Hebrew law, gave to the father an almost unlimited authority over his children, and to the master despotic power over his slaves. One very natural result of the coming of Christianity into a home was to beget in a child, or in a slave, some indications of this domestic tyranny. Christ makes His people free; Christ views all men as fundamentally equal; Christ vindicates for every one the full rights of a spiritual being and of redeemed manhood. The converted son was very likely, therefore, to dispute the interference of a parent with the new allegiance he had learnt to pay to his Father in heaven. The baptized slave was very readily tempted to resent the mastership of a heathen lord, now that he knew himself to be a free man of Christ. Hence it became necessary to warn believing children against unruly behaviour, and to charge bondsmen to be obedient still, and more than ever, to their own masters, otherwise the new teaching of the gospel would be not adorned, not commended, but discredited in the eyes of the heathen population, and the Word of God blasphemed.

Now, a danger precisely similar arises in political life. The rule of Rome which then lay upon all the lands where the gospel was being preached was a rule which rested upon the sword. Everywhere ancient nationalities had been subjected; venerable constitutions had been overthrown; the freedom of the commonwealth had been ruthlessly suppressed; and though it was Rome's policy to leave the old forms of administration untouched, wherever possible, yet it was impossible to conceal from the conquered peoples the degrading tokens of their conquest, as it is with us to-day, for example, in the case of our Indian Empire. Roman troops surrounded the palaces where Roman proconsuls sat in the seat of dethroned kings; Roman judges administered Roman law; taxes were paid in Roman kind; and the military power that pressed on the neck of once haughty and mighty nations, was but at best a heavy yoke. The Imperial laws were, on the whole, just, yet they were stern and could be merciless. Nor were the Imperial courts above the imputation of corruptness. The imposts were very heavy, and provincial revenues were drained off to feed the monstrous dissipation of the capital. For the most part, therefore, the provinces groaned beneath the burden which the strongest were unable to cast off, yet beneath which the weakest were sometimes goaded into turbulence. It is very easy for you to see that into a society thus honeycombed with political disaffection and threatening to break into revolt, the entrance of Christianity with its new conceptions of human dignity and human freedom, must have added one more element of ferment. It could not fail to quicken in men's souls that sense of injustice which oppression brings, to deepen the irritation they felt at wrong and insolence in the dominant race, to intensify their longing for a happier era, when the kingdom of God which they had received into their hearts now, should become also a kingdom of God in society, and the State—a kingdom with social equity, liberty, and brotherhood. Hence, you see, it became an object of necessity with the first preachers of the gospel to warn their early converts against political restlessness. Do as they might, they could hardly hope, under such a government as that of Nero, to escape suspicion. They were pretty sure to be reckoned in the bureau amongst those dangerous forces which every day exist in society, heaving with discontent. To do anything to give the authorities an excuse for repression would have been foolish as well as wrong. It would have compromised the progress and success of the gospel by mixing it up with the department of human affairs with which the gospel has only indirectly to do. The most successful and resolute resistance which has ever been offered to arbitrary power in this world has been offered by men whom the truth made free, and who carried their Bibles beneath the same belt on which they hung their sword. But personal and political liberty are the secondary effects of the gospel after it has penetrated the whole structure of society, and has had time to remake nations on its own new lines. For the individual private convert in an age like Paul's, or in a state of society like that of the later Roman Empire, to fling himself against the State, or to run away from his master, would have been to act falsely to the principles of his own faith, and utterly to misrepresent it to his contemporaries. The question, at what time or in what way a Christian community is justified in deposing a tyrant in order to organize itself into a free commonwealth, is a question which belongs to the Christian community, when such a community exists, and can only arise under another condition of society altogether. The time for that was by a long way not yet come. What the gospel enjoined, therefore, on the private citizen or subject, so long as the government stood, was to discern Divine ordinance underlying and dignifying all authority, even while authority is abused, so long as that authority is legitimate, and to render that obedience which is due to the magistrate as such for conscience sake towards Him who is the supreme Magistrate of all.

It is curious that the two Churches to which St. Paul addresses the most explicit instructions on this head were the Church of Rome and the Church of Crete. Rome itself was the only focus for the dissatisfied and the lawless. There the sensuality of the aristocracy and the corruption of justice were most conspicuous. In its purlieus every conspirator could lurk most secure. Some years before Paul wrote his warning to Rome, the Christians were, as yet, mingled and confounded with the Hebrews. In Crete, likewise, there were local reasons which called for a similar warning, for it, too, was a great nest of Jews. Nor did the native Cretan population stand in any need of foreign intervention. Many years before this their constitution had been abolished by the Roman general, and their island placed under officers from Rome; but the people never took kindly to their new masters, any more than they have to this day taken to their Turkish conquerors. In Paul's day, as in our own, Crete was a restless dependency of Greeks, struggling at intervals to regain their lost privilege of self-government. Were these people to see the reminder in the opening verse? "Put them in mind," said Paul to his delegate, "to submit themselves to principalities and powers, to obey magistrates, to be ready to every good work."

But even of greater consequence for the honour and repute of our holy religion, and of greater consequence for our own guidance, perhaps, are the instructions in the second verse. These refer to the spirit in which a Christian should act towards his unbelieving neighbours in social life. A handful of converts in the midst of a swarming, heathen population, sustained everywhere a peculiar responsibility. The case of modern mission Churches, as in China or in India, for example, very closely resembles that of Paul's converts in the primitive age. They are imperfectly cured of old, ingrained, rough habits; the vices characteristic of Paganism are scarcely yet eradicated; they cannot escape contact from bad examples everywhere around; they must breathe a vitiated moral atmosphere; they are pressed on every hand by the customs of idolatry, and by the modes of thought proper to an unchristian community. More than that, these converts are daily exposed to rude remarks, to unkindness, even to abuse, for the singularity of their religion; petty acts of hostility are perpetrated at their expense, for which no remedy can be had; occasionally even grosser outrage occurs which has to be borne as best it can; even where the government is tolerant and the magistrates indifferent or not unkindly, the public dislike of a new and foreign superstition is at no loss to express itself in a number of disagreeable and vexatious ways. All this is hard to bear, and it comes specially hard on men just struggling out of heathenism—men used to give a loose rein to the tongue. Now, the Cretans of the lower orders were a passionate people, rude in their manners, easily provoked to a brawl, quick to take offence, and ready in their employment of vituperation and blows. It was hard work, you will admit, to teach such men Christian meekness, patience under provocation, and to repay good for unprovoked and undeserved evil. Yet notice the responsibility under which those Cretan believers lay. If the Cretan Christian were to show himself not less quick to resent an insult than he ever was; if in the wine shop he went into a passion, and used his knife as readily as his comrade that swore by Jupiter; if the ready blow was not exchanged for the demeanour more becoming the sons of God, what the better was the man for his Christianity, or how could his neighbours be ready to respect his new law or to imitate his new faith? The graces, therefore, Paul told his delegate to impress above everything else on these converted islanders were those characteristic of the graces of the gospel, and that formed the greatest contrast to the society around them. They were never to let a word of abuse pass their lips; they were to keep clear of brawls and quarrels; they were to give way to the insolence and wrong-doing of others rather than resent it; in short, they were to display towards all sorts of persons every form of

Christian meekness—for on that word lies the emphasis. *Meekness:* what is it, brethren? It is the quality which heathenism everywhere has scouted as mean-spiritedness, but which the gospel of Christ has canonised. It is that one condition of soul which, springing out of genuine penitence for sin, a profound sense of personal unworthiness, and a profound appreciation of the Divine mercy, predisposes a man to forbearance under provocation and forgiveness for injury. It has nothing in common with pusillanimity, but it has its origin in the religious experience which we call conversion; for it is when the tap root of human pride is broken by a thorough crushing down of the soul under the discovery of its sinfulness before God; it is when the strong man reduced to cry for mercy at the hands of Infinite Justice, is fain to receive forgiveness, and hope, and peace with God as unmerited gifts from the very grace of his Redeemer; it is then, and through that religious change, that the heart grows susceptible of true meekness. Then humbleness enters — humbleness, the child of penitence, and mild charity, too, for all men, and a tender feeling—a feeling that one who has himself done so much evil in his day ought to bear with the evil doing of other men; that one who owes everything to mercy should be, above all things, merciful. Brethren, it might well seem a difficult undertaking to persuade the quick, passionate heathen of a Mediterranean harbour to check the biting words upon their tongue, to bear with the gibes of a tipsy comrade, or the deliberate insult or rudeness of some fanatical Jew. It was a difficult undertaking — so difficult that one could only say, in the words of Christ, "What is impossible with men is possible with God."

But Paul knew how that change was to be wrought. He knew what change, stranger than magic, had already come over these men since they had welcomed Christ's gospel. He knew what constraining power lay in that religious change to remodel their moral nature and turn the lion into a lamb; and therefore he did not despair of making them, to the astonishment of their neighbours, models of an unheard-of virtue, if only they would give to the facts of their own conversion, and to the facts of the gospel they believed, a due influence over their daily conduct. The splendid sentence which opens with the third, and only closes with the seventh verse, comprises a great deal of teaching which cannot be unfolded now. It is so packed full of precious, central, evangelical truth as to sparkle among the minor epistles of St. Paul as one of their most conspicuous and memorable passages. You notice that the argument supporting his plea for meekness, is introduced by the word "For." It gives the reason why the Apostle expected his Cretan friends to exhibit so rare a gentleness before their Pagan neighbours; and to this argumentative value of the sentence let us try to do justice. The sentence is in form a contrast. It sets the former condition of the believer over against his present condition. The words of time are emphatic—"then" and "now." It reminds the Cretans of what they had been in their unconverted and unbaptized state, and it grandly magnifies the grace which had now made them so wonderfully different.

Now, out of this little historical sketch—for such it really is—a sketch of their past life and conversion, there grew up the arguments for a meek behaviour. In the first place the argument runs like this. "These heathen neighbours of yours, whose conduct is so very provoking, who irritate, abuse, and try to quarrel with you, are not at all different from what you yourselves used to be, if you remember. Look back a few years and see what you were before God's grace found you. Precisely such as they are to-day. You did not then see your own foulness any more than they do, before the light came to you; neither do they see it now; you cannot expect them to; and yet contemplate you the hateful picture of what you were. What is Pagan life? Life unrenewed, life unregenerate—so dark on religious subjects as to have no true knowledge of Christ such as you now have,—no just apprehension of spiritual truth; as the result, in part, of this ignorance, disobedient in practice to all the requirements of Divine law and duty—deluded, in fact, misled—a prey to false conceptions of right and wrong, and false superstitions in worship; nay, worse, enslaved to your own desires after pleasure, given over to self-indulgence and the mere pursuit of what seemed to you to be an advantage, what seemed to you delectable, even if immoral, socially leading a life too sensual to be either just or generous to other men—a life, therefore, of malignity and enmity, cherishing rancour against one another for imagined slights and jealousies on account of superior advantages—is that a true picture of the natural life? Is that a picture of the unregenerate as it now mirrors itself in the enlightened Christian conscience? To sum it up in a word, are not such men repulsive as well as repellent, hateful as well as hating? Yet such were you; now, better than your poor heathen fellow-townsmen continue this day to be. Oh! by the memory of your own forlorn and guilty state; by the memory of the faults you used to share with them; by the old darkness out of which you have been led, bear with them tenderly, think of them kindly."

So runs the first argument, and to this argument a second joins itself. "Out of that universal depravity of mankind how came you to be delivered? How? By your own effort, or by another's kindness? Nay, not as you were; not through any righteous actions of your own or meritorious struggles to become better men, sheerly and only was it not through the unmerited mercy, the cleansing and renewing power of God our Saviour, by the Divine salvation which came to you, and found you helpless, surprised you with its benefactions, and made new men of you in the day you turned from idols to become the heirs of eternal life through Jesus Christ our Lord? Saved by the philanthropy of heaven, have you none for your unsaved brother? Changed through Divine mercy, where is your mercy? They are as you were—these unconverted and unlovable neighbours. Treat them as you were treated, do to them as He did to you. How if God had been resentful against you—hard, quick to take offence, ready to strike in His anger? Oh, how ill it becomes a Christian to speak evil of others, to brawl, to give back word for word and blow for blow! By the kindness your Saviour has shown in returning you good for your wrong, show to your still wrongful fellows what is that kindness of God, that love of God for men which has been manifested to you, which might now be manifested to them if they only received it. Show by your example that they, too, may taste and see that God is good." So I read Paul's argument.

My brethren, the argument holds good to this day. I

have tried to bring back into the Apostle's reasoning a
little of its original force, addressed, as it was, to a few
converts from Greek idolatry, for, thus read, the words
may give a certain freshness to your mind, and the edge
of the argument be somewhat whetted. But to us, if we
have been converted from a selfish and ungodly life, the
appeal carries just the same force. Brethren, there is
nothing in which a holy, chastened, renewed—if I may
so say—*christened*, temper, displays itself so unmistakably
and with such charm as by bearing with sweet patience,
and repaying with gentle kindness, the unreasonable or
the angry opposition of irreligious people. Still, as with
the Cretan, my brethren, meekness will sit well on forgiven
and redeemed men. Still the philanthropy of God our
Saviour breathes with inspiration, and prescribes a model
for our brotherly kindness. By the memory of what we
were till God came to us, and of the spontaneous grace
from heaven which has made us what we are, oh! let us
reach after that crown of saintliness and meekness which
makes us the bearers of all things, and the forgivers of all
things, for Christ's sake. Amen.

J. O. D.

XXIX. Perfect through Suffering. Heb. ii. 10

"*For it became Him, for whom are all things, and by whom are all things, in bringing many sons unto glory, to make the Captain of their salvation perfect through sufferings.*"

AT first sight, my brethren, the passion of the Son of God
may very well affect us with an uneasy sense of incon-
gruity. We are, indeed, too familiar with the cross, of
which we have been singing the praises; and we have been
too long accustomed to make it our boast to feel what is
called in the New Testament the "offence" of it, as vividly
as the ancient world felt it. In the days when our religion
was pushing its way into public notice, the Greek and
Roman world ridiculed, as the height of folly, a God who
had been executed upon the cross. The rude rabble
wrought and scribbled revolting caricatures; but Pilate
wondered at the information, and took it as the curious
vagary of Eastern fanaticism.

Over this difficulty which lay upon the threshold of the new faith, even dishonest inquiry might well stumble. On the one side there was the young Jew, crucified and no more heard of; and on the other side there was the obscure faith of obscure men that this very Jew was Eternal God, winning by the sacrifice of His life eternal salvation for men; and in this very view there lay an inconsistency which might very well be hopeless. It was not easy for an adherent of the new faith to retain his confidence in this; it was still harder to persuade anybody else to accept a creed which had appearances dead against it.

Every one in those days who tried to allure men to the faith of Jesus might have felt this difficulty. There was an awkward look about the doctrine; there was an unlikelihood in the very first article of the creed, such as all explanation failed to remove, and which put it in the way of every sinner to turn the laugh against every Christian as the worshipper of a crucified Divinity. Brethren, it could be nothing else than the power of truth itself, joined to the passionate enthusiasm of profound moral conviction, which carried conviction.

But, of course, time has changed all that. Christianity, did, so far, turn the world " upside down," as they said at Thessalonica; the very thing which in the first century was the mark of opprobrium came, in the nineteenth century, to be the symbol of honour and victory.

By the cross the Church prevails, and therefore in the cross she has a good right to boast. No one, in a civilised world, at least, will to-day make mockery of the Redeemer because He suffered under Pontius Pilate. His passion has been stripped for us of those associations which made crucifixion revolting and disgraceful.

Yet, while this outward unbecomingness has been got over, there are still deeper difficulties in regard to our Lord and Saviour which time cannot solve.

There remains a strangeness in the destiny of the Divine Person and a suspicion of unsuitableness in the fearful destiny of a Deity, in regard to pain and shame, which is as hard for us to believe as it was for His first disciples. The sacrifice to justice of the second Person of the Trinity and ever blessed Godhead is a fact, and so completely is it out of analogy that, to look at it at first sight, it will give any man pause.

How is it possible for any human man to say, "God is a man, and lived the suffering life He led, as represented in the Gospel, without resigning the attributes of His Godhead, and yet doing nothing that was unworthy of Him?" Was there nothing in all that season of eclipse which severed, with a clean cut, the glory before from the glory to follow? Nothing in that interval?

It is very natural that Christ's perfecting through sufferings should stir questions like these in unredeemed men; and to some of them, at least, Holy Scripture helps us to no answer. But yet as to the mode in which the Divine assumed a human life, as to the fitness or unfitness of the act of God, its worthiness of it, it seems to us that Scripture does offer us certain materials for the answer; but the wonderful question, I think, revelation has opened to us as to the character of God has so corrected our false image of what is and what is not God-like, that it suggests to us the vindication of this, which is the darkest of the dark passage of the history of the Son of God. For, you will observe, without going further, that it is within the Divine nature itself that the vindication of Jesus' passion as a suitable experience of a Divine person as worthy of God must be sought for. This writer to the Hebrews is very pointedly reminding us in my text that we cannot explain it by any restraint from without. He of whom we presume to reason as the absolute source and end of everything, the first and the last, seen, even although it be a monstrosity and of God's own making, is not a thing which could surprise at a disadvantage Him who sees the end from the beginning, so as to compel Him into a position, ever so slightly noticeable, to excuse the atonement as if it needed an excuse, as a double or second thought. It is inadmissible to apologise for the death of the Son of God, as good and well meaning persons are apt to do as an infinite necessity of the Divine procedure. It is quite in another direction the explanation may be sought. Rather this act of God— this supreme act—this wondrous act of God which we know nothing about, must wear, if we can only find it, a profound propriety. The humiliation of the second Person must be not only a device to which He was reduced by a painful necessity for which He needs to apologise—not something unlike God, but rather something so very like Him and so worthy of Him that I should conceive any glorious archangel of His court, perfectly knowing his neighbour—that one might be the one to expect such a manifestation of the Divine character. In a word—to emphasize one of the profoundest expressions of Holy Scripture, "It *became* Him for whom are all things, and by whom are all things."

Now, before we try, as we are about to do, to get such a view of the Divine nature as will make this passage understandable to us, let us try to see where the difficulty lies. It does not lie in the treatment to which the Son of God was pleased to subject Himself after He had clearly accepted the responsibilities of sinful men. It may be a difficulty with some, even when He became the Captain of our salvation by the birth of a woman, that He did well to be made "perfect through sufferings" of which my text speaks; but of that I am not making any difficulty.

I take it for granted, therefore, here that it "became" God, in the profoundest sense you can attach to that word, it "became" God, the righteous Judge, to require satisfaction for sin, and to stigmatise it before it could be forgiven by pain and death; then whosoever undertook to pay the ransom for guilty men, must pay it through his suffering. Justice can make no respect of persons. She is to be pictured, as all men know, blindfold, with her balance which hangs straight, and her sword which cuts deep. Finding this person, whether He be the highest—as He is—finding Him there in the fashion of a man, and in the place of guilt, "numbered with the transgressors," she simply extends her sceptre over His crowned head, and lets her sword drink His sacred blood. Nay, I will go further. When a party is accused on whom iniquities are asked to concentrate themselves, who makes Himself responsible for them, when He stands so supreme in rank, and in affection so close to the King, there is surely a greater call to do justice, and regard not the person. The slightest withdrawal of the command here, the faintest suspicion of partiality, would be fatal to the vaunted equity of heaven's administration. Where were justice on the earth if a panel like this escaped at a human bar because he was the king's son, while meaner offenders must die?

That is not the real difficulty. It lies further back than that. Who will be the Saviour of men through this life of suffering and trouble? Let us think. Who is it? It was the Son, sent by the Father, girded and shod for the dealing by the Father's hand; in other words, it is God who qualifies Himself for the tasting of death, and becomes perfect Himself through obedient suffering. And the question is, "Is that fitting?" Had it been any minor victory it might have been; but is not this too much? Not as if there could have been the slightest semblance of wrong to the innocent sufferer when we remember who He was. He was willing, so might any creature have been, but His was not a creaturely will. When He chose to take upon Himself "the form of a servant," He did so by a choice as sovereign as the Father's will; He did not sacrifice another, but the sacrifice He gave was Himself. But it is just here that the wonder lies—that Father, Son, and Holy Ghost should conquer in stooping to the fallen nature, of the God-head, to such an abyss of suffering and of shame.

Brethren, it was not after this fashion that any other of the Almighty's most glorious deeds were done. When He made this fair earth it was by the breath of the word out of His lips; when He makes spring He regarnishes the fields and woods afresh, and makes all things laugh for gladness; it costs Him nothing. When He set Israel free from Egypt, it was by a stretched out arm of strength; when He gave His law it was in thunder and lightning, while bare-faced Horeb rocked and shook beneath it. "Yes, those things became Him," you would say. And could He have set us free, and washed out our sins, and led us safe and forgiven to the land of our eternal rest, without descending from His proper glory, or, if He stooped at all, splitting the heavens beneath Him as He reached down His strong right arm that made the heavens—had it been possible by sheer strength, and in the majesty of a God to achieve the overthrow of Satan as He overthrew Pharaoh, and to loose men from bonds of sin as He loosed the captive children of Israel, then it would have been in the line of all we know of God, and all we ever pictured to ourselves of the manner and the ways of the Great Jehovah.

Surely it would have become Him then, all men being witnesses. But to stoop to limit Himself to live in a cottage, and be suckled by a woman, to toil, to learn, to grow, to be weak and faint, to strive, to pray, to suffer, to sink, to die. Ah! do these sound to you like Godlike achievements? Is that like a ray from His glorious beams? Brethren, is not the cry of our human hearts against such things—that of indignity done to the Lord of heaven and earth, that which one day broke from the lips of an apostle, "That be far from Thee, Lord; this shall not be unto Thee." Now in this exposition of what we call our difficulty, I think we have almost touched the answer to it. Brethren, the difficulty roots itself in false conceptions of God. We know all these are measuring God-likeness and God-worthiness by a wrong line. You observe it is the physical or natural attributes of God, rather than the moral, which have impressed themselves upon the imagination of men, so as to identify themselves with our conception of Deity; and it is because the humiliation and the passion of the Son of God seems against our conceptions of God's physical glory and strength that, therefore, we feel offended by it. We look at His might, to which there is nothing difficult; and to His knowledge, which does not need to grow by experience; and to His universal presence, which no bounds can shut out; and these properties so far transcend the limitation of our mode of being, however awe-struck hearts may wonder at them, that we call them Divine; and we unconsciously liken the things above to things on the earth, and invest the seat of the Eternal with human emissaries. Here on earth we set store by wealth and ease, glittering pageantry, troops of ministers, and all that is fair and sweet to fill the eye or heart. These men think to be divinely because supremely good, and instinctively transplant these from earth to heaven. We robe the Eternal with such trappings; and just because it would argue in an earthly prince that some decoration in his honour was something that was due to his earthly rank, were he to forsake the court and expose himself in a mean incognito to be insulted by the basest of his people, so we shrink from the humiliation of the Son of God, and can hardly dare to read those terrible verses of the Gospels where we are told He was mocked and spat upon and buffeted by mean and wicked men.

For a throne, we see, He comes to fill the manger; He parts from the regal seat of empire and the ministry of interest, if such there be in heaven, to get here on earth no obeisance except from the angel; for ease and comfort He consents to a limitation of His earthly fulness, and the future for a time becomes servitude. So far as we can see of that life in Palestine, it means the renunciation of what we call Divine. It means a limitation within creative conditions, that He could give nothing, say nothing, do nothing, but what the Father gave Him, taught Him, told Him. Who could redeem such a life from the charge of being unfit for Him?

Now, there is only one thing that can redeem it; it is moral beauty. It is not power, not ease and pleasure, not rule, not will, much less the homage of the world which makes up the supreme nobleness of the supremely noble one. It is goodness. "Show me Thy glory," said Moses —who, perhaps, of all the ancient saints saw deepest into God—"show me Thy glory"; and Jehovah said in answer, "I will make all My goodness to pass before thee." It is an old lesson, therefore. It is one which God has long been teaching to our hearts. We are so blind to the loveliness of character of God that we fall down to worship material, mental powers; but He never taught this lesson so strongly as by the life of Jesus. One might have thought we could have learnt it, brethren. One might have thought that men would have seen that even a man's true dignity does not lie in anything but virtue. It is worse than heathenish, when you think of it—this sin—to be so dazzled by material splendour as to forget moral goodness. History with her impartial verdicts, uttering her deepest judgments to the consciences of the race, might teach us better. Who does not see, to-day, more glory in the outlaw who spared his king within the shelter of a cave, than in the king who with three thousand men hunted him on the hills?

And now, my brethren, that God has come, and that we

have seen the true Divine translated into suffering, why should it be so hard for us to see that this was the true glory of the heart of God? Think of the new discoveries we have found here, of the shut-up depths of the Divine character, that any God, great as He is, resistless, awful, imperious, swaying the universe, that in Him there dwelt, nevertheless, a tender pity, and patience, and lowliness, and gentle grace, and generous forgiveness, a power and a capacity for all the meek and subject virtues, a will to suffer rather than to see others suffer, and a magnanimity of charity that would die for the saving of those that hated Him! I doubt very much if any creature who knew most of God knew so much of Him as this before. I do not doubt that at the amazing discovery of such qualities in God the wisest angels forget other revelations of Him in His universe and desire to gaze into this, because, when once a pure soul sees this glory, the glory of the meek suffering of love, all other glory grows dim beside it.

This is Godlike; this "became Him." Material splendour, as of the green earth and star-lit sky, is but a robe of His, which perishes when He folds it up. To make, to unmake creation is a less thing even than to rule it well; and yet His common ruling providence and His judgment seems but a poor thing to the Divine task of conquering sin in the human heart by patience and love.

Never, I think, never till the Son of God measured Himself—if I dare so speak—with the task of winning back the rebel creature, did He do any work within our knowledge that was fit to develop before the eyes of creation the stupendous resources of the Divine nature. Those exterior conditions, like service and pain and shame, which look at first sight so unbecoming, are, in fact, the very conditions which alone could display the divinest attributes of God; for until man fell earth had no room for those things. Where were patience if there was nothing to suffer, where meekness if no insults, where humiliation on God's part if no need to bow and descend to men? How can faith be tested but in trial, or obedience known but through service, or love measured save by its self-denial? The depth of our Saviour's humiliation becomes the standard of His glory. The darker the night of His passion, so much the brighter does His virtue shine. The laurels which our Captain wears are laurels which He has won, and He wears them on the brow where our sins sat before.

O brethren, had you and I, whom His years of toil and passion saved—had you and I but spiritual eyes that were anointed to see with the freedom of which religion tells us, spiritual eyes which, in the light of God, could follow the path by which Christ's noble heart walked in the lowliness of His life, while He bravely held fast His purpose of mercy to mankind through all hindrances from men themselves, and meekly bore the worst that could be done by earth and hell to crush Him, until He rose through sheer endurance, through patience, to the solitary majesty of victorious love—rose from the wreck of His earthly flesh, torn and rent and ruined—rose to save the souls of men and to deliver them from sorrow—if our eyes, I say, could take in the moral splendour and the costly triumph of that spectacle, we should know, as perchance those with serener vision in the upper temple know, how such love unto death "became" God.

XXX. Sinai and Sion. HEB. xii. 18. *"For ye are not come unto the mount that might be touched."*
22. *"But ye are come unto mount Sion."*

IT is at once marvellous and beautiful to trace the unity of purpose which runs through this epistle, how every argument and every illustration is made subservient to the same practical design. The purpose of the epistle, as you are aware, was to confirm the Jewish Christians in their recent espousal of the faith of Christ, and to guard them against the apostasy to which they were sorely tempted both by false teachers, and by the corrupting influences of the external world. The design may be discovered in each succeeding chapter, and the appeals to fidelity are rendered more and more forcible by the cumulative evidence by which they are sustained. The magnificent contrast, for example, that is drawn in the verses, part of which we have read, between the Christian dispensation and that which it had superseded, while it could not fail to rouse the most fervent gratitude in the bosom of the heirs of the new and better covenant, was mainly intended to point the solemn warning which follows—" See that ye refuse not Him that speaketh, for if they escaped not who refused him that spake on earth, much more shall we not escape if we turn away from Him that speaketh from heaven." There is, as you will perceive, an artistic finish in the construction of the passage. The comparison is ably drawn; the elaboration of the effect is grandly defined. But while we admire it, it has done its work, and lodged its warning in the wavering soul. It is like the deadly shell; we watch it as it issues from the mortar and admire the superb rapidity with which it cuts through the air, but while we follow it an explosion far off in the enemy's earthworks attests at once its gunner's purpose and unerring aim. With like design we would remind you of your privileges that we may the more effectually insist upon your duties. We would impress upon you and endeavour to arouse you to a sense of the greatness of your advantages in that we "have not come to the mount that might be touched," but we are "come to mount Sion." The Apostle sets forth the dispensation of the gospel—your dispensation and mine—as very much superior in certain important particulars to the dispensation of the law—Mount Sinai, or the mount that might be touched, being put for the law that was given upon it; Mount Sion, literally the southern part of the city of Jerusalem, where David fixed the court and Solomon built the temple, being put for the newer revelation of God in the days of Jesus Christ. Some expositors understand that term, Sion, as having reference to heaven. It is not impossible that in those inner and deeper meanings that we find shining through many parts of Scripture, like Arcturus through the tail of the comet, covered but not hidden by it, there may be some such reference, but the main allusion is obviously to a state of higher privilege than that—a state which is *now* enjoyed; for the Apostle says—" Ye *are* come unto this state already." It is not a matter of promise, but of experience; not a future dimly apprehended, but a present actually and consciously realized.

There are several thoughts suggested by the passage that indicate the superiority of Sion over Sinai, and which will impress you, if you will only think of them, that your facilities are greater and your responsibility by consequence greater than that of any in former times to whom the messengers of God have come. The two great points of contrast are, that Sinai was the emblem of a sensuous, and Sion of a spiritual economy, and that Sinai was a system of rigour, and the gospel is a system of love. Sinai is represented as the mount that might be touched, that is, something palpable, the emblem of a material framework, or a system of gorgeous ceremonies and local shrines, and of impressiveness of external appearance. I need not tell you that this was very largely characteristic of the system of Judaism. The giving of the law for example, was an overwhelming address to the senses of the awed multitude. The eye was arrested by darkness that defined the gaze, by the lightning and the tempest which played about the summit of Sinai; the ear was thrilled by the trumpet blast, and was appalled by the thunder. Such was the majesty of the voice which spoke that the listeners crouched beneath its tones, and entreated almost with tears that it might not speak to them again. All the ritual services of the temple, the furniture, every ceremony and every sacrifice of the dispensation, were surrounded with accessories all intended to impress the senses either with sublimity or with terror. Of course there was an inner life in all this —at least in the palmy days of Judaism—a vital heart pulsing beneath that drapery of symbol. But in the time of the Saviour—the incarnation—the religion of too many had become only a rubric and a creed; the shadow was still grasped tenaciously, but the substance was gone; the whole system was like a corpse awaiting its embalmment, all ready for burial, so that the sepulchre were but in a garden. And this very sensuousness of the Jewish economy necessitated, so to speak, the appointment of sacred places, and a central temple of worship. Hence, all those journeys to Jerusalem in times of special festival which were binding upon the masses of the people. Jerusalem was the centre of the system from which all its light was understood to radiate, and to which the best affections of its people converged as to their chiefest joy. Hence, when the swarthy chamberlain of the African queen heard in the defiles of his native wilderness of the God of the Hebrews, he must go up to Jerusalem for to worship. Hence, in after years of exile, long enough to have trampled out the last spark of nationality, the Israelite turned to this his home as the fire-worshipper to the sun; and Daniel kneeled down three times a day with his lattice open towards Jerusalem. That was, so to speak, the depository of the dispensation's power. There might be many synagogues; there was only one temple. Hence the oracle of Divine wisdom spoke. From this fountain the streams of healing flowed, and all Judea was fertilized and blessed. Here, and here only the atonement could be offered and the sin forgiven; and there was not a patriot in the tribes, as before his solemn fancy rose up the loved image of Sion, but would invoke upon himself the imprecation—"If I forget thee, O Jerusalem, let my right hand forget its cunning; may my tongue cleave to the roof of my mouth if I prefer not Jerusalem above my chief joy."

But now, in contrast with this pomp of ceremonial and localization of interest, ye are come to the spiritual Sion, filled with the inner man, and with lively human stones building up a spiritual house. God on Sinai gave to the Hebrews a law; God on Sion hath given to His people a life, and now that the age of visible symbol has passed away, the Lord speaks no longer from the lips of seers, or from any chosen or exclusive lawgiver. We are not restrained from impiety by any palpable excitements. The Shechinah has departed from its accustomed habitation in the temple, and there is no process of wholesale and central lustration by which a congregation can be simultaneously forgiven. We have got a temple yet, but it is for worship, not for sacrifice. We have the ministry of reconciliation yet, but it is not a priesthood by any means in the midst of us; it is just a body of the men who are the messengers in the Churches, and the glory of it. We have the sacraments, the Godly sacraments which the Saviour ordained in His Church, but they are commemorative, not regenerating; not powers to constrain or to meeten for a covenant, but seals of a covenant that has been already made. Religion, as the gospel sets it before you, and asks you to receive it, comes, so to speak, in the bareness of the

Saviour's incarnation. No pomps attend it, no patronage commends it to our regard; its glory is not of this world; it stands alone upon the banks of our modern Jordan, unattended by any retinue of circumstance; a living, holy, independent stranger. Without form or comeliness to the beauty-seeking eye of nature, it is loved and it must be loved for itself alone. It has no preferments in its gift, save those that are beyond the grasp of human hands. It calls men to no reluctant duty, and it offers to mortal weakness no compromise; it only offers the succour of a grace that will stoop down from heaven to help it up.

Now, my brethren, what do you think of such a religion? It goes straight into the inner man, and as it finds there not merely fancies vagrant and prodigal motives blemished and alloyed, but idols lurking in the secret places of the heart, revelry with some unclean rites, with some cherished Ashtaroth or Baal, it says—" I must have these things cleansed. Drive out those money-changers of spiritual usury; I want this temple to be holy, completely holy unto God." Look at that religion, as, perhaps, for the first time in his life, it introduces a man to himself, strips him of the flimsy disguise with which he would veil his own deformity, compels him to introspection, turns him off from the excuses of his neighbour's complicity, or from complicity in his neighbour's error; and sets him searching, hunting, so to speak, after the discovery of his own vileness, not, as in former times, trying to hide it from his coward eye. Look at him, as it opens up to him a vista of still increasing purity, all perfect with a glory that streams upon him from the hill of sacrifice, as it urges him from one spiritual mastery to another, until, brave wrestler as he is, he has thrown the world, and humbled the flesh, and spoiled all the goods of the devil! I ask you, is not there in this a recognition of the spiritual faculty of man, in this directness of appeal to him, in this noble scorn of sensuous motives, in this wounding of the flesh, in this attack upon the heart and conscience by motives that are congenial, and that are sublime; is not there a majesty, a grandeur and a divineness that you could not get in any costly externalism whatever; and does not there come a paleness upon the lustre of all former dispensations when there shines out in all its brilliancy the lustre of the glory which excelleth?

And then this religion, thus spiritual in its aim, must surely have that element of commonness which will adapt it to us. The gospel river of life does not branch out into divers streams. There is not there, a broad sweep of water for the rich, and for the intellectual, and for the cultivated, and here a little scant runnel, where the poor may now and then come and get healed by the side of its precarious wave. There is no costly sanatorium beneath whose shade patrician leprosy may get by itself to be fashionably sprinkled and healed. Naaman, with all his retinue watching, must come and dip, and plunge like common men in Jordan. There is no sort of salvation, except the one ransom and deliverance, that is purchased for rich and poor together by the influences of the Lord Jesus Christ; and the poor beggar—his garment ragged from the havoc of a hundred storms, and his flesh bleeding from the ulcers of a hundred wounds—may dip eagerly into the same Bethesda, and emerge unscarred, and comely as a child. Oh! there is a hopefulness, a keen, loving, winsome insight, so to speak, in this religion of Jesus which constrains it to furnish the very amplest and most bountiful provision. It comes to you therefore, to every one of you, and it says, "God is a spirit and you are a spirit; you are therefore in God's likeness, and you are therefore capable of God's service." You have divorced yourself from His moral image; it does not flatter you, it says, "There is family likeness still, but it is bloated with intemperance—fallen away from the beauty in which it was once comely and lovely exceedingly." But from your possession of the spiritual nature, it tells you that you can never divorce yourself. Wherever the prodigal wanders, it does not matter how far off, he always—he cannot help it—must carry his father's blood in his veins. And, it is this spirituality of the nature, this identity of the nature, upon which rests the hope of the gospel for you. You have sinned, but you can rise; nay, you have sinned, *therefore* you can rise. The very thing that damns you, saves you, so to speak; the very thing—the spiritual nature—that makes you able to sin, is that royal possession which makes you capable of God; and just as the rags dredged out of earth's meanest refuse-places, become the glossy paper upon which may be traced the words that burn, and just as the savage cannibal colony may become the mission colony, the Christian colony, and join loudly in strange and unwonted hosannahs, so there is the spiritual nature in every man that furnishes a sort of leverage by which you can raise him heavenward, that furnishes that path within him by which he may be reached, impressed, and saved.

And then the same spirituality necessitates that the gospel shall be catholic; that there shall be no shrine more sacred than another; that the old feud between the Jews and the Samaritans shall be altogether discarded as a meaningless thing. Who would think of vaunting his own small synagogue, when he stands beneath the grand arches of the universal temple? So there is allied with this commonness—it is necessitated that there should be —a universality too. The Jewish economy was a noble law for a people, but if you look for the people now, you cannot find them, therefore the law is obsolete. The people are scattered everywhere; there are no elements of a nation at this moment in the holy city. True, there are those that take pleasure in the stones of Jerusalem, and that favour the dust thereof; and there is a grand future for the Hebrews yet, when they shall look on Him whom they have pierced, and hear Him proclaim for them an Easter and a jubilee; but at present for the masses of mankind there is no binding law in Judaism, nor any pulse of vigorous life. It would be a bitter day, don't you think, for the world's poor pilgrims, if they had to go to Jerusalem to worship, like that Ethiopian eunuch of old? It would be a bitter day if they had to prostrate themselves before the shrine of the prophet in Mecca, or if they had to visit any other exclusive place of sacredness. Why, with our diversities of language, and national peculiarities, and jealousies of government, that mar the freedom of intercourse, half the world would have to live in the neglect of religious ordinances for ever, and the other half might die unpardoned on the journey before they could reach any of those places of healing and of life. How glorious then the revelation, at once the rebuke of the intolerant and the charter of the needy—God is a spirit, and wherever two or three are gathered in His name there He is! How utterly does this unalterable promise silence the dogmas of all rabid ecclesiasticisms, and fill the souls of the true worshippers with a very flood of joy! Neither Gerizim nor Jerusalem have any haughty exclusiveness of privilege now. Of course means are not superseded—they are yet used and sanctified. The Book has not yet lost its authority, nor the Sabbath its obligation, nor the house of God its sacredness. All that is seemly and decorous in external worship is preserved and left, "but the hour cometh, and now *is*," when the Father "seeketh" in every clime His true and spiritual worshippers. Oh, the beauty of that phrase! It is not the worshipper seeking the Father, it is the Father seeking the worshipper—looking down from heaven to find where the really contrite ones are that in sincerity and truth adore. "The Father seeketh such to worship Him." The blessing is hidden no longer in the temple's inner shrine; it has belted the broad world as with a zone of glory; the veil no longer shrouds the holiest from the view, the inner radiance hath found its way through the outer covering, and now shines in the face of all people, "A light to lighten the Gentiles, and the glory of Thy people Israel." Oh, do not think for a moment that by frequenting places that have an odour of peculiar sanctity you can alone acceptably worship God. Have you got a contrite heart? Then that can consecrate the meanest place on earth. It does not matter where the congregation may gather, only let them be a congregation of faithful men, yearning for truth, ready to make any sacrifice to obtain it, and that God who is everywhere present will reveal Himself in blessings wherever they may choose to assemble. They may crowd into the solemn Minster, and while the organ peals out its alternate wail and psalm, to them it may be a spiritual service, and their hearts may glow in purer light than streams through painted windows. They may draw around the hearth of the farmer's homestead, and while the frost-king reigns outside, their spirits may burn with a warmth that may defy the keenness of the sternest winter. For them there may be a spiritual harvest more plentiful than the garnered store in the barn that has been lent for worship; or a season of refreshing beneath the thatch through which the penitent soul can filter up its sighs for heaven. On the gallant vessel's deck, with no witnesses of the service but the sky and sea, there may be the sound of many waters as the Lord of Hosts comes down. And in the Alpine solitudes, where the spirit, alone with God mid murmuring streams, and bowing pines, and summits of eternal snow, uplifts its adoration, there may be a whisper stiller, and sweeter, and more comforting than that of nature, saying, "Peace, peace be unto you." Oh! it is a beautiful thought, that in this, the last of the dispensations, the contrite heart can hallow its own temple! Wherever the emigrant wanders—wherever the exile pines—in the dreariest Sahara, rarely tracked save by the Bedouin on his camel—on the banks of rivers yet unknown to song—in the dense woodlands where no axe has yet struck against the trees—in the dark ruin—in the foul cell—in the narrow street—on the swift rail—there where business tramps and rattles—there where sickness gasps and pines—anywhere, anywhere in this wide, wide world, if there is a soul that wants to worship, there can be a hallowed altar and a present God.

"Ye are not come to Sinai, but to Sion"—the spiritual temple where God is ever ready to bless His people with the fulness of His life and of His grace. Brethren, think of that! These are your privileges, how have you improved them? Oh, if those of meaner opportunities and of scantier means are punished at last because they come short, surely the many stripes and the wrath even to the uttermost must be reserved for the unfaithful ones who have inherited the privileges, and "not come to Sinai but to Sion."

I can hardly dwell upon the other thought, but if you could think of it—and you may—at home, it will enhance the estimate of your own superior position.

The Sinaitic was a rigorous discipline; the gospel is a system of love. If you think of all the accessories in the giving of the law, you will find that it gendered bondage; that though the mountain was a material one, yet the people might not touch it; if a beast touched the mountain it was to be stoned or thrust through with a dart. They stood afar off. There was darkness; there was tempest; there was a voice majestical even to terror; when the utterance did come it was a command and precept altogether; not a word of mercy, not the faintest intimation of recovery for the erring, or of salvation for the sinner. Even when the provision of sacrifice was introduced, the privilege was restricted, and the access was difficult. Only the High Priest could come into the holiest—he only once a year; at all other times it was jealously closed. Then not without blood in acknowledgment of his transgressions and in deprecation of the wrath that he had deserved; and whenever the worshippers went into the temple, there was the veil, thick and shrouding and impenetrable, concealing from the view the presence of God. It was a glorious dispensation, notwithstanding; glorious in itself, far above human desert; glorious, inasmuch as it gave access to God, and the means of impression and salvation. But it was introductory, rudimental; an infant stage of God's purposes, which their development has left far behind; only the strict corrective discipline which, like a stern schoolmaster, was intended to bring us to Christ. The system under which it is our privilege to live is very different, and very superior. Our God is not remote but near. He does not shroud Himself in Divine darkness, and from some inaccessible summit of fire address us in thunder and in flames. We do not come to a solitary mountain, but to a peopled city, gay with the rapture of life and social with the hum of men, the city of the living God. Our law is the gospel—mercy is the very essence of religion. Our very threatenings are fringed with sunlight. Our every precept has a promise. In its heart our sacrifice has been once offered, and does not need any repetition, but preserves through countless years its efficacy and its power. Our blood fadeth not in its crimson, our voice falters not in its advocacy; but through all time and for all enormities of crime the blood of sprinkling yet speaks and pleads, all prevalent for the help of man. The holiest is not now concealed, the veil is rent. The privileged priesthood has died out as an order in the Church, and each one of us, grasping the hand of his Divine Daysman, may go right in without misgiving and without fear, and be bold in his access to the throne. Brethren, the service to which Christianity invites you is not a drudgery, but a healthful and lucrative labour. When the love of God is shed abroad in the heart; when the man is come to Sion, and is happy

T

in its citizenship, he rejoices that glorious things are spoken of his city. He takes the yoke upon him in all humbleness, but he is never galled or fretted by it. And you can hear him singing in his happy toil—" Thy commandments are not grievous, Thy service is perfect freedom." When the voice speaks, he does not shudder at it, he is not oppressed with it, much less does he intreat that it may be hushed and not speak again. He says, rather, as he listens to catch and devour every Divine syllable—" Thy word is more precious than rubies, sweeter also than honey and the honeycomb." Everything about him is congenial, not constrained; intimacy, not distrust and distance; the calm of a soul that revels in sunshine, not the unrest of a spirit where tempest mutters and broods. He is satisfied with God's likeness, his delight is in the law of the Lord. Oh, it is a happy thing to have come to Mount Sion.

And then, only think of the companionship. I cannot enlarge upon it. The Apostle takes you very rapidly through it in the verses in connection with the text. The most exalted associations in the universe become yours if you are faithful in the improvement of your privileges. When you come to Mount Sion there will be an innumerable company of angels. Heaven and earth are reconciled and united in the new covenant, and an innumerable company of angels smile down upon the Church of the firstborn, upon the earliest regenerated, upon the predestined heirs of that heaven in which they abode from the beginning. The chariots of God on Sinai were twenty thousand, even thousands of angels, but they terrified the people then, and the poor multitude quailed down on the plain, stricken with the consciousness of sin. The angels live yet, and are bright in the glory of their first estate, but they minister to the people now, they bear in their hands some helpless child of grace lest in the world's rugged and wayward pilgrimage he should dash his foot against a stone. And they look on, for there is no envy in the angels now. There was once, when one of them fell because of it, but they look on now, sympathetic and unenvying, while poor ransomed mortals are lifted up into a glory that is higher and brighter than theirs. And then, besides this, you come into union with all that believe, all that are professors of the same precious faith, and whose names are written in heaven—your hallowed confederacy. You can claim help from sufferers everywhere; it is a commonwealth. Your wants and sorrows are the wants and sorrows of all. The sympathy of the Hebrew was a very contracted sort of thing—bounded by kindred and clanship, and so on. Hence the priest and the Levite could not come down from the proprieties on the other side of the way and assist the poor plundered stranger. But the sympathy to which you are entitled is a sympathy catholic as the heart of Christ, and universal as the brotherhood of man. "Ye are come to God, the *judge* of all." He was the special lawgiver to the Hebrews, and yet they dared not come to Him; but the energy and force of this passage in reference to the Christian is, that through Christ he may come straight up to the *Judge*, not to the Father but to the Judge, and claim by virtue of his substitute, acquittal, and smile, and recompense, and reward. And then, "Ye are come to the spirits of the just made perfect." For them the tears are shed—for them the crown is won. But you are linked to them yet—by covenant, and by struggle, and by faith you mingle with them. Across the dark waters which separate you there are mutual interests and a hearty oneness of feeling. They look down—a cloud of witnesses—in loving and helpful encouragement of your strife, for they know what it is. They have struggled themselves, and have themselves overcome; and you at the heat of the battle, gaze wistfully upwards towards them where they are in their brightness, and in their beauty, and—

> "E'en now by faith you join your hands,
>   With those who went before;
> And greet the blood-besprinkled bands
>   Upon the eternal shore."

And then, crown of all other privileges—we could not leave that out—the reason why all other privileges are inherited—"Ye are come to Jesus the Mediator, and to the eloquent blood of sprinkling that speaketh better things that that of Abel." The Hebrew's day of atonement only came once a year—Jesus is ever nigh. In all your lapses and short-comings, your sudden yieldings to temptation, your unworthy acts of compromise to evil, there is heaven and the Divine advocate; here on earth is the open fountain; your means of propitiation are ever at hand. The voice that pleads for you does not know how to be silent. The tired sun may pause, sometimes, perhaps in his march; the light may drop upon weary wings; there may come a shadow upon the bright hues of the ocean, and a tremor of age upon the everlasting hills; but through all times and through all change, the atonement retains its efficacy, and the speaking blood yet pleads with its glad tidings before the throne. "Ye are not come to Sinai but to Sion."

Brethren, the subject is not done, but my time is, and I want you just to know why it is that I have brought the matter before you. Why is it, sinner, why is it I have brought this matter of lofty privilege before you, who have nothing in the world to do with it? Why, that I may just unfold before you the wealth that you are refusing and the unsearchable riches that you are casting away; the patrimony that once belonged to you, but from which you have been disinherited in consequence of your transgressions. Why, O *believer*, have I brought this matter before *you?* Why, that you may take a look at your treasure—that you may revel in the riches that there is no fear of exhausting, and that you may find a force coming from the Saviour's admonition, upon the conscience of every one of you— "Except your righteousness *exceed* the righteousness of the scribes and Pharisees, ye shall in no case enter into the kingdom of heaven." W. M. P.

XXXI. A Model Layman. 3 JOHN 5-8.

"*Beloved, thou doest faithfully whatsoever thou doest to the brethren, and to strangers; which have borne witness of thy charity before the Church: whom if thou bring forward on their journey after a godly sort, thou shalt do well: because that for His name's sake they went forth, taking nothing of the Gentiles. We therefore ought to receive such, that we might be fellow-helpers to the truth.*"

"THE elder" speaks these words. The definiteness of the article seems to indicate that the distinction was one which might be rightfully assumed, and that the person who thus designates himself was of riper age, or of more distinguished office, than any other in the Christian Church at the time. This consideration goes far to fix the authorship of these epistles. None surely could write thus but that venerable apostle, latest of the band to linger, who was closing his beloved life in Ephesus, and whose last counsels were of the love which he had never ceased to cherish since he drank it in upon the Master's bosom. It is the outpouring of one loving Christian heart to another. "The well-beloved Gaius," or Caius as the Latins would call him, may or may not be identified with the Gaius who figures among St. Paul's salutations in the sixteenth of Romans, though there was a kinship at any rate in the virtue of Christian hospitality, as St. Paul describes him "My host, and of the whole Church;" but he stands as the winsome type of a thorough and whole-souled Christian man—a model layman of the early Church. He may have been in feeble health—many of God's jewels are framed in a frail setting. We do not gather that he was exceptionally wealthy, but he was affluent in the riches of a liberal spirit, the savour of his charity was borne abroad by the testimony of strangers, he rendered ungrudging and helpful service to the missionaries among the Gentiles, and he did it not for ostentation's sake, but "faithfully," as part of a recognised stewardship of which he must give an account. Then, further, he was not merely hospitable, making his generosity, after the fashion of some, to "cover a multitude of sins;" he had a firm persuasion of the truth, he walked in it with consistent footsteps. He was spiritually-minded, an active helper in all works of faith and love. No wonder his name had a charm in it which won upon the heart of the Apostle. No wonder that he embalms him in his epistle, and hands down his name to immortality for the stimulus and benefit of the Churches of all time. The Church has need of men like-minded still. The scriptural types of lay helpfulness need to be reproduced amongst us. The modern Apollos needs Aquila and Priscilla to "show him the way of God more perfectly." There is yet room for Dorcas and her "garments of praise," for "the spirit of heaviness" still hangs upon the poor. There is deaconess's work in other spheres than at Cenchrea. We want our local ensamples, who like Demetrius, "have good report of all men and of the truth itself;" Obed-Edoms, with the ark in the house; Mnasons, mellow with their "fruit in old age;" Simeons waiting in the temples; Gaiuses "bringing" their pastors "on their journey after a godly sort"—we need them in the midst of us to-day. In these days especially, when there is such a blessed quickening in the sense of personal responsibility and service—when ears, formerly dull, are strained to catch the Lord's whispered summons—when the whole Church as with one voice, and that a mighty voice, is asking the Lord, "What wilt Thou have me to do?" it cannot be amiss to urge upon ourselves, whatever our sphere or the measure of our influence, to become "fellow-helpers to the truth." Amongst the holy solemnities which our annual conference brings, none is more interesting and more solemn than the reception of candidates into the ministry, and their ordination to that sacred office. If we are spared for the services of the coming week, crowds will gather to hear their testimonies for the truth and to witness their public separation to their sphere of life-long service. It is proper that the members of our Churches should be deeply and profoundly stirred, for their own souls' prosperity, and the prosperity of the commonwealth of the faithful are largely bound up with the good or evil influence of these men. It will be my duty, in connection with their designation to the fulness of their office by the laying on of the hands of the presbytery, to address to their heart and conscience seasonable truth, as God may enable me to speak it. I believe it to be equally my duty to remind you—the people—that you have duties to your ministers of which you cannot rid yourselves, and which it were folly and sin to disregard. If Joshua is to fight manfully with the foe in the plain; if Moses, on the slopes of the hill, is to offer his princely and prevailing prayer; Aaron and Hur must inspire the warrior's valour by holding up the intercessor's hands. Will you bear with me, therefore, while I urge you, with all plainness, that if you would be fellow-helpers to the truth "you must take heed how you hear"—you must "esteem" your ministers "highly in love for their works' sake"—you must, as this same apostle elsewhere expresses it, "look to yourselves lest they lose their full reward."

The minister and the people make up the Church. A Church is not only "a congregation of faithful men," who live and are glad in the riches of abundant privilege. A

Church is a school of testimony. A Church is an organised force for the propagation of the truth which has been entrusted to it. It is of the essence of the constitution of a Church, therefore, that there should be fellowship, control, and well-adjusted division of labour. The minister has his sphere and his work—his relations to his flock and to his Master. These are well-marked and intelligible, and if he fail in his duty, he must answer it when the assize is held, and before the Judge from whom nothing can be hidden, But he cannot do his people's work, and it were useless and foolish to try. They have personal duties and services which they cannot transfer. He cannot watch and pray in their stead, nor "mortify the deeds of the body," nor evolve from them the radiance of a holy character, nor buy on their behalf a sort of vicarious right to heaven. And just as their experience in the Christian life must be personal, their activities in the Christian service must be personal also. They must dwell in the mount if they would act upon the multitude for good. If they would be approved servants, they must be ready and strong, as those who are commissioned from the King. They must absorb the sun's rays if they would "let" their "light shine before men." In a word, no solitary duty of the Christian life can be performed by proxy. The call is not upon the mass, but upon the individual. It is not you—the community; it is "thou"—the man. "I have chosen *thee*." "Go *thou* and work in My vineyard." "Be *thou* faithful unto death." And this is one distinguishing excellence of Protestant Christianity. I know of no other system in the world which has no priests. There are none in Protestant Christianity. When men call themselves priests, their Protestantism commits suicide in the utterance of the word. When the charge of priestcraft is brought against the ministers of Christ, it is brought in ignorance of the nature of their office; for the differences between the priest and the pastor are so many and so radical that they cannot be honestly confounded. A priest offers sacrifice; a pastor points to a complete sacrifice which has been offered once for all. A priest assumes to be a mediator; a pastor relies, both for himself and for his people, upon the sole and sovereign mediation of Christ. A priest derives his power over conscience from his supposed knowledge of occult mysteries from which the people are excluded; a pastor's power over conscience is in direct proportion to the truth which he enforces and reveals. A priest retains the key of sacred knowledge in his own hands, and doles out the treasure to those who propitiate or pay; a pastor summons all men, in Christ's name, to "search the Scriptures" that they may live. In fine, when we think of a priest, we think of one who does certain duties in another's stead—when we think of a pastor, we think of one who is set apart to urge upon all men to do their own duty, and to "work out" their "own salvation" through faith, and in the sight of God. Now there is some danger lest those who have renounced the theory should in practice subside into the comfortable heresy of priesthood, by leaving the minister, unsupported, and often discouraged, to do all the work of the Church. This is precisely the evil against which I wish to warn you. The current talk now-a-days is of the people's rights. Suffer me to beguile you into a consideration of their duties. You are called, each of you who has put on Christ, to a sphere of personal service. No solitary member of the Church is exempt from this paramount obligation. It is by this interpenetration of effort and sympathy that Churches live and grow. God has called the ministers into their work, but their work links itself with yours, and requires yours as its complement and perfectness. It has been said of the prayers of the former time that "all the intercessions which ever rose, Adam's for the race, Abraham's for the Hebrew, Paul's for the Gentile, Christ's for the world, are delayed in their fullest influence until we complete them." And it is true of effort as of prayer. The minister's service without yours "cannot be made perfect." Carry your thoughts back among the Israelites, roused from their criminal apathy by the prophet's appeals. What a description of zealous and united labour for God! "And the Lord stirred up the spirit of Zerubbabel the son of Shealtiel, governor of Judah, and the spirit of Joshua the son of Josedech the high priest, and the spirit of all the remnant of the people: and they came and did work in the house of the Lord of Hosts, their God." There is also a beautiful illustration of mutual encouragement and blessing in Psalm cxxxiv. It consists but of three verses, the first two of which are a benediction invoked upon a band of watchers, the last of which is the response of the company to the blessing of the friendly singer. Those who are thus commended in blessing are the Levites, who are the guardians of the temple in the night, who hold their eyes from slumber lest some thief should filch the treasures, lest the lamps go out, or lest the fire upon the altar of burnt-offering be suffered to die. The singer is the officer who closes the gates of the temple. As he takes his leave he sings his vesper hymn, " Behold ! bless ye the Lord, all ye servants of the Lord, which by night stand in the house of the Lord. Lift up your hands in the sanctuary, and bless the Lord." Refreshed and strengthened for their night-watch, they sound out the responsive music, " The Lord that made heaven and earth bless thee out of Zion." Now it is this—shown not in the lip-song merely, but in the calm consistency of the life—to which I would urge you to-day. You are Christians ? Then you are bound to work for Christ. You are members of the visible Church. You have realised that central idea, that first necessity of churchmanship—union with your Saviour? Then, emulous of His example, " For Zion's sake you will not rest, and for Jerusalem's sake you will not keep silence, until the righteousness thereof go forth as brightness, and the salvation thereof as a lamp that burneth." But you are more than this. You have not only enlisted in the army —you have chosen the regiment under whose banners you are to serve and war. The social law which works all nature through has drawn you into fellowship with Christians of like views and preferences for the mutual maintenance of faith, and for the more effectual out-working of your plans of holy toil. It may not be out of place to say here that the existence of the denomination—an inner circle within the Church—is neither without use nor without warrant. It springs indeed from the very liberty of Christianity, and is an almost necessary adjunct of a free Church-life. Sects, of course, ought not to be needlessly multiplied, and they should keep at the heart of them all the life-blood of divinest charity ; but they are not in themselves evil, nor are they incompatible with the essential and catholic unity for which the Saviour prayed. They may be but as the graceful varieties of nature, tributary to her grand central harmony; and the prismatic colours, preserving their individual distinctness, and yet melting into each other to form the bow which spans the cloud. Then if you have identified yourselves with the fellowship which you prefer, *that* is your sphere of service. Its members are your brethren. Its ministers your pastors. Its fortunes your charge in a sense in which no other can be. You are not to be so wonderfully loving to all that you have no particular affection for any. You are not to beat the wasteful air in profitless energy. You have home-ties, home-duties, home-work, and, "standing in your lot," you are *there*, to be "fellow-helpers of the truth." I solemnly believe that you, as representing the laity of the Methodist Church, have its prosperity largely in your own keeping. I am the more urgent, therefore, that you be "co-workers" with your ministers for God. You are summoned, then, to hold up your ministers' hands—to help them in the doing of their work by the conscientious doing of your own. The great requirement to this end is *sympathy*—the penetration of your whole nature with love of the truth you are to help, and of your fellow-helpers in the glorious mission—the enlistment in the service of every force and feeling, chastened but not weakened by the grace of God—the enkindling of strong affection for the work, and for the workers also, "for the work's sake." This sympathy is the secret of all active Christian helpfulness—and where it "flows as a river" there will be many branching streams. It will prompt to *charity*, to *liberality*, to *enterprise*, to *prayer*.

I. *It will prompt to charity*—a generous construction of motive, aim, and conduct. If your ministers are sent of God, you will receive them "in the name of a prophet" that you may "receive a prophet's reward." But who is a prophet? Simply a man to whom God has given a voice and a message. He does not cease to be a man because he has been lifted into an office, the burden of whose duties his own strength is too feeble to sustain. Rather is his humanness weighted with abnormal conditions of disadvantage because he is compelled to the front, and must live in the fierce light of the world's eye. There has been a half-acknowledged heresy on this matter which has done immense mischief. Men have come to imagine that a minister is invested with separate and almost alien sanctity, is lifted above the temptations which assail ordinary men, is sheltered in some nook of grace from the stern onset of evil. There can be no more baneful mistake. Ministers are not angels, but men—with the same besetting dangers, the same wearful restlessness, the same traitorous hearts. They have natures as perverse and wills as rebel, and sorrow crushes them as readily, as the poorest of their flock ; they need as urgently as any to be weighed in merciful scales of judgment. Beloved brethren, do not err in this regard. Look into your own hearts, those of you who have experience of the Christian life. Remember how your trials have multiplied—how your duties have tried you, so that you have often done them in weariness and trembling—how your sufferings have tried you, so that the "shrinking flesh must needs complain, and murmur to contend so long"—how your surroundings have tried you, and you have felt it difficult, amid many entanglements and under all conditions, to be brave for Jesus. Think of the boding fears and sad misgivings and giant hindrances which have haunted and harassed you, and made your heavenward progress so often a warfare and a struggle ; and then, when these memories are most vivid, remember that all of trial which you have felt presses upon your ministers in equal measure, and that they have discouragements peculiar to their office, of which you know nothing, but which make their burden heavier to bear. They have resigned some of their personal liberty, and put themselves under a self-imposed restraint, that they may be the ministers of God to you for good. Their service, their endowments, their reputation, their life, they have put, so to speak, into the Church's hands. It is your duty to guard faithfully that which they have in good faith entrusted to your keeping, and to see to it that you suffer no anxieties which you can ward off to consume their life, nor any slander which you can repel to whisper venomously their good name away. Be tender and loving in your judgment of their public doings. If a sermon seems to you feeble, remember how many other sermons have been strong, and how, even from the feeblest and faultiest, you can gather more gospel teaching than you are prepared to carry out into the life. Remember the close connection between this body of our humiliation and the mind which it enshrines, and how the aching head, or the deranged digestion, or the bruised and paining nerves, may rob the spirit of its self-possession and of its power. Ask yourselves whether there may not have been untoward influences in the congregation which have sometimes hindered his vigour and freedom. He is not insensible to the stare of the thoughtless, and the laughter of the trifling, and the impatient rustle of the wearied, and the noisy intrusion of the late comer—not to mention that very poor help to pulpit power, the equivocal approval of the slumberer's assenting head. Nay, do not hesitate to search your own hearts. You blame him that he was not sufficiently experimental, or plain, or doctrinal, or practical, as the bias of your criticism may happen to incline. You thought him in a sickly condition to preach; are you quite sure that you were in a healthy condition to hear? Had you cooled from the fitful fever of the week? Had you quite washed the gold-dust from your busy fingers? Did no thought of sale and bargain mingle with worship, song, and sermon? Were your lips warm with the prayer which you had just offered that he might be able to speak strong words, and heal sick hearts, and stir the consciences of men? Brethren, there are proprieties of hearing as well as of preaching; and if our congregations must wait for acceptance until they had graduated into proper dispositions for the heedful hearing of the Word, there are perhaps some even here who would be kept a long time upon trial. Brethren, give me a censorious Church—hard, stern, keenly critical, exacting its requirement of service like an Egyptian taskmaster, and I need look no further for the cause of many an apparent ministerial failure. Give me a loving, hearty people, generous in their judgments, considerate in their claims, even like the Master, slower to censure than to encourage, and for such a people any minister whose soul is in his work will not grudge the costliest he can render, even if it should involve the offering of the life and of the blood.

II. *This sympathy will prompt to liberality*—that is, an adequate and liberal provision for your ministers' support. They have a right to expect this at your hands. They have foregone the chances of business, trusting to your faith and honour. The same ability which fits them for their high office, if exerted in other spheres, might have made them as wealthy, or even wealthier, than yourselves. The care of the soul is certainly as important, and should be as well recompensed, as the care of the health or the care of the estate. The minister's claim to his stipend rests upon a law of heavenly appointment, and it is the same law which regulates the salary of the statesman, the returns of the merchant, and the wages of the poor. "In all labour there is profit." It is the right of every man to live by sweat of brow or brain, and "they who preach the gospel" are to "live of the gospel," according to the Word of God. There are high spiritual reasons, reasons affecting the prosperity of the cause of Christ, why the appointment of the minister's stipend should be liberal, and the payment of it prompt and kindly. He has a great work to do, and he ought not to be called down from it by the comfortless pressure of financial cares. He needs the Tabor-experience and the Tabor-communion. Don't cloud his brow with the disquiet of straitened means and of a dubious equality between the winner and the spender. If he is to do your souls good, he must be bold to reprove you if you need it. Let him not be ground into an unworthy dependence, destructive of his self-respect. That were at once the meanest and cheapest way to turn the rebuke of a prophet into the unheeded anger of a child. If the Churches value the manliness and spiritual power of their teachers, they will lift them above present embarrassment and the dread of penury; for when want, either personal or relative, looms upon the soul, it is the deadliest destroyer of the energy, and the surest tempter to evil. If the ministers are men of Christ's choosing they will have trampled out of their hearts the love of money, but they have a rightful claim that a just and generous award shall be made to them, not with the airs of a patron, "not grudgingly nor of necessity," by the people of their charge. "Who goeth a warfare at any time at his own cost? who planteth a vineyard and eateth not of the fruit thereof? or who feedeth a flock, and eateth not of the milk of the flock?" "If we have sown unto you spiritual things, is it a great matter if we shall reap your worldly things?" These sentences which you listen to in your heart's tenderest moments, when with wishful longing you await the Lord's coming to the feast, embody the teaching of the Word, and your duty in this behalf, and He, the highest whom you serve, has joined in a wedlock which no man may divorce the liberality of earth and the spiritual bountifulness of heaven. "Bring ye all the tithes into the storehouse, that there may be meat in Mine house, and prove me now herewith, saith the Lord of Hosts, and see if I will not open you the windows of heaven, and pour you out a blessing that there shall not be room enough to receive it."

III. *This sympathy will prompt to enterprise*—a warm and willing co-operation in all that tends to the glory of Christ, or the extension of His kingdom. We cannot too often remind ourselves that spiritual prosperity cannot be achieved by a minister's unaided effort, but must result from the intelligent and hearty work of the whole Church. If a leader has no followers, how shall he gather to a head of power? If a captain has no army, or his soldiers be mutinous or craven, what avails his generalship in the field? In this age, especially, of quickened desire and zeal, there is no room for idlers in the temple of the Lord. That figment of old and foolish Popery, which absorbs the work in the pulpit, and bids the people stand listlessly by, has no place in the sympathy of the true minister, nor in the heart of the living Church. Christ has something for each of His members to do. The meanest and the mightiest—the disciple who has just taken the free yoke upon him, and longs to prove his loyalty by service—the veteran who from the summit of his honoured age looks back upon a long life of happy toil—the child whose dawning gaze has fastened on the Saviour—the patriarch of years, who waits in the Beulah-land the summons to the King in His beauty—for each there is an allotted field of toil, and a promised recompense of honour. It may be that your sphere is contracted, and your influence small; but He who inspired the stripling shepherd-boy to smite the Philistine, and gained the victory for Gideon's army without the handling of sword or bow, and subdued the nations by the invincible tenderness of *the Name* in which the apostles preached, can use a worm to thresh a mountain still, and can make your unostentatious work a power for the creation of other powers which may avail to win the world. Without this enlistment of personal service, it is impossible that there should be permanent success. The minister may preach well and faithfully, and individuals may profit and be saved, but there can be no glorious ingathering to awaken and to justify the joy of harvest. Without personal service the most perfect systems are mere cumbrous machinery, useless for saving purposes unless there be the "Spirit in the wheels." How is it with you, dear brethren? Are you working? Are you putting forth the energy and self-denial of the fellow-helper to the truth? Your fathers did noble work—held up the hands of God's ministers without fear or faltering—have earned a good degree among those worthies of renown who fearless "for their Master stood." You cherish their memory. Their traditions live with you. You mourn their loss, but are you only to be mutes at the funeral? Did you bury your own spiritual manhood in their graves? Are you so enamoured of their memory that you have no heart to imitate their example? Dear brethren, ponder these questions, I pray you. Are there not some of you who were somewhile very willing helpers, but whose activity and zeal are matter of history now? You fell out of the ranks, you hardly know how or why—perhaps on the plea of increasing business, or municipal honours, or fancied infirmities, or advancing years—or perhaps in times of recreancy and of peril you grew despondent and out of heart. You essayed to embody the revelation angel, and you flew forth with your gospel through the azure and in the sunshine, but when the storm came you furled your timorous wing; or perhaps in the midst of your usefulness there came a little cloud, not, alas! of blessing, but of shadow.

> "A something light as air—a look,
> A word unkind or wrongly taken,
> And love which tempests never shook,
> A touch, a breath like this, hath shaken."

And the slight, or the opposition, or the calumny (all of them parts of the believer's heritage) overcame your old attachments, and you left the city for the wilderness, and are useless and solitary now. Brethren, come back and do your first works, and feel your first love. Do you ask for a call to duty? Gather the lesson from the experience of the incarnate Saviour, "My meat is to do the will of Him that sent Me, and to finish His work." The doing of His Father's will was to Him as necessary food. And what is to be your call? *Hunger of heart to work for God and souls;* or, if you need others, listen to the wail of the perishing—perishing at your own doors. There's a call, as from a hundred mouths. The harvest, which the sun and the rain of heaven have combined to ripen, drooping in neglected masses, for want of reapers to gather it in. There's a call; and He, the Lord of the harvest, issues to you His rebuke and His encouragement. His rebuke—like thunder in a clear sky—"To him that knoweth to do good, and doeth it not, to him it is sin." His encouragement—like music in the interval of storms—"Inasmuch as ye did it unto one of the least of these, ye did it unto Me."

IV. *This sympathy will prompt to prayer.* You are well enough instructed in the Christian's life to know that, however lengthened it may be, there is no moment of it when he can cease from the cry of helplessness, from the invocation of new grace, from the expression of the longings of spiritual desire. If you have thought otherwise, you will be let into some humbling secrets by-and-by. And if you think that a cause of Christ can be built up by one man's labour in the pulpit, and by many men's labours in the Church, you will find your mistake full soon. Confusion of tongues will be the token of heavenly displeasure, and in the ruins of your prostrate Babel the vaunt of your atheism will be seen to be a discarded lie. The danger perhaps in this age of unflagging activities is to the forgetfulness of our utter dependence, and to the presuming trust in our systems or in our efforts rather that in the Divine Agent who alone can make them mighty. The nerveless limb stiffens into catalepsy, I know, but there is such a thing as an arm palsied through excessive use; and while we are to be as active as if the success depended upon our unaided strength, we are always to remember that we can do just nothing at all in real transforming work "until the Spirit be poured out from on high." We spread the sails, but the breath of God must fill them, and waft the vessel of our hopes to its haven by the shining shore. Now, dear brethren, you are summoned to pray, to hallow your gifts by prayer, to energise your efforts by prayer, to bring "free course" to the Word, and a glory on it by that which makes the people wonder—by prayer. You expect your minister to pray You think you can discover the measure of his individual devotion by the halo that is round him, or by the halting of his speech and spirit. But is the prayer to be all on one side? Are you under no obligation too? Think you there is no difference felt when you come prayerless to the sanctuary, with dull face and leaden feet; and when you come from the summit of the mountain, with shinings on your forehead and fragrance in your breath, and your faces glad as with pleasant memories of a friend? I tell you it makes all the difference between barrenness and blessing. Give us praying Churches, and we shall have the commanding ministry and aroused sinners, and communities aflame with zeal for God and souls, and a very gracious rain, and an opened and peopled heaven. Oh, if the millennial time of the Church is ever to dawn, if ministers are to be free from shallow conceits and questions which gender strife, if the old gospel is to swell grandly forth from lips which are strong to speak it; in a word, if Pentecost is ever to triumph over Babel, and the world's many tongues merge into the one language of praise and worship, it will be when every believing heart is a praying heart, and shall set itself to prayer with its whole desire absorbed for its fulfilment; and when there shall be such a concert of mighty and prevailing supplication that the feeblest shall rise into the strength of David, and David, purified from all shame and weakness shall be as an "angel of the Lord."

And now, dear brethren, suffer this word of exhortation. The mission which God has given to us is not yet fulfilled. Our Church is still needed for testimony and for aggression. We, its ministers, humble before God for our numerous shortcomings, which we feel more painfully than you can do, are yet inflamed with intensity of desire to covenant afresh, and to go forth to our work with greater earnestness than ever, and with a baptism of the Holy Ghost. We want all our Churches to join us in the hallowed compact. Whatever your past may have been, whether lukewarm like Laodicea; or, like Ephesus, that you have languished from your first espousal's ardour; or, like Sardis, that you have been living the life of the paralysed—now with a little strength, and now just ready to die—let us all gird ourselves anew for warfare and for triumph. To the most corrupt and slothful, He, the All-merciful, speaks, "As many as I love, I rebuke and chasten." Then He loves us still. He begins to address the blameworthy by marking anything which He can find to commend. He closes in each case by a starry promise to the conquerors. The tree of life—the hidden manna—the white stone—the white raiment—the confessed name—the established pillar—the new and more glorious name—the share of the throne. Oh, ravishing fulness of blessing! *even* as the Saviour shares the throne of His Father—all these in store for "him that overcometh." Then let us grasp these promises. By the blessing of God they may be ours, and under their inspiration let us pay our vows—more solemn, more self-denying, more complete in their whole-hearted surrender of ourselves to Christ, than we have ever done before—that so, to the last courses of the sun, our system, if God need it, may be a witnessing unity—an earnest ministry made strong by the fellow-helping of an earnest Church.

W. M. P.

INDEX OF SUBJECTS.

Apostles' Alternative, The, 233.

Christ, The Ascension of, 127.
Christ Speaking in Parables, 32.
Christ Washing the Disciples' Feet, 120.
Christian Meekness, 248.
Christmas, The Festival of, 65.
Coin, The Lost, 86.

Devils, Casting out, 80.

Easter, The Lessons of, 38.

Fig Tree, The Barren, 45.

Giver, A Cheerful, 196

John the Baptist, 12.
Joy and Tribulation, 183.
Justification, The Results of, 178.

Layman, A Model, 276.

Moralist, The Petition of, 57.
Mother, The Virgin, 1.

Nain, The Story of, 72.

Paul and Festus, A Contrast, 134.
Paul, The Life of St., 142-159.
Paul's Messages to Individuals, St., 189.
Perfect through Suffering, 256.
Prayer and the Answer, St. Paul's, 204.
Prodigal Son, The, 105.

Sainthood, 223.
Silvanus, 241.
Sinai and Sion, 264.
Spiritual Blessings in Christ, 213.

Trusting in Jesus, 23.

Where are the Nine? 93.

INDEX OF TEXTS.

MATTHEW.

	PAGE
i. 22, 23	1
ii. 7	12
„ 25–30	23
xiii. 1–3, 10–36	32
xxviii. 5, 6	38
xxi. 19	45

MARK.

x. 17	57

LUKE.

ii. 15	65
vii. 11–15	72
viii. 35	80
xv. 8	86
xvii. 17	93
xv. 11–32	105

JOHN.

	PAGE
xiii. 12–15	120

ACTS.

i. 9	127
xxvi. 25	134

ROMANS.

v. 1–12	178
„ 2, 3	183
xvi. 12	189

2 CORINTHIANS.

ix. 7–15	196
xii. 8, 9	204

EPHESIANS.

i. 3	213

	PAGE
i. 1	223
v. 3	223

PHILIPPIANS.

i. 21–26	233

TITUS.

iii. 1–4	248

HEBREWS.

ii. 10	256
xii. 18, 22	264

1 PETER.

v. 12	241

3 JOHN.

i. 5–8	276